COME OUT OF HER MY PEOPLE

COME OUT OF HER MY PEOPLE

The Encouragement and Exhortation of the Book of Revelation Chapters 1-3

Tony Kessinger

Copyright © 2003 by Tony Kessinger.

ISBN :	Hardcover	1-4134-2660-3
	Softcover	1-4134-2659-X

All rights reserved. No part of this book may be reproduced or transmitted in any form or by any means, electronic or mechanical, including photocopying, recording, or by any information storage and retrieval system, without permission in writing from the copyright owner.

This book was printed in the United States of America.

To order additional copies of this book, contact:
Xlibris Corporation
1-888-795-4274
www.Xlibris.com
Orders@Xlibris.com
21126

CONTENTS

Preface 7
Introduction 11
Chapter One
    The Patmos Experience 27
Chapter Two
    The Development of the Early Church 75
Chapter Three
    A Matter of Interpretation 91
Chapter Four
    Ephesus: The Church That Left Their First Love 96
Chapter Five
    Smyrna: The Fragrant Church 118
Chapter Six
    Perganum: The Church Where Satan's Throne Is 134
Chapter Seven
    Thyatira: The Tolerant Church 155
Chapter Eight
    Sardis: The Attention-Deficit Church 171
Chapter Nine
    Philadelphia: The Church of the Open Door 197
Chapter Ten
    Laodicea: The Church of Disingenuous Belief 222

Bibliography 243

PREFACE

God calls for His people to love Him with all their heart, soul, mind, and strength. He is a jealous God and unwilling to share the love of His people with anyone or anything. In Revelation 18:4, He calls out, "Come out of her, my people." This verse, like similar verses in the Old Testament (Jer. 51:6, 45), is a summons issued to the people of God to disentangle themselves from the allure of the world.

The people of God today are very much like Lot in Genesis 19. Lot knew he lived in a decadent city. Yet, he remained there. When the angels came to deliver Lot from the ravages of God's judgment on Sodom, Lot lingered (verse 16), not wanting to go. The angels were forced to take Lot, his wife, and his two daughters by the hand to lead them out of their house and the city. Even then, it was too much for Lot's wife to apprehend as she longingly looked back to the city as it was being destroyed. Lot was enmeshed in the world around him.

Believers in the first century faced similar circumstances. The people of Ephesus left their first love. It is reasonable to assume that if they left one thing, they gravitated to something else. The people of Pergamum compromised with the world around them. The people of Thyatira tolerated false teaching. The people of Sardis lived on reputation. The people of Laodecia operated from a wrong premise. In each case, God called out to them using the same phrase, "He who has an ear, let him hear what the Spirit says to the churches."

This book takes the position that God is calling His people to come out of the world. Coming out of the world should not be taken to mean the physical universe. Jesus prayed, "I have given them Your word; and the world has hated them because they are not of the world. I do not pray that You should take them out of the world, but that You should keep them from the evil one" (John17: 14, 15). The world Jesus referred to was the system of evil dominated by Satan that has surrounded all people since the fall of man in the Garden of Eden. About this world James writes, "Do you not know that friendship with the world is enmity with God? Whoever therefore wants to be a friend of the world makes himself an enemy of God" (James 4:4).

The allure of the world is strong and oftimes irresistible. The Lord continues to exhort His people to disentangle themselves from the web of the world's deceit. He doesn't expect the believer to accomplish this on their own strength, but enables all who appropriate the power of the Holy Spirit to be victorious.

The material contained in this book is the first part of a continuing work. Part one covers chapter one through three of the Book of Revelation. There is also a chapter dedicated to the development of the early church. The purpose of this chapter is to allow the reader to get an idea of what the early believer experienced and the impact of the separation of the church from its Judaistic roots. It also helps explain how and why the church and Judaism reached the level of animosity that has endured even to this day.

Future work will focus on chapters four through twenty-two.

It would be inappropriate on my part if I did not acknowledge the many people who encouraged me and made this work possible. A sincere thank you goes to: My wife, Diane, who lovingly tolerated the study and research time, needed to write this book. My son, Tory, who edited the pictures in the book. My daughter, Tonya, who has always encouraged my writing. My daughter, Tai, who helped create the PowerPoint presentations as I taught the material. The most wonderful and loving Sunday School class a teacher could ever hope to have. Carolyn Justice, a member of that Sunday School class, who so graciously caught the many mistakes in spelling, grammar, and construction that appeared in the first drafts of the manuscript.

Finally, it is only fitting to acknowledge all those scholars in the past who have laboriously researched and written so that we have a record of their efforts. Some of those scholars have been quoted in this manuscript. If there are any thoughts or ideas or quotes or footnotes that have not been properly credited or that are deemed to be inappropriately used, I offer my most sincere apology.

It is my fervent prayer that, as you read this book and interact with the Scripture, you will experience the encouragement and exhortation that only God through the work of the Holy Spirit can bring to your understanding.

Tony Kessinger
July 2003

INTRODUCTION

Prerequisites of Bible Study

Before undertaking the privilege of delving into the Word of God, certain preparations need to be made. The single most important prerequisite is prayer. Prayer that the Holy Spirit, who moved holy men of God to write this word (2 Peter 1:21), would teach the reader all things and bring back to memory (John 14:26) those things that have been made known. Prayer is the tilling of the soil of the mind and heart so that the implanted seed of the word can burst forth in a fruitful life.

The second prerequisite is the discovery that God gave His word to counsel (Psalm 119:20) and to illumine the way of the believer (Psalm 119:105). The Word of God "gives understanding to the simple" (Psalm 119:130). It is the source of spiritual nourishment. It is described as "pure milk" (1 Peter 2:1-3), solid food (1 Cor. 3:3; Heb. 5:12-14), and as sweet as honey (Psalm 119:103; Ezekiel 3:3). It was given as instruction so that "the man of God may be complete, thoroughly equipped for every good work" (2 Tim. 3:17).

Pilate sardonically asked Jesus, "What is truth?" (John 18:38). Pilate was confused. But the believer needn't be because it has been revealed that God's word is truth (John 17:17). It is the ultimate reality. "God is not a man that He should lie," spoke Balaam (Num. 23:19) nor can He lie wrote Paul to Titus (Titus 1:2). Therefore, what He has spoken is certain.

Given these facts, does it seem probable that God would, through the ministry of the Holy Spirit, inspire the writers of Scripture to give His creation a book of riddles, puzzles, or conundrums? Or does it seem probable that the Holy Spirit inspired the writers to convey exactly what He intended for His creation to understand? If the first proposition is true, then Scripture is a maze through which God's creation must attempt passage. This would be an example of spiritual survival of the fittest. On the other hand, if the second proposition is true, Scripture was given in order to be understood and thereby become crucial to the life of the believer.

In studying the first three chapters of the Book of Revelation, the reader encounters real people who lived real lives in a real place in real time. Chapters 6-22 examine real people who live in a real place in a future time. But make no mistake about it, what chapters 1-3 record as history past, chapters 6-22 record as future certainties. The events described will most assuredly transpire.

Scholars study these future events and classify them in a category known as *eschatology*. The term is derived from the Greek word *eschatos*[1] combined with the English word *logy*[2] to mean the study of last things. Some view it as the study of future events. Indeed, eschatology examines what the Christian anticipates in the future but it is based on what has been promised and on what has occurred in the past. "What comes under discussion in eschatology is not a knowledge of the future but first of all an acknowledgement of God as the One who is coming."[3] The key event in eschatology is the Second Coming of Christ ushering in the consummation of history. The Apostle Peter wrote that in the last days there would be people saying, "Where is the promise of His coming?" (2 Peter 3:14). He refers to those making such statements as scoffers and how they have forgotten that by the Word of God the heavens and the earth were spoken into existence. Although the coming events tarry, they will surely ensue according to His promise (2 Peter 3:9-13). Berkouwer writes,

---

[1] According to Spiro Zodhiates, the word means "with reference to time, the last, generally that which concludes anything. Spiro Zodhiates, *The Complete Word Study New Testament*, (AMG: Chatanooga, 1991), p. 916.

[2] The World Book Dictionary defines *logy* as "doctrine, study or science of."

[3] G. C. Berkouwer, *The Return of Christ*, (Grand Rapids: Eerdmans, 1972), p. 19.

> So this expectation of the future is unlike expectations that are grounded in either empirical historical events or relative and uncertain speculations. This expectation does not permit itself to become a mere hypothesis, a postulate, or the projection of human guesswork. It is and remains based on the word and the sure promise of God.[4]

Gordon Thomas writes,

> Biblical scholarship might do better justice to the material in Scripture by defining eschatology as the doctrine of ultimate things. Ultimate reality is not just what will transpire at the end of time, but that which has always existed in the heavenlies and which God apparently has always sought to make a present reality, according to the Law and the Prophets.[5]

In the final analysis "it is not the unknown of the future but the known in the future that is decisive for eschatological reflection."[6] "The real question is whether the biblical expectation is dubious or sure, uncertain or immovable."[7]

Eschatology is both personal and general.[8] The personal aspect is composed of death and the intermediate state.[9] The general tells of the Second Coming of Christ, the millennium, the final judgment, eternal punishment and reward, and the new heaven and the new

---

[4] Ibid., p.10.
[5] Gordon J. Thomas, "A Holy God Among a Holy People in a Holy Place: The Enduring Eschatological Hope," in Kent E. Brower and Mark W. Elloitt eds., *Eschatology in Biblical Theology*, (Downers Grove: Intervarsity, 1997), p. 55.
[6] Berkouwer, p.13.
[7] Ibid., p.24.
[8] Sometimes referred to as individual and cosmic.
[9] The intermediate state is that place or state which believers and unbelievers experience between death and resurrection. Believers experience the presence of God while unbelievers experience the absence of God.

earth. The personal is individual while the general is universal. This dual concept is not without debate. Some view the personal concept as being to narrow a perspective with the salvation of the individual subordinating the broader dimension of the end times. Others view the general as dwelling on the future events and subordinating the present. Berkouwer had it correct when he stated, "The universal encapsulates the personal; and during the time when the Lord has not yet returned, attention must also be focused on the life and death of the individual."[10] Study of future events must not be so focused that the believer overlooks the application of the expectation in the present.

Eschatology is dealt with in several ways. In his book *Christian Theology*, Millard Erickson discusses two opposing viewpoints. The first he labels as *eschatomania*. This describes a person with an intense preoccupation with eschatology seeing it behind every bush and tree making it the whole of theology. "As a result, some preachers and teachers have been caricatured as having the Bible in one hand and the newspaper in the other."

The opposite of this view Erickson calls *eschatophobia*. "This describes a person with a fear or aversion or at the very least an avoidance of discussing the topic. Because many of the issues of eschatology are obscure and difficult to deal with, some teachers and preachers choose to ignore the subject altogether."

These two extremes need to be avoided and a position that neither exalts eschatology above all else nor a position that seeks to hide from the topic can be acceptable. The Apostle Paul wrote to the Thessalonians and told them to comfort each other with the words he sent to them. Much of what Paul wrote to the Thessalonians involved eschatological issues. The believer must keep a balance regarding eschatology and not allow what is future to overshadow the present and not allow the present to diminish future expectations.[11]

---

[10] Berkouwer, p. 62.

[11] Millard J. Erickson, *Christian Theology*, (Grand Rapids: Baker, 1985), p. 1152, 1153.

Key Issues in Determining a View of Prophecy

There are several issues that must be considered in developing a view of prophecy in order to have a consistent understanding. The first issue is to determine an interpretive distinction. That means that the believer needs to determine how Scripture is to be interpreted. Is it primarily allegorical/symbolic or is it literal?

The allegory/symbolic method of interpretation understands that beneath the letter or the obvious of what is written is the real meaning intended. *Allegory* is defined by some as an extended metaphor. This method of interpretation was pioneered in the early church by Clement of Alexandria (ca A.D.150-215) and continued on by Origen (A.D. 185-254). Both of these men were influenced by Philo (25 B.C.-A.D. 45), a Hellenistic Jewish philosopher from Alexandria.

> Philo attempted to correlate the Old Testament revelation with philosophy and Greek piety by means of the allegorical method, thus opening the way to the Christian school of Alexandria, which preserved his works.[12]

"Clement saw . . . that if the church permanently shut itself off from Greek intellectual tradition, it would have to give up its mission to the educated classes."[13]

> Clement's great merit is that he saved the church from intellectual alienation from culture. With a sure grasp on the fundamental Christian realities, his comprehensive mind brought all the human learning of his day into the service of the church. He may have lacked some perspective and he may have overdrawn certain positions, but he made Christianity a religion that could stand on its own

---

[12] Jerald C. Brauer, ed. *The Westminster Dictionary of Church History*, (Philadelphia: Westminster Press, 1971), p. 657.
[13] Ibid, p. 212.

intellectually and compete with the rival claims of the other philosophical and religious positions of his time.[14]

Clement believed that God intentionally placed stumbling blocks to the reader in the literal meaning to awaken people's minds to find the hidden truths buried beneath the surface of the text.[15]

Origen spiritualized virtually every Christian doctrine . . . [His] method of exegesis was so subjective that it allowed for an almost infinite number of symbolic meanings and interpretations of the biblical text, most of which bore little resemblance to the plain meaning of the words.[16]

He acknowledged the existence of the literal method of interpretation but relegated it to the mass of Christians in general whom he considered to be weak in intelligence. He writes,

Then, finally, that the Scriptures were written by the Spirit of God, and have meaning, not such only as apparent at first sight, but also another, which escapes the notice of most. For those (words) which are written are the forms of certain mysteries, and the images of divine things. Respecting which there is one opinion throughout the whole Church, that the whole law is indeed spiritual; but that the spiritual meaning which the law conveys is not known to all, but to those only on whom the grace of the Holy Spirit is bestowed in the word of wisdom and learning.[17]

Origen's allegorical interpretation was widely accepted and

---

[14] Ibid, p. 213.
[15] Mal Couch, ed. *Dictionary of Premillennial Theology*, (Grand Rapids: Kregel, 1996), p.144.
[16] Ibid, p. 213.
[17] Origen, De Principiis, *www.newadvent.org/fathers/04121.htm*. Preface para. 8 7/12/2003.

deeply influenced Augustine whose influence is still felt today.[18] Mounce writes,

> In the Alexandrian church a spiritualizing approach was developing, in part because of the influence of Greek thought, the fact that centuries had passed without the establishment of the awaited kingdom . . . Origen played a major role in the rise of an allegorical method of exegesis. The mysteries of the Apocalypse can be learned only be going beyond the literal and historical to the spiritual. The spiritualizing method was greatly advanced by the work of Tyconius, who interpreted nothing by the historical setting or events of the first century. Augustine followed Tyconius in his capitulation to a totally mystical exegesis. For the next thousand years this allegorical method was normative for the interpretation of Revelation.[19]

In the third and fourth centuries A.D., reacting to the Alexandrian thought process of an allegorical interpretation of Scripture, early church leaders in the town of Antioch, Syria, emphasized a literal approach to interpreting Scripture. The literal method is that method that gives to each word the same exact basic meaning it would have in normal, ordinary, customary usage, whether employed in writing, speaking, or thinking. It is called the *grammatical-historical method* to emphasize the fact that the meaning is to be determined by both grammatical and historical considerations. Dr. David L. Cooper coined a statement regarding this method of interpretation known as Cooper's Golden Rule. It states,

> When the plain sense of Scripture makes common sense, seek no other sense; therefore, take every word at its primary,

---

[18] Couch, p. 289.
[19] Robert H. Mounce, *The Book of Revelation*, (Grand Rapids: Eerdmans, 1977), p. 25.

ordinary, usual, literal meaning unless the facts of the immediate context, studied in the light of related passages and axiomatic and fundamental truths, indicate clearly otherwise.

Dr. Cooper wrote,

By following this rule we avoid the many pitfalls of attempting to read into the text something that is not there, and failing to see what is actually expressed in the Sacred Word.[20]

The literal method of interpretation began to lose influence within the Church in the fourth and fifth centuries. The allegorical method became prevalent and remained that way until the reformation and the modern period.[21] The literal method of interpretation is the method used in this book.

Israel and the Church

The second issue that needs to be addressed is the distinction between Israel and the Church. The issue is whether the Church has superseded Israel in the eyes of God and thereby inherits all the promises made to Israel in the Old Testament or there is yet a future for Israel and God will keep His promises to them. The issues are as follows:

A. **The promise made to Israel in the Old Testament will be fulfilled in the Church.**

　　1. The Jews rejected Christ as their Messiah and continue to do so thereby forfeiting the right to be called the people of God.

---

[20] Biblical Research Study Group, www.biblicalresearch.info/page47.html.
[21] Couch, p. 149.

2. Jewish believers will be absorbed into the Church based on Paul's teaching that all distinctions between Jews and Gentiles ended in Christ.
3. The Old Testament is to be interpreted in light of the New Testament.
4. God's original plan was to establish Israel's earthly kingdom at the first coming of Christ.

Wayne Grudem could summarize this theory. He writes, "The church incorporates into itself all the true people of God, and almost all the titles used of God's people in the Old Testament are in one place or another applied to the church in the New Testament."[22] An important passage in Grudem's conclusion is 1 Peter 2:4-10. About this passage, Grudem writes,

> Peter says that God has bestowed on the church almost all the blessings promised to Israel in the Old Testament . . . What further statement could be needed in order for us to say with assurance that the church has now become the true Israel of God and will receive all the blessings promised to Israel in the Old Testament.[23]

B. God will yet fulfill His covenants with Israel.

1. God's promise is certain and irrevocable.
2. A key factor in Jesus' message was His future coming. It was not an afterthought but God's original plan.
3. The New Testament should be seen as the climax of the plan of God that unfolded in the Old Testament. The New Testament can not be understood without the basis that is established in the Old Testament. For example, how is Jesus to be understood as the Lamb of God who

---

[22] Wayne Grudem, *Systematic Theology*, (Leicester: InterVarsity Press, 1994), p. 862.
[23] Ibid., p. 863.

>   takes away the sin of the world without an understanding of the sacrificial system established in the Old Testament?
> 4. Paul concludes his forceful argument regarding the Jews in Romans 9-11 by saying "All Israel will be saved."

Edwin Blum counters Grudem's argument above regarding 1 Peter 2: 9,10. He writes,

> Peter applies to the church various terms originally spoken concerning Israel. But this does not mean that the church is Israel or even that the church replaces Israel in the plan of God. Romans 11 should help us to guard against that misinterpretation . . . In the future, according to Paul, God will once again use Israel to bless the world (cf. Romans 11:13-16, 23-24).[24]

After having reasoned through chapters 9-11 of Romans with a series of twenty-seven questions, Paul ends his discourse by dictating to Tertius a doxology of praise. He is overwhelmed with the wisdom and knowledge that God has given to him and has allowed him to convey to his first-century readers and subsequently to every other reader since. "Has God cast away His people? Certainly not! . . . all Israel will be saved . . . for the gifts and calling of God are irrevocable" (Romans 11:1, 26, 29). "How unsearchable are His judgments and His ways past finding out!"(Romans 11:33b). He must have shouted these words in excitement to Tertius. For as brilliant as Paul was, he did not conclude that God was finished with Israel but that God was yet to use them in a mighty way. This book takes the position that God yet has a plan for Israel and He will carry it out.

The Millennium

The third issue necessary to determine a prophetic view of Revelation is the millennium. The word itself, just like the words *rapture* or *trinity*, does not appear in Scripture. The word means

---

[24] Edwin A. Blum, "1, 2 Peter," *The Expositors Bible Commentary*, ed. Frank Gaeblein, vol. 12. (Grand Rapids: Zondervan, 1981), p. 231.

one thousand years. Revelation 20 mentions this time frame six times in the first seven verses. There are three basic positions regarding the millennium

Amillennialism

Much controversy has surrounded this time frame. Those who interpret Revelation using the allegorical/symbolic method see the millennium as an indefinite period of time. This view is often referred to as *amillennial*. The word means no millennium. The prefix *a* means not or without. It is of Greek origin and is called the alpha *privative*. The *a* stands for *alpha* which is the first letter of the Greek alphabet combined with *privative* which means to take away. The *a* corresponds to the English prefix *un*. An example would be the word apathy (*a* without + *pathos* feeling). In English a synonym would be *unfeeling*.[25] Amillennialists believe that the millennium is spiritual and not physical. There are two schools of thought among amillennialists. The first school believes that the millennium is being fulfilled only in heaven as Christ reigns over the glorified saints. The second school believes the millennium is being fulfilled in the present age in the church and is on the earth.[26]

Postmillennialism

Another millennial position is known as postmillennialism. As the name implies, those holding this view see the Second Coming of Christ as being post or after the period known as the millennium. Postmillennialists see this time frame as being "the entire period of time between the two advents of Christ."[27] Postmillennialist Kenneth Gentry defines postmillennialism this way.

> Postmillennialism expects the proclaiming of the Spirit-blessed gospel of Jesus Christ to win the vast majority of

---

[25] See The World Book Dictionary, 1981 p. 1.
[26] Paul N. Benware, *Understanding End Times Prophecy*, (Chicago: Moody, 1995), p. 105, 106.
[27] Ibid., p. 121.

human beings to salvation in the present age. Increasing gospel success will gradually produce a time in history prior to Christ's return in which faith, righteousness, peace, and prosperity will prevail in the affairs of people and of nations. After an extensive era of such conditions the Lord will return visibly, bodily, and in great glory, ending history with the general resurrection and the great judgment of all mankind.[28]

Premillennialism

Those who interpret Revelation using the literal method see this millenium as a literal one thousand years that will begin after the Second Coming of Christ and will usher in a period of righteousness where Christ will rule the world with a rod of iron. This is a time period yet in the future. The prefix *pre* in this designation indicates that Christ will return prior to the time known as the millennium. This book takes the position that the one thousand years is a literal one thousand years. More discussion on this topic will occur in the discussion of Revelation 20.

The Four Systems of Interpreting Revelation

There are generally four schools of thought concerning the interpretation of the Book of Revelation. It is important to at least have some familiarity of these different interpretive methods even if a person has been taught only one.

The Preterist View

The word *preterist* comes from the Latin word *praeteritus* meaning gone by, past, past and gone, departed.[29] This view holds that the events described in the Book of Revelation took place during the time of the author and thus has already occurred. Preterist Kenneth

---

[28] Kenneth L. Gentry, Jr., "Postmillennialism," in *Three Views of the Millennium and Beyond*, ed. Darrell L. Bock, (Grand Rapids: Zondervan, 1999), p. 13-14.

[29] Carlton T. Lewis, *An Elementary Latin Dictionary*, (New York: Harper and Brothers, 1891), p. 644.

Gentry writes, "Preterism holds that the bulk of John's prophecies occur in the first century, soon after his writing of them. Though the prophecies were in the future when John wrote them and when his original audience read them, they are now in the past."[30]

The Historical View

This view teaches that God revealed the entire church age in advance through the symbolic visions of the Apocalypse. "For example, the breaking of the seven seals (chapters 6-7) is often said to be barbarian invasions that sacked the western Roman Empire. The scorpion/locusts that come out of the bottomless pit (chapter 9) are the Arab hordes attacking the eastern Roman Empire, followed by the Turks, represented as the horses with serpents for tails and flamethrowers for mouths. The beast (chapter 13) represents the Roman papacy."[31] Many leaders of the Protestant Reformation including Martin Luther held this view but the majority of modern commentators are not in agreement.

The Idealist View

Those holding this view see the events in the Book of Revelation as being timeless. There is no sequence of events nor are there illusions to actual historical situations. Everything in the book is taken symbolically. It describes a spiritual conflict and not a physical experience.[32] This system can't really be defined, but it can be described. Idealist Sam Hamstra, Jr. describes it this way,

> Scholars describe this pictorial presentation of truth as apocalyptic, a style of communication and writing

---

[30] Kenneth L. Gentry, Jr., "A Preterist View of Revelation," in *Four Views on the Book of Revelation*, ed. C. Marvin Pate, (Grand Rapids: Zondervan, 1998), p. 37.

[31] Steve Gregg, *Revelation Four Views A Parallel Commentary*, (Nashville: Nelson, 1997), p. 34.

[32] Tim Lahaye, *Revelation Illustrated and Made Plain*, (Grand Rapids: Zondervan, 1975), p. 4.

characterized by bold colors, vivid images, unique symbols, a simple story line, a hero, a happy ending. Thus, in Revelation you meet angels, animals, and numbers. You see lightning and hear thunder. You witness earthquakes and battles. You see the sparkle of jewels and a woman clothed with the sun facing a terrifying dragon. You see a rider on a white horse and hear the lyrics of the Hallelujah Chorus.

You approach apocalyptic literature differently than you would a letter or one of the gospels. In Revelation, words take the place of pigments and brushes to create a portrait designed to visualize great principles, not particular incidents. Resisting the temptation to dissect the portrait described in each vision, you let the vision as a whole impress you.[33]

The Futurist View

This view understands the events in Revelation chapters 4-22 as being future events. The futurist interprets Revelation literally except where the clear meaning is symbolic. Robert Thomas comments, "The futurist approach to the book is the only one that gives sufficient recognition to the prophetic style of the book and a normal hermeneutical[34] pattern of interpretation based on that style. It views the book as focusing on the last period(s) of world history and outlining the various events and their relationships to one another."[35] John MacArthur writes, "Anything other than the futurist approach leaves the meaning of the book to human ingenuity and opinion. The futurist approach takes the

---

[33] Sam Hamstra, Jr., "The Idealist View of Revelation," in *Four Views on the Book of Revelation*, ed. C. Marvin Pate, (Grand Rapids: Zondervan, 1998), p. 97-98.
[34] *Hermeneutics* is the study of the principles of interpretation.
[35] Robert L. Thomas, *Revelation 1-7 An Exegetical Commentary*, Chicago: Moody, 1992), p. 32.

books meaning as God gave it."[36] This book is based on the futurists' interpretation of Scripture.

It is the purpose of this introduction to establish in the reader's mind the issues that need to be addressed in order to have a deeper understanding of the Book of Revelation. However, it should be pointed out that there are "disputable matters" (Romans 14:1 NIV) in the church. Warren Wiersbe writes, "There are certain truths that all Christians must accept because they are the foundation for the faith. But areas of honest disagreement must not be made a test of fellowship."[37] All of the views mentioned above believe in the literal bodily return of Christ. Each system of interpretation, however, sees that event happening differently. Daniel Lewis writes,

> The various eschatological systems superimposed upon the text of Scripture attempt to provide interpretations of the biblical data that are cohesive, logical, and plausible. Since these systems sharply differ at various points, it is clear that they cannot all be right. In fact, we must recognize the possibility that while they can't all be right, they all could be wrong . . . I suspect that when everything has come to an end, and when every knee bows before Christ to proclaim Him as Lord to the glory of the Father, none of us will be looking around to see if our neighbors are wearing the wrong eschatological hat.[38]

---

[36] John MacArthur, *Revelation 1-11*, (Chicago: Moody, 1999), p. 11.
[37] Warren Wiersbe, *Be Right*, Colorado Springs: Victor, 1977), p. 160.
[38] Daniel L. Lewis, *3 Crucial Questions about the Last Days*, Grand Rapids: Baker, 1998), p. 130, 133.

CHAPTER ONE

The Patmos Experience

The opening verse of the Book of Revelation answers four very important questions concerning the remainder of the book: (1) Verse one tells the reader what the book is about. It is the revelation of Jesus Christ. The word translated *revelation* "means an uncovering of something hidden, the making known of what we could not find out for ourselves."[39] God gave this revelation to Jesus who in turn sent His angel to deliver it to John.

The question that immediately comes to mind is what or who is revealed? Hendricksen writes, "It is a revelation or unveiling of the plan of God for the history of the world, especially of the Church. It is called the Revelation of Jesus Christ because Jesus Christ showed it to John and through him to the Church."[40] In other words, it is revelation from Jesus Christ. Thomas concurs when he states, "it refers to data that Jesus Christ was inspired by God to reveal to His servants."[41] Gregg refers to this revelation as presenting a certain ambiguity with Jesus being either the subject being revealed or the one doing the revealing.[42] Walvoord writes "It is a revelation of truth about Christ Himself, a disclosure of future events, that is, His Second Coming when Christ will be revealed. It is as well a revelation which comes from Christ."[43]

---

[39] Leon Morris, *The Book of Revelation*, (Grand Rapids: Erdmans, 1999), p. 46.
[40] William Hendricksen, *More Than Conquerors*, (Grand Rapids: Baker, 1998), p. 51.
[41] Thomas, p. 52.
[42] Gregg, p. 52.
[43] John F. Walvoord, *The Revelation of Jesus Christ*, (Chicago: Moody, 1966), p. 35.

The Book of Revelation reveals or uncovers many divine truths. But, according to MacArthur,

> Supremely, overarching all those features, the Book of Revelation reveals the majesty and glory of the Lord Jesus Christ . . . While this book is certainly revelation from Jesus Christ, it is also the revelation about Him. The other New Testament uses of the phrase *apocalupsis Iesou Christou* (Revelation of Jesus Christ) suggest that John's statement in this verse is best understood in the sense of revelation about Jesus Christ.[44]

Prior to the writing of this book, Christ had been revealed in person during the forty days between His resurrection and His ascension to heaven, in oral tradition as the first-century Christians shared what they knew personally of the Risen Lord, and in writing through the efforts of Matthew, Mark, Luke, and John. Christ had been revealed as the savior, the Lamb of God who takes away the sin of the world. John, the writer of this book, was well aware of the revelation of Jesus in this way. He experienced it personally and wrote about it.

So the question arises that if John had already seen the Risen Lord on numerous occasions, preached the Risen Lord to those he ministered to, and wrote about the Risen Lord in his gospel, why was he afraid to the point of passing out when he saw the Risen Lord on Patmos? The obvious answer is that what he saw on Patmos was a manifestation of the Risen Lord that he had not experienced before. Instead of seeing Jesus as the Lamb of God who takes away the sin of the world as he wrote in John 1:29, he sees the Jesus described in Revelation 6:15,16. This Jesus is depicted as the Lamb of God that has the kings of the earth, the great men, the rich men, the commanders, the mighty men, every slave, and every free man begging for the mountains and rocks to fall on them to hide them from the wrath of the Lamb.

---

[44] MacArthur, p. 15,16.

John falls at the feet of the Risen Lord as dead because he has never seen the victorious Lamb prepared for His Second Coming in order to judge those who dwell on the earth and to deliver those who have been in bondage to Satan. This is the revelation of Jesus Christ in all His glory and majesty. The plan of God that Hendricksen refers to is surely revealed. So too, the data that is passed on to John through His angel about which Thomas speaks. It is also the disclosure of future events as stated by Walvoord. But overshadowing all the events depicted in the book is the revelation of Jesus Christ and Christ alone as sovereign and Lord. This is what John saw and this is what John conveyed to his readers.

Verse one tells the readers (2) the mode of delivery of the message. The revelation that is about to be unveiled is given by God. In the high priestly prayer of Jesus recorded by John in chapter 17:9 of his gospel, Jesus says, "For I have given to them the words which you have given Me" (New King James Version). While on earth, Jesus conveyed to His disciples the words, which God the Father wanted Him to convey. The result was that "they have received them and have known surely that I came forth from You, and they have believed that You sent Me" (NKJV). The same pattern is established in the last book of the New Testament. God gives Jesus the revelation to give to John.

The only information that we have about God is that which He chooses to reveal to us. In Matthew 16:15, Jesus asks His disciples "Who do you say that I am?" (NKJV). Peter answering for the group says, "You are the Christ, the son of the living God." Jesus replied, "Blessed are you Simon-Bar Jonah, for flesh and blood has not reveal this to you, but My Father who is in heaven" (NKJV). When God wants His people to have spiritual knowledge, He reveals it to them; thus, God gives the revelation.

Verse one tells us (3) why God gave the revelation. The phrase "which God gave Him to show His servants things which must shortly take place" indicates that God wanted the followers of Christ to know something they had not previously known. God is willing and ready to reveal Jesus Christ to whoever is willing and ready to discover Him. The things which must shortly take place will add to the revelation that John and his subsequent readers will experience. Those things will reveal the glory and majesty of the victorious Lamb.

Unfortunately the Book of Revelation has received a bad rap. David Reagan writes that when he was growing up, his pastor taught the church that the Book of Revelation was like a Chinese puzzle. "Nobody can understand it. Nobody ever has." This thought process articulated to the congregation did not enhance anyone's appreciation for the study of the book. As a matter of fact Reagan states,

> The effect was to create a psychological barrier in my mind. I have since discovered that this mental barrier against the book exists in the thinking of most professing Christians, regardless of what church they grew up in.[45]

In the very first verse of the book the author states that not only is the message understandable, but that God has given it for that very purpose. The book was

> Not designed to mystify, but rather to explain the truth of God more clearly. For this reason one should approach it with the expectation of learning, and not with the expectation of being confused.[46]

Verse one tells us (4) to whom the revelation was given. The verse simply says that John was the one to whom the angel communicated Christ's message. In John's day he was known and revered. The mention of the name John in the area of Asia Minor would have alerted the Church as to the exact identification. Were there more men in Asia Minor at that time named John? Certainly. But by this author identifying himself simply as John three times

---

[45] Dr. David Reagan, *Wrath and Glory*, (Green Forest: New Leaf, 2001), p. 18.
[46] Merrill C. Tenney, *Interpreting Revelation*, (Peabody: Hendricksen, 1957), p. 28.

in the first chapter of the book and once in the concluding chapter, he leaves little room for the possibility that his readers will not know his identity. He is recognizable to them as authoritative. They know who he is.

If you heard the following statement would you, by any reasonable standard, understand clearly to whom the statement refers?

> Elvis is an icon for the last half of the twentieth century. Identify which Elvis is referred to in this statement.
>
> A) Elvis Grbac
> B) Elvis Costello
> C) Elvis Presley

You would immediately rule out the first two choices even though they are real people living during the same time frame and are celebrities in their own right. You would select Elvis Presley because of his renown. The same premise holds true for identifying John the apostle as the one to whom this revelation was given.

Beginning with Justin Martyr in about 130-165 and continuing through Hippolytus, who died in 236, the testimony was nearly unanimous in favor of John the apostle as the author of this book. However, in the middle of the third century, Dionysius, bishop of Alexandria and a man of exceptional rhetorical skills, began questioning the authorship and suggested that there was another John who lived in Ephesus at this time and that it was one known as John the Elder who was the author of the book. Dionysius gave as evidence of the differences in the style of the writings between John's gospel and letters, which he considered authentic, and the writing of Revelation. He writes,

> Therefore that he is called John, and that this book is the work of one John, I do not deny. And I agree that it is the work of a holy and inspired man. But I cannot admit that he was the apostle, the son of Zebedee, the brother of James, by

whom the Gospel of John and the Catholic Epistle was written. For I judge from the character of both, and the forms of expression, and the entire execution of the book, that it is not his. For the evangelist nowhere gives his name, or proclaims himself, either in the Gospel or Epistle.[47]

Perhaps the best argument for apostolic authorship was given by Guthrie when he wrote,

> In the second and early third centuries, the following writers clearly witness to their belief in apostolic authorship: Justin, Irenaeus, Clement, Origen, Tertullian, Hippolytus. Indeed they assume it without discussion. So strong is this evidence that it is difficult to believe that they all made a mistake in confusing John of the Apocalypse with John the Apostle. The usual treatment of this evidence by those who deny apostolic authorship is to suppose that these early fathers were unaware of the true origin of the book, and, therefore, guessed that John must have been the well-known son of Zebedee. This has frequently been based on the theory of two Ephesian Johns, who could quite easily be mixed up, or else on the theory that the only John of Ephesus was the elder who was later mistaken for the apostle. If all this evidence is due to a mistake it would be an extraordinary case of mistaken identity. It must be concluded that taken as a whole it points very strongly to the probability that the John of the Apocalypse was, in fact, John the Apostle.[48]

At this point, the question arises as to what difference all this debate makes. Does it matter that John the Apostle or John the Elder or some other John wrote the book? Does the authorship change the message? No, the book says what it says. It is not the

---

[47] Eusebius, *The History of the Church*, (London: Penguin, 1989), 7.25.2.

[48] Donald Guthrie, *New Testament Introduction*, (Downers Grove: Intervarsity, 1990), p. 933.

message but rather the authority behind the message that becomes important. Rejection of apostolic authorship led to severe questions about canonicity.[49]

> The Greek word *kanon* literally means a reed. It was a tool used by a carpenter or builder, and thus referred to a straight rod or bar. The term gradually came to signify written laws, which serve as rules of behavior. Later, it came to mean a list or catalogue, which is close to our usage of the term. Since a canon was the general rule of doctrine or practice, the Scriptures that were generally recognized by the Church could be described as canonical or canonized. Thus a canon is a list of writings considered to be God's revelation to His people and which serves as the authority for their faith and practice.[50]

The Book of Revelation has not always enjoyed the acceptance of all scholars. In 140 Marcion who is described as a defector from the orthodox strain of Christianity by the *Westminster Dictionary of Church History* rejected the book in its entirety.[51] In the third century, Gaius, a presbyter of the church, was a militant opponent of a heretical movement known as Montanism.[52] Montanus was a priest of Cybele who appeared in Asia Minor claiming to be sent from the Holy Spirit to bring into the Christian Church the final stage of revelation. The prominence of prophetesses and ecstatic language led church leaders to the conclusion that pagan practices and thought were trying to make their way into the Church. Montanus was using Revelation to foster his movement.[53] Gaius hoped to discredit the movement by denying the canonical status

---

[49] Mounce, p. 23.
[50] Clayton Harrop, *History of the New Testament in Plain Language*, (Waco: Word, 1984), p. 105.
[51] Brauer. p. 524.
[52] Ibid., p. 349.
[53] Ibid., p. 569.

of Revelation. As already mentioned, Dionysius tried to discredit the book. Eusebius, writing in the fourth century, quotes Dionysius:

> Among Spurious books must be placed . . . the Revelation of John, if this seems the right place for it: as I said before, some reject it, others include it among the Recognized Books . . . These would all be classed with the Disputed Books, but I have been obliged to list the latter separately, distinguishing those writings which according to the tradition of the Church are true, genuine, and recognized from those in a different category, not canonical, but disputed, yet familiar to most churchmen; for we must not confuse these with the writings published by heretics under the name of the apostles, as containing either Gospels of Peter, Thomas, Matthias and several others besides these, or Acts of Andrew, John and other apostles. To none of these has any churchman of any generation ever seen fit to refer in his writings. Again, nothing could be further from apostolic usage than the type of phraseology employed, while the ideas and implications of their contents are so irreconcilable with true orthodoxy that they stand revealed as the forgeries of heretics. It follows that so far from being classed even among Spurious Books they must be thrown out as impious and beyond pale.[54]

The early attempt to deny apostolic authorship was for the express purpose of insuring the book to be considered non-authoritative. Only authoritative books were read in the churches at that time. Books were not plentiful and those writings that were considered authoritative were read to the congregations as they met for worship. Revelation contains a blessing for those who read and those who hear the message. If the book were non-apostolic, it would not be read and consequently would have gone the way of other non-canonical writings.

---

[54] Eusebius, 3.25.2

The book was accepted as authoritative in the West from the second century. However, the Eastern Church took a little longer to endorse it. By 680 when the Council of Constantinople ratified it, the Apocalypse received formal acceptance as New Testament literature.[55]

Even though the New Testament canon was closed there remained critics of Revelation as being rightfully accorded canonical status.

> The Reformation period witnessed a renewal of the earlier questions concerning its apostolic authorship and canonical status. Thus Luther, offended by the contents of Revelation, declared that he regarded it as neither apostolic nor prophetic.[56]

> Luther, for instance, relegated it to secondary status in his New Testament, saying, "My spirit cannot accommodate itself to this book. There is one sufficient reason for the small esteem in which I hold it—that Christ is neither taught nor recognized.[57]

What criteria were used to determine the acceptance of writings into the canon? What separated some writings from other writings? First, and perhaps most important, was the idea that the writing was written by an apostle or the follower of an apostle.[58] If in fact the dissenters from the early church view regarding apostolic authorship were correct, then Revelation does not belong in the New Testament canon and should be rejected as non-authoritative. Luther and other reformers of the 1500s would be pleased at such

---

[55] Mounce, p. 24.
[56] Alan F. Johnson, *The Expositors Bible Commentary*, ed. Frank Gaebelein Vol. 12," (Grand Rapids: Zondervan, 1981), p. 404.
[57] D. A. Carson, Douglas J. Moo, and Leon Morris, *An Introduction to the New Testament*, (Grand Rapids: Zondervan, 1992), p. 481.
[58] Harrop, p. 127.

a turn of events. However, Revelation still holds its place in the canon and is properly looked to today as a life jacket in a sea of hopelessness.

> The inclusion of Revelation in the canon indicates that it was recognized by the majority of the church as a genuine disclosure of prophetic truth and that it deserved a place with the Gospels and the other writings, which constituted the written platform of the new covenant in Christ.[59]

Verse two tells us John's response to having received the revelation. He bore witness to the Word of God and the testimony of Jesus Christ, to all things that he saw. It was not God's intent for John to experience the fullness of the revelation and then bask in that afterglow. It was His intent that John share that experience with as many people as he could, up to and including, readers as far removed as the twenty-first century. John was a witness and he testified to what he saw.

John was not selective in his witness. It would have been very easy for him to share the wonder of the Risen Lord. How majestic and awesome the images must have been to him. But, verse two says that he bore witness to all things that he saw. The majestic and awesome were mixed in with the gruesome and grotesque. John was faithful in sharing the entire context of his experience on Patmos. John was a servant of Jesus Christ. A servant does what his master commands. John was given this task of communicating this prophecy because he was a servant. He had already served his master for more than sixty years. Now, as a result of his faithfulness, he is given another opportunity to serve the Risen Lord. He had been faithful in the past and he would be faithful again in bearing witness to all that he saw.

Verse three introduces the first of the seven beatitudes found in Revelation. A *beatitude* is a literary form, which begins with the word *blessed*, and anticipates some appropriate reward from God.[60]

---

[59] Tenney, p. 17.
[60] Emory Stevens Bucke, ed. *The Interpreter's Dictionary of the Bible*, 4 vols. (Nashville: Abingdon, 1962), p. 369.

In the Sermon on the Mount Matthew records nine beatitudes. Paul records three in his letter to the Romans, and John records one in his Gospel. Beatitudes in Revelation are found in 1:3; 14:3; 16:15; 19:9; 20:6; 22:7,14.

The beatitudes represent the first set of sevens found in Revelation. There is the seven—fold Spirit, the seven churches, the seven lampstands, and the seven stars in the first chapter alone. Seven in Scripture is one of the perfect numbers along with three, ten, and twelve. It is the number of spiritual perfection.[61]

> In Hebrew seven is shevah. It is from the root, which means to be full or satisfied, have enough of. Hence the meaning of the word "seven" is dominated by this root, for on the seventh day God rested from the work of creation. It was full and complete, good and perfect. Nothing could be added to it or taken from it without marring it . . . It is seven, therefore, that stamps with perfection and completeness that in connection with which it is used.[62]

In the New Testament and especially in Revelation, the number seven denotes in general the final eschatological appearance of God, encompassing everything.[63]

> This number seven indicates completeness. It harmonizes very well with the idea that the symbols refer to principles of human conduct and of divine government that are always operative especially throughout this entire dispensation.[64]

In this first beatitude, John is pronouncing a blessing on the one who reads the prophecy and the one who listens and keeps the prophecy. In the first century, church scrolls were not plentiful as

---

[61] E. W. Bullinger, *Number in Scripture*, (Grand Rapids: Kregel, 1967), p. 23
[62] Ibid., p. 167-168.
[63] Verlyn D. Verbrugge, ed. *The NIV Theological Dictionary of New Testament Words*, (Grand Rapids: Zondervan, 2000), p. 464.
[64] Hendricksen, p. 42.

our Bibles are today. Since most people in this era were unable to read, in order for the church to hear the prophecy, someone would have to stand before the congregation and read it to them. Each church may have had one copy, providing someone took the time to copy it before it went to the next congregation. The reader would in effect get a double blessing, one for reading the book and another for hearing and keeping the words found in the book.

The thought of keeping the words found in the book echoes the words of Jesus in Luke 11:28 where He states, "Blessed are those who hear the word of God and keep it." The words John wrote were not merely foretelling what was to happen in the future, they were an admonition to better behavior on the part of the hearer.

Verse three tells us what type of book with which we are dealing. Within the beatitude John identifies his writing as prophecy. Not only does John identify the book as prophecy in verse 3 but he makes the same claim four times in the concluding chapter (22:7, 10, 18, 19). Vine's defines prophecy as "signifying the speaking forth of the mind and counsel of God."[65] A *prophet* is one who proclaims a message, which he received via direct communication, a messenger, or through visions or dreams. Prophecy is both foretelling of future events and a forth telling taken from that which is already revealed.

Much has been made about the genre of the Book of Revelation. *Genre* is from the French meaning type or category. Today we have fiction and non-fiction. Within the fiction category there are Western novels, romance novels, science-fiction etc. Studies have been made analyzing literary features such as structure, style, and content among others. Scholars have been unable to agree upon an acceptable conclusion.

The debate centers around a literary genre known to exist from the first century B.C. through the second century A.D. categorized

---

[65] W. E. Vine, Merrill F. Unger, William White, Jr., *Vine's Complete Expository Dictionary of Old and New Testament Words*, (Nashville: Nelson, 1985), p. 492.

as apocalyptic. This type of literature flourished in periods of undue difficulty and defeat. It was characterized by its imagery, symbolism, and visions. Since Revelation was written during this same period and in a time of serious persecution and conflict for the early believers, it is assumed that the writing is apocalyptic.

In the early church this type of writing was prolific. However, much of this work was written for a specified audience who would understand the symbolism the author was trying to convey. Because its purpose was to mask the real message from unintended readers, the meaning is virtually incomprehensible to readers far removed from the original audience.

Perhaps an example would clear up the confusion. Project yourself one thousand years into the future working on an archaeological dig. You discover a fragment of a manuscript containing ten pages. The fragment speaks of a large population suddenly disappearing from planet earth without notice. They are just gone. Those remaining on earth are perplexed as to where this large population group went and why they went there. Those remaining on earth were simply left behind. The more you read, the more obvious it becomes that the material you discovered is similar to the Book of Revelation. You have unearthed a fragment of the *Left Behind Series* authored by Tim LaHaye and Jerry Jenkins. Now despite the fact that this series is based on Scripture, it is not Scripture. It is fiction. It is the imagination of two men who are trying to convey in a literary format how the end times could occur. Would you compare this with Scripture in order to determine truth? Of course not! Yet, that is exactly what those who hold to structural criticism maintain. They want to compare the fiction written during the time period 200 B.C. to 100 A.D. with the Word of God.

Revelation claims for itself to be prophetic. If it was in fact communicated by God to Jesus to John via an angel, the choice of literary style was chosen by God and not by John. The other writings compared to Revelation as being of the same genre were writings whereby the author himself chose the style and method of his writing. These writings to which Revelation is compared were not considered authoritative by the early Church in the days when they were written nor have they been considered authoritative through the course of church history. Trying to fit Revelation into a genre replete with works deemed spurious seems to be a non-productive task given the clear message that the book is prophetic in nature.

John concludes verse three with the phrase "for the time is near." The blessing associated with the keeping of the prophecy takes on somewhat of an urgency. This phrase coupled with the phrase "things which must shortly take place" have led many to assume that the prophecy of Revelation must have taken place in the first century in order for the initial readers of the work to derive any meaning.

> The events of Revelation "must soon [Gk. Tachos] take place" (v. 1) because "the time is near" [Gk. Engys].
>
> Greek lexicons and modern translations agree that these terms indicate temporal proximity. Throughout the New Testament *tachos* means "quickly, at once, without delay, shortly." The term *engys* ("near") also speaks of temporal nearness . . . The inspired Apostle John clearly informs his original audience nearly two thousand years ago that they should expect the prophecies to "take place" in their lifetime.[66]

The argument follows that in order for John's original audience to have any meaning from the book, the things prophesied in it must come true within the generation of those receiving the initial prophecy. Gregg proposes the question as to whether the original human readers of Revelation would share the perspective that events occurring two thousand years in the future would be viewed by them as near.[67]

---

[66] Pate, p. 40-41.
[67] Gregg, p. 53.

Johnson writes concerning this issue of *shortly*:

> That soonness means imminency in eschatological terms. The church in every age has always lived with an expectancy of the consummation of all things in its day. Imminency describes an event possible in any day, impossible in no day.[68]

Herschel Hobbs writes,

> John speaks of things "which must shortly come to pass" . . . What does shortly mean? Some say it means suddenly. Others say that it means certainly. Some say it means both. I think it means that whatever is going to happen is certainly going to happen, and when it does happen it will be suddenly.[69]

Ray Summers writes,

> The closing statement of the third verse, "for the time is at hand," is a restatement of the truth that the message is an unveiling of events which are to take place shortly. This does not mean that every detail of the book is to see an immediate fulfillment. The interval of time between the beginning of relief for the Christian and the final consummation was not revealed to John; neither he nor the other Christians needed to see that. They needed the assurance of immediate relief and final and complete victory. That is exactly what was given to them.[70]

In Genesis 3:14-19, God addressed the serpent, Eve, and Adam regarding the disobedience in the Garden of Eden. Each played a part. In 3:15 God says to the serpent, "And I will put enmity

---

[68] Johnson, p. 417.
[69] G. R. Beasley-Murray, Herschell H. Hobbs, Ray Frank Robbins, *Revelation: Three Views*, (Nashville: Broadman, 1977), p. 77.
[70] Ray Summers, *Worthy Is The Lamb*, (Nashville: Broadman, 1951), p. 100.

between you and the woman, and between your seed and her Seed; and He shall bruise your head, and you shall bruise His heel." Commentators consider this passage as the "first gospel" or the embryonic promise of the Messiah. However, the Messiah didn't come for some four thousand years depending on the date used to determine the time of Adam and Eve. Since this represents so long a period of time would we argue that the promise meant nothing to the people to whom it was delivered?

God promised Abram His blessing to be a great nation living in a land of his own whereby those who blessed him would be blessed and those who cursed him would be cursed. Yet, that promise didn't see fulfillment initially for hundreds of years later when Joshua led the Israelites into the Promised Land. Did this promise mean nothing to the people to whom it was delivered?

The Book of Hebrews answers this question when it states, "Now faith is the substance of things hoped for, the evidence of things not seen. For by it the elders obtained a good testimony." By faith Abel, Noah, Abraham, and Moses experienced the fulfillment of the promise but, "Having seen them far off were assured of them, embraced them, and confessed that they were strangers on the earth."

If God worked in this manner in the "men of old," why would we not expect Him to work in the same way in the Book of Revelation? The promises made to the first readers of this revelation given by God to Jesus and communicated through His angel to John was given to assure those readers and every reader of every age thereafter, that God is sovereign and in control. Believers in the early Church, believers today, and believers in future time until the Lord comes can rest in the assurance that God is in control and can look forward with wonder and expectation of being in the very presence of the God that makes and delivers such wonderful promises.

In verse four, John introduces his first audience. He is writing this communiqué to the seven churches, which are in Asia. The Asia he is referring to is the land of western Asia located between the Black Sea on the north, the Mediterranean Sea on the south, and the Aegean Sea on the west. Throughout history the area has been called by many names. Anatolia being one. Probably the most prominent name, however, is Asia Minor. Today it is known as Turkey.

A knowledge of the geography of the region opens the readers' mind to the rugged life travelers faced in this area. Because of the natural divides, a cultural distinction can be seen often ending in a fragmented society composed of diverse tribes competing for dominance.

> The major part of Anatolia's interior consists of relatively level terrain, but the border regions show far greater differences in relief. The sharp contrast between the central and border areas is the most striking geographical feature of Anatolia or present day Turkey. Going from north to south, one first passes a high mountain range. Then barren undulating or flat plateaus, interrupted only by low mountain ridges, and in the south again a high mountain chain. The mountains in the north and south reach an altitude ranging from 2000 to 3000 meters (9000 feet). The highland plateau between the two mountain zones is about 1,000 meters above sea level and increases in height toward the east.
>
> It must be taken into account that the natural road network is oriented mainly in an east-west direction rather than on a north-south axis. The Anatolian rivers although unnavigable often determined the course of roads for trade and routes for military campaigns and frequently played an important role in political history as boundaries.
>
> In spite of the essentially favorable sea borders, the mountains on the northern and southern coasts and the innumerable large and small valleys that characterize parts of the central plateau—surrounded by low mountain ridges and often traversed by a river—tend to promote a fragmentation of political power and perhaps linguistic diversification.[71]

---

[71] Jack M. Sasson, ed., *Civilizations of the Ancient Near East*, vol. 1, (New York: Simon & Schuster MacMillan, 1995), p. 259-261.

All seven churches are located in the western coastal area of Asia Minor. A look back at the history of this area of the world is helpful in beginning to understand the significance of where this country came from and where it is today.

According to Turkish tour guides, the first mention of the country goes back to Genesis 2:10-14 where Moses describes the area of the Garden of Eden. The two rivers that are mentioned in those verses, the Tigris and the Euphrates, have their source in eastern Turkey. The Tigris winds southeasterly for approximately 1,150 miles through what is now Iraq and joins the Euphrates about 120 miles from the Persian Gulf.

The water that forms the Euphrates River originates in the Turkish highlands and flows to east central Turkey. From there it flows approximately 1,799 miles until it joins the Tigris near Al Qurnah in Iraq. The ancient land of Mesopotamia was so called because it meant the land between the rivers. The Tigris and Euphrates flow roughly parallel and are never more than 100 miles apart.

In light of the fact that scholars are not certain where the four rivers of Genesis 2 were located, we can't be dogmatic about the location of the Garden of Eden. However, we cannot simply dismiss the notion that Eden actually existed in this part of the world.

Genesis 8:4 tells us that the ark which carried Noah, his wife, his three sons and their wives came to rest on the mountains of Ararat. Mount Ararat's highest peak is 16,940 feet and is located in eastern Turkey near the modern borders of Armenia and Iran. When Noah and his sons disembarked from the Ark, God instructed them to "Be fruitful and multiply, and fill the earth" (Gen 9:1). They were fruitful and did multiply. However, they did not fill the earth. Instead, their descendants found a plain in the land of Shinar or Sumer and made this their home. This area is generally acknowledged as the world's first civilization. It was here that cities were built and dominated by pyramid type or stepped buildings called *ziggurats* that honored their gods. All spoke one language. God confused their language and caused them to be scattered over the face of the earth. Lud, a descendant of Shem, settled in western

Asia Minor. Javan, a descendant of Japheth, settled in the coastal area of southwestern Asia Minor. Gomer, a descendant of Japheth, settled in the central plateau area of Asia Minor. Togarmoth, a descendant of Japheth, settled in the mountainous area of eastern Asia Minor close to the modern day border of Iran. Finally, the Hittites, descendants of Ham, settled in the central plains area of Asia Minor.

The Hittites were the first dynasty to subdue much of Asia Minor. They arrived in Asia Minor then called Anatolia, in about 2000 B.C. Their empire flourished in the fourteenth-thirteenth-century B.C. era. In 1286 B.C. they battled the Egyptian king, Ramses II, at Kadesh. A description of that battle survived. Both the Egyptians and the Hittites claimed victory in this battle. The result was the first known recorded peace treaty in the world having occurred in 1284 B.C.

The Hittite Empire came to an end at the hands of a group called the "Sea People." This was a migrating group of people who settled in the central plain area known as Phyrgia.

In the eleventh century B.C. a growing population in what is modern-day Greece began competing for cities. The Ionians were one of these groups who occupied the southern peninsula of Greece known as the Peloponnesus. When the Dorians, another of the competing factions, attacked the Ionians, they fled the country. Androklos, the son of Kodros, the king of Athens, was leading a group to migrate to Anatolia. They settled in the central part of the western coastland. The area became known as Lydia. This region first achieved prominence under the reign of Mermnad in 680 B.C. However, its most famous ruler was Croesus who ascended to power in 561 B.C. and was defeated by Cyrus the Great in 547 B.C.

The Persians ruled Asia Minor until the campaign of Alexander the Great in 331 B.C. Alexander died in 323 B.C. and control of his empire was divided among his top four generals. Ptolemy was given control of Egypt. Seluecus was given control of Syria and Palestine. Cassander was given control of Greece and Lysimachus was given control of Asia Minor. Rome eventually conquered the region and Anatolia remained at peace under the Pax Romana for the next four hundred years.

The Apostle Paul taking Jesus seriously when he said, "Go therefore and make disciples of all nations, baptizing them in the name of the Father and of the Son and of the Holy Spirit, teaching them to observe all things that I have commanded you; and lo, I am with you always, even to the end of the age" (Matt 28:19,20), began missionary journeys in A.D. 46. He and Barnabas were commissioned at Antioch which today is in Turkey. Their first journey took them by sea to the island of Cyprus and then to the cities of southern and central Asia Minor. In A.D. 49 Paul again set out on his second missionary journey. This time he traveled with Silas overland from Antioch probably following the Royal Road through south central Asia Minor into Phyrgia and on to the coast of the Aegean Sea at Troas. There he traveled by ship to Greece and back by ship to Asia Minor via Corinth. He stopped in Ephesus for a brief time then set sail for Caesarea and back to Jerusalem.

A third time Paul visited the sites where churches had been established in Asia Minor and Greece. In A.D. 53, Paul again left Antioch and traveled through central Asia Minor until he settled in Ephesus for a period in excess of two years. From Ephesus he traveled by ship to Greece. He traveled on foot as far north as Illyricum and as far south as Cornith before returning to Philippi in the same manner. From Greece he traveled by ship to Miletus where he called for the Ephesian elders to join him for a farewell. From Miletus he sailed to the islands of Cos and Rhodes before landing again at Patara on the southern tip of Asia Minor. From Patara he returned across the Mediterrean Sea to Tyre and on to Jerusalem. Paul would land in Myra in the province of Lycia on his trip to Rome after appealing to Caesar in the case brought against him by the Jewish leaders in Jerusalem.

Paul's initial efforts were carried forth by his disciples. The area of Asia Minor was the springboard to shape the future of western civilization. By the year 100 there were an estimated eighty thousand believers concentrated in Asia Minor. It was at about this time that the Apostle John received his vision on Patmos. His messages to the seven churches encouraged and exhorted them to live their lives in a manner consistent with what they claimed to believe. Part of that belief was the continuation of the missionary work that Paul had earlier modeled for them.

Verses four and five constitute a typical letter format of a normal Greek letter written in the first century.[72] John identifies himself as the author or sender of the letter and identifies the seven churches of Asia as the recipients. He further follows Paul, who in every one of the epistles attributed to him, in greeting the readers with the phrase, "grace to you and peace." Just as Paul, John understands and passes along to his readers that the bestowal of grace by God results in peace in the life of the receiver of the grace.

John identifies the giver of the grace as coming from (1) Him who is and who was and who is to come, (2) the seven spirits of God who are before His throne, and (3) Jesus Christ.

1) Him who is and who was and who is to come. This reference to God stresses His eternal nature. God is always the God who is, rather than a god who was in the past or a god who will yet be in the future. When Moses encountered the burning bush, he asked, "Indeed when I come to the children of Israel and say to them, 'The God of your fathers has sent me to you,' and they say to me, 'What is His name? What shall I say to them?' And God said to Moses, 'I AM Who I AM.' And He said to Him, 'Thus you shall say to the children of Israel, I AM has sent me to you" (Ex 3:13, 14). God identified Himself as the Self-Existent One. He is the One who is. The designation who was and is to come further signifies God's eternal presence "which underlines the dynamic unfolding of God's plan."[73]

2) The seven spirits who are before His throne. This is a reference to the Holy Spirit. John makes reference to the seven spirits of God here and in 3:1, 4:5, and 5:6. Seven is the number of completeness and refers to the fullness of the

---

[72] Vern S. Poythress, *The Returning King*, (Phillipsburg: P&R Publishing, 2000), p. 72
[73] Ibid. p. 73

Holy Spirit. Isaiah 11:2 talks about the (1) Spirit of the Lord, (2) the Spirit of Wisdom, (3) the Spirit of Understanding, (4) the Spirit of Counsel, (5) the Spirit of Might, (6) the Spirit of Knowledge, and (7) the Spirit of the fear of the Lord. This description of the sevenfold Spirit is said to present the seven modes of operation of the Spirit.[74] Thomas sees a more satisfying explanation in Zechariah 4:1-10 where the prophet speaks of seven lamps and seven pipes that are the eyes of the Lord which scan to and fro throughout the whole earth.[75] In any event it seems as though this verse is referring to the fullness of the Holy Spirit.

3) From Jesus Christ. Whereas the first two designations may have differing understandings, this one is obvious. However, John further identifies attributes of Jesus. He is described as the Faithful Witness. In John 18:37 Pilate was interrogating Jesus. Jesus said to him, "For this cause I came into the world that I should bear witness to the truth." He came for that purpose and faithfully carried out this assignment even unto death. Christ is not only faithful in carrying out that assignment, but He is faithful in all that He says and does. He is the firstborn from the dead. This does not mean that He is a created being. It does mean that He is the preeminent One, "the One to whom first place and honor belong."[76] He is the first in a great company who will follow.[77] The ruler over the kings of the earth refers to Jesus' rule over all earthly monarchs regardless of whether we see it or not. John was affirming that even though Jesus is not physically present and the earthly monarchs appear to rule, in reality it is He not they who rule over all.[78]

---

[74] L. Morris, P. 49
[75] Thomas. p. 68
[76] William Barclay, *The Revelation of John*, vol. 1, (Westminster: Philadelphia, 1976), p. 32.
[77] Johnson, p. 421
[78] Ibid., p. 421

John can hardly contain himself after writing these things. Immediately, he bursts into a benediction of praise for the work of Christ in loving us, washing us, redeeming us, and coronating us. For all His work John ascribes to Christ the glory and dominion that are due Him. He ends his praise with a hearty Amen! So be it!

The anticipation of Christ coming again is so certain in John's mind that he exhorts his readers to be continually on the lookout for His coming. MacArthur writes,

> The exclamation *idou* (Behold) is an arresting call to attention. It is intended to arouse the mind and heart to consider what follows . . . it suggests that Christ is already on the way, and thus His coming is certain.[79]

The allusion to coming with clouds refers back to Daniel 7:13 as well as Matthew 24:30. It depicts the manner in which Christ will come again. In Acts 1:9-11 Jesus ascends to heaven. As the disciples witnessed this event, they saw Jesus taken into heaven and a cloud received Him. Two angels standing by asked the disciples why they were staring into the sky. They told them, "This same Jesus who was taken up from you into heaven, will so come in like manner as you saw Him go into heaven." Daniel, Matthew, and Luke all mention the presence of clouds associated with the return of Christ. Acts 1:12 says that the disciples returned to Jerusalem from the Mount of Olives also known as Olivet in Luke 19:29. The city of Bethany is located on the eastern slope of the Mount of Olives. Luke 24:50 tells us that "Jesus led them out as far as Bethany, and He lifted up His hands and blessed them. Now it came to pass, while He blessed them, that He was parted from them and carried up into heaven." If Jesus was on the Mount of Olives when He ascended to heaven and He will return in like manner, then He will return to the Mount of Olives. Further proof of His return to the Mount of Olives is in Zechariah 14:4 where the prophet states, "And in that Day His feet will stand on the Mount of Olives which faces Jerusalem on the east."

---

[79] MacArthur, p. 28

Somehow, every eye will see Him when He comes, even those who pierced Him. Those who pierced Him are the Jews who failed to recognize Jesus when He came and presented Himself to them as their Messiah. In describing Jesus' triumphal entry into Jerusalem, Luke writes,

> Now as He drew near, He saw the city and wept over it, saying, "If you had known, even you, especially in this your day, the things that make for your peace! But now they are hidden from your eyes. For days will come upon you when your enemies will build an embankment around you, surround you and close you in on every side, and level you, and your children within you, to the ground; and they will not leave in you one stone upon another, because you did not know the time of your visitation (Luke 19:41-44).

John 1:11 says, "He came unto His own, and His own did not receive Him." In Matthew 23:37-39 Jesus says,

> O Jerusalem, Jerusalem, the one who kills the prophets and stones those who are sent to her! How often I wanted to gather your children together, as a hen gathers her chicks under her wings, but you were not willing. See! Your house is left to you desolate; for I say to you, you shall see Me no more till you say, "Blessed is He who comes in the name of the Lord."

Zechariah 12:10 tells us that those who pierced Him will also mourn for Him. The Jews, who rejected Christ, pierced Him and will mourn for His return. But He will not return until they say "Blessed is He who comes in the name of the Lord." This will mark their repentance and acceptance of Christ as the Messiah.

Not only will the Jews mourn, but the tribes of the earth will also mourn. There is however a distinction to be made in the reason for the mourning. The Jews mourned because they longed for their Messiah and repented for His return. The tribes of the earth will mourn not from a repentant heart but out of fear. For there is a time coming when Christ will come again in wrath to judge the world. This judgment will be terrifying and the people of the world who do not belong to the Lord will mourn because of their rejection of Christ. They will not be mourning due to repentance but from the fear of facing the returning Lord who will be coming in wrath.

As another expression of the eternality of God, John quotes the Lord saying, "I am the Alpha and the Omega." This is the first and last letters of the Greek alphabet just like our expression from A to Z. It is comprehensive and exhaustive. The Lord is the alpha or the originator. Everything has its origin in Him. He is also the omega or the terminator. He is the Beginning (Creator) as well as the End (Finisher). He is the God who is. The attribute of His that God chooses to express in this scenario is His omnipotence. He is all powerful and can and will do all that He says He will. God is sovereign and in control of all facets of the life of His creation.

Patmos

World Book Online defines *exile* as banishment from one's own land. It was a common form of punishment for crimes and political offenses in ancient Palestine, Greece, and Rome.[80] Thucydides, a Greek historian, was banished from Athens in 424 B.C. for failing to protect the city in a battle of the Peloponnesian War. He returned from exile twenty years later. In literature, the backdrop of Shakespeare's *The Tempest* is a mysterious island inhabited by a witch who had been exiled there.

Perhaps the most known incident of exile occurred in Genesis 4 where Cain was said to be "a restless wanderer on the earth" and "went out from the presence of the *Lord*" (NIV). Cain was banished from the land and from the presence of the *Lord* and found his punishment "more than I can bear" (NIV).

---

[80] Anthony D'Amato, Ph.D., *Exile* World Book Online Americas Edition, http://aolsvc.worldbook.aol.com/wbol/wbPage/na/ar/col1888460, March 14, 2002.

In the Roman world of the first century A.D., exile was a common form of punishment. The Roman historian Tacitus writing in A.D. 109 speaks of banishment as a punitive measure taken by the Roman Senate for crimes. Sometime the exile was merely from Rome where the recipient of the sentence was not allowed access to the city. In Book IV of the Annals of Tacitus, he writes about the punishment of one Cassius Servis who was banished to the island of Crete.[81]

Eusebius was a Greek Christian writer often referred to as the "Father of Ecclesiastical History." He lived from A.D. 260-339 and wrote prolifically about the early church and the conditions that prevailed at that time. About the reign of the Roman Emperor Domitian (A.D. 81-95) he writes,

> Many were the victims of Domitian's appalling cruelty. At Rome great numbers of men distinguished by birth and attainments were, for no reason at all, banished from the country and their property confiscated.[82]

Bust of Domitian from First Century.
Picture taken at the Ephesus Museum

---

[81] Tacitus, *The Annals, http://classics.mit.edu/tacitus/annals.4.iv.htm.*
[82] Eusebius, 3.17.

Exile was common in the reign of this emperor for those who opposed him politically even those of noble birth and standing. Banishment to an island was a common and accepted penalty.

> The duration of the sentence was life long; it ended only with death. The exile was allowed to live in free intercourse with the people of the island, and to earn money. But he could not inherit money nor bequeath his own, if he saved or earned any: all he had passed to the state at his death. He was cut off from the outer world, though he was treated with personal cruelty or constraint within the limits of the islet where he was confined.[83]

During the reign of Domitian, Christianity was considered a crime against the state. Ramsey suggests that the penalty for being convicted as a Christian underwent a type of evolution.

> In the first stages, before it was regarded as a crime, some Christians were subjected to comparatively mild penalties like scourging; but in such cases they were punished, not for the crime of Christianity, not for the "name," but for other offenses, such as causing disorder in the streets.[84]

Even though Christianity was considered to be primarily composed of the lower class of Roman society, Eusebius writes about the conviction and exile of the niece of a Roman consul:

> Indeed, so brightly shone at that time the teaching of our faith that even historians who accepted none of our beliefs unhesitatingly recorded in their pages both the persecution and the martyrdoms to which it led. They also indicated in

---

[83] W. M. Ramsay, *The Letters to the Seven Churches*, (Peabody: Hendrickson, 1994), p. 60.
[84] Ibid., 61.

precise date, noting that in the fifteenth year of Domitian Flavia Domitilla, who was the niece of Flavius Clemens, one of the consuls at Rome that year, was with many others, because of the testimony to Christ, taken to the island of Pontia as punishment.[85]

John tells his readers that he was sent to the island of Patmos "for the word of God and for the testimony of Jesus Christ." During his imprisonment on Patmos, John took refuge in a cave located in what is now called Hora. The cave was approximately 850 feet above sea level and overlooked the eastern portion of the island. The opening of the cavern faces east toward Ephesus. From his vantage point, John stared yearningly toward the city to which he longed to be resident. Despite this yearning there was a great sea separating him and the people with whom he longed to commune.

Today, the cave is enclosed by the Monastery of the Apocalypse which has been built around it. The interior of the cave is dark gray rock with an uneven ceiling so low in places that the tour guides constantly warn the pilgrims to watch where they are walking so as not to bump their head on the rock ceiling.

On the ceiling of the cave is a triple fissure said to have occurred as a result of an earthquake that accompanied the appearance of the Risen Lord when He appeared to John. In the form of a triangle, the fissure is thought to be symbolic of the Trinity.

---

[85] Eusebius 3.18.4

John's view from inside the cave looking east toward Ephesus. The harbour is in view and just over the hills is the Aegean Sea which separates John from Ephesus.

Patmos is a small Greek island off the coast of Asia Minor approximately 40 miles from the city of Miletus. It is part of a chain of twelve islands known as the Dodecanese. The word *dodeka* in Greek means twelve. The island is approximately 10 miles from north to south and 6 miles east to west. At the port of Skala the island is indented and the width is approximately one mile. It is composed of three volcanic swells of land connected by two small isthmuses, and appearing in a horseshoe shape. The highest point is over 850 feet.

The island produces small crops of grapes and wheat and suffers from a lack of water, firewood, and food. There is no fresh water source, meaning that rainwater must be gathered in the winter rainy season for use in the summer.[86] The climate is moderate, aided in the summer by the northerly wind known as the *meltemia*. In the winter months temperatures can drop into the mid-forty-degree-Fahrenheit range.

---

[86] Dr. Joochan Kim, *Seven Churches in Asia Minor*, (Okhap: Korea, 1999), p. 168-69.

Patmos was populated by the Dorians approximately 500 B.C. followed by the Ionians up to the second century B.C. when Rome expanded its empire. A temple to Artemis has led some etymologists to believe that the name Patmos is derived from Latmos which is a mountain in Asia Minor where the goddess Artemis was worshipped.

> Patmos was a place of exile for criminals during the Roman era where they were forced to work in stone pits. This was very painful for the criminals, because they had to work hard without water in the summer and shivered with cold during the winter. The Roman soldiers guarding them had to endure the same conditions, so only the most unwanted soldiers were stationed there.[87]

Tradition records that John had left Jerusalem some time after the Jerusalem Council of A.D. 49 mentioned in Acts chapter 15. In Galatians 2:9, Paul writes about going to Jerusalem and meeting with James, Cephas, and John "who seemed to be pillars" of the Church. Acts 21 records another visit by Paul to Jerusalem after his third missionary journey approximately eight years later. At this visit he meets with James and all the elders (v18). Since no mention is made of John at this meeting, it is assumed that he was no longer in Jerusalem.

Fox's Book of Martyrs states that "the churches of Symrna, Pergamos, Sardis, Philadelphia, Laodecia, and Thyatira were founded by him."[88] Whether this is true or not, it certainly places John in Asia Minor where it is said that he resided at Ephesus having arrived there in A.D. 68 after Paul had been beheaded.

The phrase "for the word of God and the testimony of Jesus Christ" that John uses in Rev 1:9 could have at least three interpretations. The phrase could be taken to mean that John while

---

[87] Ibid., p. 169.
[88] Fox's Book of Martyrs, *http://www.ccel.org/f/foxe-j/martyrs/fox101.htm* 3/12/02.

in Asia Minor felt lead to go voluntarily to Patmos to evangelize or minister to the prisoners and soldiers there. It could mean that he needed some time to be alone after a long period of ministry in Asia Minor and chose Patmos as a place of solitude to be in closer communion with the Lord. Or it could mean that John was banished there as a result of being convicted of some crime.[89]

The probability of the first two options is not likely since John identifies himself in verse 9 as being a brother and companion to his readers in the tribulation and kingdom and patience of Jesus Christ. John was on the island of Patmos as a result of a prison sentence for doing what his Lord and Savior commanded him to do the last time he saw Him. In Acts 1:8 just before ascending to the Father, Jesus spoke to those gathered on the Mount of Olives saying,

> But you shall receive power when the Holy Spirit has come upon you; and you shall be witnesses to Me in Jerusalem, and in all Judea and Samaria, and to the end of the earth.

John was there and heard the words of his Lord and was busy about that task when he was arrested and subsequently sentenced for his crime. Legend has it that John was sent to Rome where he was convicted. His punishment took place at a time when the "penalty for Christianity was already fixed as death in the severer form (i.e., fire, crucifixion, or as a public spectacle at games and festivals) for persons of humbler position and provincials, and simple execution for Roman citizens."[90] Tradition says that John was cast in a cauldron of boiling oil but escaped without injury. Doubt has been cast as to the authenticity of this account but given what we know about the reputation of Domitian and the severer forms of capital punishment at that time the account is not that unlikely. In any event, not being able to end the apostle's life, Domitian banished him to hard labor at Patmos.

---

[89] Barclay, p. 42.
[90] Ramsay, p. 61.

This form of punishment presented even more difficult obstacles for a man of John's age who was by now approximately eighty years old. Banishment would have been preceded by scourging, and it was marked by perpetual fetters, scanty clothing, insufficient food, sleep on bare ground in a dark prison and work under the lash of military overseers.[91] There is a legend which says that John being aged at the time of his banishment would not have been expected to do the work of an exiled criminal on the island. Instead, he was given freedom on Patmos to go where he pleased. Customarily, prisoners lived in camps and were confined to work in quarries. John, however, was exempt from these conditions due to his age. Regardless of whether John was exempt from the work and confinement or he participated in the work and confinement is secondary to the fact that he was on the Island of Patmos and could not leave there.

Jerome writes concerning John:

> In the fourteenth year then after Nero, Domitian having raised a second persecution he was banished to the island of Patmos, and wrote the Apocalypse, on which Justin Martyr and Irenaus wrote commentaries. But Domitian having been put to death and his acts, on account of his excessive cruelty, having been annulled by the senate, he returned to Ephesus under Pertinaxand.[92]

John was banished to Patmos by Domitian in A.D. 95. Domitian was assassinated by a member of his household staff on September 18, 96 A.D. Upon his death, Nerva became emperor and ultimately set aside John's conviction and released him from his exile of eighteen months.

> After fifteen years of Domitian rule, Nerva succeeded to the throne. By vote of the Roman Senate Domitian's honors

---

[91] Ibid., p. 61
[92] Jerome, *De viris illustibus*, http://www.newadvent.org/fathers/2708.htm 3/12/02

were removed, and those unjustly banished returned to their homes and had their property restored to them. This is noted by the chroniclers of the period. At that time too the Apostle John, after his exile on the island, resumed residence at Ephesus, as early Christian tradition records.[93]

The recipients of the messages that John sent would have known the circumstances of his banishment. So, there was no need for John to elaborate on his present conditions. Furthermore, in all likelihood John wrote the messages and sent them to the seven churches via a messenger. Perhaps someone from Ephesus came to Patmos to check on John and delivered the messages upon his return. There are different understandings as to when John wrote the Book of Revelation. Some believe that he wrote the book while on Patmos while some believe he wrote the book after his sentence was commuted and he had returned to Ephesus.

Those who believe that John would have waited until he returned from Patmos might argue (1) that John's usage of the past tense "was on the Island of Patmos" indicates that he was there once but he is no longer there as he writes; (2) the spartan conditions of the island would not have lent itself readily to writing materials; (3) John was sentenced to hard labor and would not have the time or the inclination to write.

Those who believe that John wrote on the island might argue (1) the appearance of the Risen Lord and His command to write would have overridden any lack of motivation John might have suffered; (2) If John had been released, he would have gone personally to the churches to deliver the messages; (3) when God gives His servants a task, he provides them everything they need to complete that task.

The imperative that John was given by the Risen Lord to write what he saw would seem to militate against any other possible argument for delaying the task. If the image John saw was sufficient to cause John to collapse in fear as though dead, surely it would

---

[93] Eusebius, 3.20.5.

have been sufficient to cause John to immediately obey any command that would be issued.

There is an interesting legend in the Orthodox Church concerning the writing of the Book of Revelation. The contention is that John dictated what he experienced on Patmos to an amanuensis named Prochorus. In Acts 6, Prochorus was the name of one of the seven servants, sometimes referred to as *deacons*, selected by the brethren and appointed by the apostles to care for the needs of the Greek-speaking widows. Prochorus was selected because of his good reputation, the attestation of the Holy Spirit in his life, and wisdom which he demonstrated.

The Prochorus tradition states that he first accompanied Peter on his journey through Pontus, Galatia, Cappadocia, Asia, and Bithynia as alluded to in 1 Peter 1:1. As a result of his loyalty and good standing, Peter appointed him bishop of Nicomedia, a city in northwest Asia Minor near the Bosphorus today called Izmit.[94] After the death of Mary in Ephesus, Prochorus became a coworker of the Apostle John. Both John and Prochorus were banished to Patmos and John dictated to Prochorus his vision in the cave which became the Book of Revelation. Pilgrims to the island of Patmos will be shown the cave where John reclined to receive the visions and the podium where Prochorus stood to write what the aged apostle spoke.

As charming as this story may be, the internal evidence, i.e., the evidence contained in the Scripture text itself, speaks against the probability of this being factual. Nowhere in the Book of Revelation does Prochorus appear, nor is his participation in the writing of the book alluded to. In 1:19 John is told to write the things which he has seen. Dutiful to that command, John wrote and in 10:1-4 was prepared to report what he heard the seven thunders utter. As he was about to write what he heard the seven thunders utter, he heard a voice commanding him, "Seal up the things which the seven thunders uttered, and do not write them." Clearly, John was given the command and John is the one who was

---

[94] Columbia Encyclopedia, Sixth Edition. Columbia University Press, 2001.

about to write. There is no indication that John was dictating what he saw and experienced on Patmos.

What benefit does any of this information have on the readers of Revelation? In reading any literary work, in order to understand the author's message, one needs to see what the characters of the work are experiencing. What is the setting of the scene? How did the character get there? What are the circumstances surrounding the scene? What senses are being employed? What are the potential outcomes?

The Bible was written for the readers to respond to its message. Does it matter to know that the character of John in the book was a real person, suffering real persecution, in a real location, in a real time in history? It matters if we try to understand what implication the story has in our own lives.

John was doing what he thought the Lord wanted him to do. If he is doing the Lord's will, how could evil befall him in this manner? John had served the Lord faithfully. He is called a servant of the Lord. In the gospel of John he is called "the disciple whom Jesus loved." Yet John found himself in circumstances that he didn't understand. Arguably, he wasn't expecting the Risen Lord to show up that day on Patmos. Certainly he wasn't expecting him to show up in the manner that he did. When John did see the Lord he fainted in fear. Jesus needed to reassure John that he was in control of all circumstances in life whether John was able to understand them or not. "Do not be afraid," He tells him. Jesus then reassures John that He is the "First and the Last," and the "One who was dead, and behold I am alive forevermore." Furthermore, He tells him that He has "the keys of Hades and Death."

This phrase is particularly interesting. John must have had assurance of his salvation. He had been teaching, preaching, and pastoring for at least sixty years. He had written his gospel assuring his readers that "these are written that you may believe that Jesus is the Christ, the Son of God, and that believing you may have life in His name." Furthermore, he had written in 1 John 5: 12, 13 "He who has the Son has life; he who does not have the Son of God does not have life. These things have been written to you who believe in the name of the Son of God, that you may know that you have eternal life, and that you may continue to believe in the name of the Son of God." So why then does Jesus tell him to not be afraid because He has the keys to "Hades and Death"? Surely John would not have feared being in Hades. After all didn't Jesus promise him in John 14:1-3, "Let not your heart be troubled; you believe in God, believe also in Me. In My Father's house are many mansions; if it were not so, I would have told you. I go to prepare a place for you. And if I go and prepare a place for you, I will come again and receive you to Myself; that where I am, there you may be also."

MacArthur writes in his notes in *The MacArthur Study Bible* on Luke 16:23,

> Hades was the Greek term for the abode of the dead. In the LXX, it was used to translate the Hebrew Sheol, which referred to the realm of the dead in general, without necessarily distinguishing between righteous and unrighteous souls. However, in New Testament usage, "Hades" always refers to the place of the wicked prior to final judgment in hell.[95]

This understanding conforms with Greek mythology. Edith Hamilton writes,

> The kingdom of the dead was ruled by one of the twelve Olympians, Hades or Pluto, and his Queen Persephone. It is often called by his name, Hades. It lies, the Illiad says, beneath the secret places of the earth. In the Odyssey, the way to it leads over the edge of the world across Ocean. In later poets there are various entrances to it from the earth through caverns and beside deep lakes.[96]

---

[95] John A. MacArthur, *The MacArthur Study Bible*, (Nashville: Word, 1997), p.1548.
[96] Edith Hamilton, *Mythology*, (New York: Mentor, 1940), p.39.

The word Hades is used ten times in the New Testament. Four of those are in the Gospels. Each of those occurrences are by Christ. Each time it is clear that the usage is as described above by MacArthur and Hamilton. The usage of Hades in Acts 2:27 and 31 by Peter is clearly a reference to a place after death.

In the Book of Revelation Hades is used four times. In 6:8, Hades is used to personify a warrior which follows Death as the rider of the pale horse. In 20:13, Death and Hades deliver up those who are contained within and in 20:14 Death and Hades are cast into the lake of fire.

Notice that the order Death first then Hades makes common sense. In life, death ultimately comes first. For the believer, absent from the body means to be present with the Lord (2 Cor 5:8; Phil 1:27). For the unbeliever, Hades awaits.

Of the four uses of Hades in Revelation, three of them (6:8; 20:13, 14) appear in order with Death first then Hades. However in the King James and New King James translations, in 1:18 Hades appears first then Death, "I have the keys of Hades and Death." *Vine's Complete Expository Dictionary of Old and New Testament Words* says of Hades, "It has been thought by some that the word etymologically meant 'the unseen [from a, negative, and *eido*, to see], but this derivation is questionable."[97] Spiro Zodhiates in his *New Testament Word Study Dictionary* also refers to this possibility.[98] In the center reference column of the New King James Version, there is an annotation regarding the use of Hades in Rev 1:18. The word is marked by a "superior numeral which indicates an alternate translation, equivalent translation, literal translation, explanatory note, language note, or textual note."[99] In this case the superior numeral indicates a literal translation for the word Hades as unseen: the unseen realm.[100] Of the other nine usages of the word Hades in the New Testament, not once do the New King James Version translators make this distinction.

---

[97] Vine's, p. 286.
[98] Zodhaites, p. 8.
[99] MacArthur, XXVII.
[100] Ibid., p. 1993.

In his Expanded Translation of the New Testament, Kenneth Wuest translates 1:17, 18 as follows:

> And when I saw Him, I fell at His feet like a dead man. And He laid His right hand upon me, saying, stop fearing, As for Myself, I am the First and the Last and the Living One, and I became dead, and consider this, I am alive forever and forever. And I have the keys to death and the unseen.[101]

The context of verses 1:9-20 is about what John is seeing and about which he is to write. Five times between verses 11 and 19 the word *see* or *saw*, or *seen* is used. In verse 11 the Greek word *blepo* is used and in verse 19 the word *oida* is used. In the *NIV Theological Dictionary of New Testament Words*, the word *oida* is defined as know, understand.[102] Vine's identifies *blepo* as meaning to have sight, is used of bodily vision[103] while *oida* signifies primarily to have seen or perceived.[104] Zodhiates defines *blepo* as to look at, to behold, whereas *oida* is defined as to know, be aware, have knowledge.[105]

In verse 11 (paraphrasing) Christ speaking to John says, "write what you visually [*blepo*] ascertain." John turns, gets a visual of this new revelation from God, and falls to the ground as if dead. In verse 18 Jesus says to him (paraphrasing), "I have the keys to what is unseen. John, you have only your limited perspective but just remember, I am in control of all things whether you see them or not." Then in verse 19, He says (paraphrasing), "Now write about that which you know [*oida*]." John gets a new perspective not just for himself, but it took that new perspective for John to articulate it to his readers.

---

[101] Kenneth S. Wuest, *The New Testament: An Expanded Translation*, (Grand Rapids: Eerdmans, 1961) p. 588.
[102] Verbrugge, p. 50.
[103] Vine's, p. 556.
[104] Ibid., p. 346.
[105] Zodhaites, p. 897.

In verse 10, John says that he was "in the Spirit on the Lord's Day." He uses this same phrase "in the Spirit" here and in 4:2; 17:3; 21:10. In 17:3 and in 21:10 John describes himself as being carried away in the Spirit. Note that in all four circumstances John was given new revelation as a result of being in the Spirit. In 1:10 he is in the Spirit, hears a great voice behind him, and turns to see the One who identifies Himself as the Alpha and Omega, the First and Last. In 4:2 John is in the Spirit and is transported to the throne room of God. In 17:3 John is carried away in the Spirit to see spiritual Babylon and her destruction. In 21:10 John is carried away in the Spirit to see the New Jerusalem descending out of heaven from God.

John's use of the phrase "in the Spirit" can be defined as a heightened state of spiritual consciousness for the purpose of receiving communication from God. Old Testament comparisons can be seen in Ezekiel 1:3; 3:14, 22; 8:1; 33:22; and 37:1. Chapter 1 verse 3 tells of the Word of the Lord coming to him as he met with his fellow captives at the River Chebar. In verse 3 he says "the hand of the Lord was upon me there." Ezekiel was in a heightened state of spiritual consciousness. In chapter 3 God gives Ezekiel further instruction to which the prophet concludes in verse 14, "but the hand of the Lord was strong upon me." In verse 22 of that same chapter, he gets further communication from God but not before he states, "Then the hand of the Lord was upon me there." Just as Ezekiel was in a heightened state of spiritual consciousness for the purpose of receiving communication from God, so too was John.

Some commentators see John in the Spirit as being in an ecstatic state comparing this verse with Acts 10:10 where Peter is said to be in a trance. The word translated as trance is the Greek word *ekstasis*. Vine's defines this word as,

> a condition in which ordinary consciousness and the perception of natural circumstances were withheld, and the soul was susceptible only to the vision imparted by God."[106]

---

[106] Vine's, p. 639.

The Merriam Webster Online Dictionary defines *trance* as,

> A half-conscious state characterized by an absence of response to external stimuli typically induced by hypnosis or entered by a medium. A state of partly suspended animation or inability to function.

John's ability to function while being in the Spirit is demonstrated by his being able to see (1:12; 17:3,6), by his ability to hear (1:17-20), by his ability to obey (2:1, 8, 12, 18; 3:1, 7, 14), his ability to write (2:1, 8, 12, 18; 3:1, 7, 14), his ability to marvel (17:6), and by his weeping (5:4). Being in a trance hardly gives the reader the real meaning of the phrase.

Some commentators see John in the Spirit as being in an ecstatic frenzy. Again, Webster defines *ecstasy* as, "an emotional or religious frenzy or trancelike state, originally one involving an experience of mystic self-transcendence." *Frenzy* is defined as, "a temporary madness. A violent mental or emotional agitation. Intense usually wild and often disorderly compulsion or agitated activity."

These words—trance, ecstasy, frenzy—give the impression that John was either euphoric or out of control. It is better to understand that John was in the Spirit so that God could impart to him information that he could get nowhere else for the purpose of sharing those revelations with his readers. John may have been amazed at what he experienced, he may have been confused by what he heard and saw, he may even have been fearful, but he was neither euphoric nor intensely agitated. He was a forthteller of what God revealed to him.

John was in the Spirit on the Lord's Day. Some commentators see in this designation Lord's Day a reference to the Day of the Lord. This view contends that John was catapulted into the future to see the time of wrath and judgment that would later be revealed to him. However, the Lord had not yet revealed anything to John and as was stated earlier, John was not anticipating what he would eventually see.

A more probable understanding of the Lord's Day is neither a period of time nor a particular event, but rather Sunday as the first day of the week. Sunday was the day the early church met and worshipped together. As early as Paul's first letter to the Corinthians (A.D. 55), there is a reference to the saints gathering together on the first day of the week.

> Now concerning the collection for the saints as I have given orders to the churches of Galatia, so you must do also: On the first day of the week let each one of you lay something aside, storing up as he may prosper, that there be no collections when I come (1 Cor 16:1,2).

Then in Acts 20:7 when Paul was ministering in Troas on his way back to Jerusalem from his third missionary journey (A.D. 57) the disciples came together on the first day of the week to *break bread*, a term commonly associated with the early church communion or Lord's Supper service.

Ignatius of Antioch writing to the Magnesians in A.D. 110 says,

> If then, those who walked in ancient customs came to a new hope, no longer sabbathing but living by the Lord's Day, on which we came to life through Him and through His death, which some deny, through which mystery we received faith, through which also we suffer in order to be found to be disciples of Jesus Christ, our only teacher.[107]

The Didache or The Teaching of the Twelve Apostles written ca A.D. 140 states "On the Lord's Day of the Lord gather together, break bread and give thanks after confessing your transgressions so that your sacrifice may be pure."[108]

---

[107] W. A. Jurgens, *The Faith of the Fathers*, vol 1. (Collegeville; Liturgal Press, 1970), p. 19.
[108] Ibid., p. 4.

In a letter of Dionysus written A.D. 164/174 he refers to Clement's epistle to the Corinthians. Quoting from Clement he writes,

> Today being the Lord's Day we kept it as a holy day and read your epistle, which we shall read frequently for its valuable advice, like the earlier epistle which Clement wrote on your behalf.[109]

In Justin Martyr's First Apology ca A.D. 148-155, he writes,

> The Day of the Sun is the day on which we all gather in a common meeting, because it is the first day, the day on which God, changing darkness and matter created the world; and it is the day on which Jesus Christ our Savior rose from the dead. For He was crucified on the day before Kronos;[110] and on the day after that of Kronos, which is the Day of the Sun, he appeared to his Apostles and disciples, and taught them these things which we have also submitted to you for your consideration.[111]

Finally, in the Apostolic Constitution Book 7.30 it states,

> On the day of the resurrection of the Lord, that is, the Lord's Day, assemble yourselves together without fail, giving thanks to God, and praising Him for those mercies God has bestowed upon you through Christ, and has delivered you from ignorance, error, and bondage, that your sacrifice may be unspotted and acceptable to God, who has said concerning His universal Church: "In every place shall incense and a pure sacrifice be offered unto Me; for I am a great King, saith the Lord Almighty, and My Name is wonderful among the heathen."[112]

---

[109] Eusebius, 4.23.8.
[110] Justin's reference to Kronos means Saturday
[111] Jurgens, p, 56.
[112] *www.ccel.org/fathers2/ANF-07/anf07-47.htm* 10/12/02

From the writings of Paul through the early church fathers, the first day of the week was set aside to worship the Risen Savior. This is what John was celebrating as he was on Patmos in a heightened condition of spiritual consciousness prepared for God to reveal to him what only God can reveal. John did not expect the revelation he received, but he was prepared to receive the revelation he got. The same condition exists today as we prepare for worship or Bible study. John's heart was prepared. The question is, are we prepared to understand the revelation John was given?

Verse 11 elaborates on verse 4 naming the seven churches in Asia Minor. These were not the only churches in Asia Minor at that time. Paul wrote a letter to the church at Colossae and the churches in Galatia. In his Colossian letter he mentions those in Heiropolis (4:13). At Troas, Paul met with the brethren and preached all night (Acts 20:7-13). Peter wrote his first letter to the pilgrims in Pontus and Bithynia which are located in Asia Minor north of the seven churches. The bottom line is that there were many churches in Asia Minor at the time John wrote Revelation.

Why then did the Lord choose these seven? The number seven is the number of completeness in Scripture. These seven churches are representative of all the churches. They represent all churches at all times. They were all located in western Asia Minor and connected via a trade route used also as a postal route. Some commentators refer to John as the "Postman of Patmos." Because these churches were used symbolically to represent all churches of all time should not lead one to the conclusion that Christ was not referring to real churches occupied by real people who had real problems to which real solutions were being offered. The members of those churches were just as real as the members of Christ's church today. The areas of encouragement and exhortation highlighted in each of the seven messages are as relevant today as they were in the first century. Circumstances may have changed but fallen human nature has not. Twenty first-century Christians are faced with the same basic concerns as their first-century counterparts.

John is told to write what he sees and send it to these churches. The voice John heard was behind him so he turned in the direction of the voice. When he turned his eyes focused on seven golden lampstands. These lampstands are an allusion to the lampstands that God had directed Moses to have fashioned out of gold for the purpose of providing light for the priest to minister in the tabernacle (Ex 25: 31-40). Aaron and his sons were to tend the lampstands morning and evening while the people were to supply oil for the lamps that they may burn continually (Ex 27: 20, 21). Exodus 25: 40 tells us that these lampstands were made according to the pattern. About this Walter Kaiser writes,

> "According to the pattern" is once again a key word warning Moses and all subsequent readers that what he was really building was only a model, not the real, or the archetype, which lay behind the model. Therefore it was only a shadow of the good things that are coming—not the realities themselves. Thus there was a built-in obsolescence in this revelation. And the models exhibited in the whole tabernacle and it service . . . The archetype remained with God while these earthly models merely pictured what was yet to come.[113]

In Zechariah 4:1-7 the prophet sees a lampstand of solid gold with seven lamps connected to seven pipes. There is similarity and difference between these two Old Testament passages. Both lampstands appear to be the same. However, the lampstands described in Exodus had to be maintained by the priests on behalf of the people. In Zechariah, the lampstand was connected to an endless supply of oil without the help of a priest. God revealed to Zechariah that it was the power of "My Spirit" that was at work.

In the midst of the seven lampstands, John sees a human form which he describes as "one like the son of man." Some commentators see a distinction in the term "one like the son of man" and the son of man[114] arguing that the use of the simile *like* should be taken to mean non-messianic. However, Thomas states, "this reasoning is unconvincing and the interpretation son of man and like the son of man should be viewed as equivalent."[115]

---

[113] Walter C. Kaiser, Jr., *Exodus The Bible Expositor Commentary*, vol 2. Grand Rapids: Zondervan, 1990, p. 458.

[114] Robert W. Wall, *Revelation*, (Peabody: Hendrickson, 1991), p. 62.

[115] Thomas p. 98.

The phrase *son of man* appears in the New Testament eighty-eight times.

> The phrase occurs frequently in the gospels, always in sayings ascribed to Jesus or in indirect discourse reporting his words, and the evangelist always understand it as a self-designation of Jesus.[116]

John was familiar with the phrase having used it of Jesus eleven times in the gospel of John and twice in Revelation.

The apparel John describes, "a garment down to the feet and girded about the chest with a golden band," is the apparel of the priesthood. Here, John pictures Jesus ministering to the lampstands, being in their midst to see that the wicks were trimmed and assuring the continuous flow of oil to keep the lamp illumined.

The description of the appearance of the Son of Man pictures His eternality. His white hair resembles the hair "white as pure wool" that Daniel describes in 7:9 as belonging to the Ancient of Days. His eyes were like a flame of fire, piercing, being able to penetrate to the very heart of a man. His feet were like fine brass representing judgment. His voice roared as the sound of a waterfall crashing to the rocks below. In his right hand He held seven stars and out of His mouth came a sharp two-edged sword. This double-edged sword should be seen as coming from the mouth as the spoken word resulting in judgment. Added to all this was an aura that caused His countenance to shine like the sun.

John saw a Jesus that he had never seen or even imagined before. He saw a picture of a warrior coming in judgment. The image was so stunning and arresting that John was paralyzed with fear and fell at the feet of this Jesus as though he were dead. In a word, John fainted. He passed out from fright. But, just as tender as He is fierce, Jesus lays His right hand on John, assuring him that everything is under His control and that he should not fear because this Jesus who is the First and the Last and is alive forevermore will

---

[116] George Archer Buttrick, *The Interpreters Dictionary of the Bible*, vol 4. Nashville: Abingdon, 1962, p. 424.

have the last word in the drama that is about to unfold. He holds the keys to the seen and the unseen, to what is apparent and to what is real, to what is perceived and to what is certain. He is omnipotent, omniscient, and sovereign over all.

After John has recovered from his fainting spell, Jesus gives him instructions. Many commentators see in verse 19 the outline for the entire book. Jesus tells John to write the things which John has seen. If He means write only what John saw as a result of being on Patmos, then John would have written about the scene described in 1:10-18. He tells him to write the things which are that would refer to the messages to the churches in chapter 2 and 3. He tells him to write the things which will take place after this referring to those events that take place in chapters 4-22.

Many commentators see the Book of Revelation as symbolic. On the interpretation of the book Herschell Hobbs writes,

> In other words, is it symbolic or is it literal? I don't know about you, but if I try to go literal, I go crazy. So I vote for symbolic. You can't ride first one horse and then another just to suit your convenience. You can't go symbol, symbol, literal, symbol. You have to go all the way, one or the other. Just make up your mind which way you are going.[117]

To be sure, symbols are employed in the book. However, when symbols are employed they are generally made apparent. David Reagen writes,

> Keep in mind that symbols are used for a specific purpose. They stand for something. They have a literal meaning behind them . . . When a symbol is used always look for the literal meaning behind it. God does not use symbols randomly, just pulling them out of the sky as if they have no meaning whatsoever.[118]

---

[117] Beasley-Murray, p. 77.
[118] Reagan, p. 28, 29.

An example of this is found in verse 20. Jesus referred to seven stars which He held in His right hand in verse 16. In verse 20, He says that there is a mystery regarding these seven stars. He tells John that the seven stars are the messengers or angels of the seven churches to whom John is to write. Furthermore, He tells John that the seven golden lampstands that he saw in verse 12 are the seven churches. Jesus used the stars and lampstands as symbols but went on to explain the symbols He used. This is not unlike His use of parables while on earth. First He told the parable, then He explained the parable to His disciples.[119]

This mystery paints a picture of Jesus ministering in the midst of His Church taking care of the needs that exist. He is ever present, available, and willing to intercede. He has the power to hold the Church securely in His mighty right hand where no one can snatch it away (John 10:28). He is the Good Shepherd taking care of His flock, protecting them and nourishing them. This was an image that John could pass on to a church that was enmeshed in persecution from many sides. An image that would raise the level of encouragement from a church that was struggling under oppression. An image that would give hope to a church that needed to know that its shepherd was on the job and would prevail against any and all adversaries. The sovereign, omnipotent One was ready to do what only He could do—deliver His people from the grip that Satan had upon them.

Perhaps you are reading this page and find yourself in circumstances that are seemingly overwhelming. The same Jesus that appeared to John on Patmos is available to you. Today you can have the same comfort and the same encouragement that John did in knowing that nothing escapes His attention. When He told John that He was the First and the Last, He wasn't just speaking of the first century. He was speaking of all time. This is the power that John wrote about when he said, "He who is in you is greater than he who is in the world" (1 John 4:4). It may seem as though the weight of the world is on your shoulders; the load so heavy

---

[119] For an example of this see Matthew 13:1-9 and 18-23.

that you are bowed over from it. Remember, "The *Lord* upholds all who fall, and raises up all who are bowed down (Psalm 145:14)." This is the same *Lord* of Revelation. He is capable and He is willing. Call on Him; rest in Him; wait on Him. Trust Him that He will do what He promises and even more than you could possibly imagine. "Let not your heart be troubled; you believe in God, believe also in Me (John 14:1)."

CHAPTER TWO

The Development of the Early Church

Too often history is distorted because it is viewed from the perspective of our own vision of the present reality. We project into the past what looks familiar to our eyes today. And under the pressure of our habits and the weight of our laziness, we cultivate clichés and prejudices and thus construct a history that better fits our natural inclination.

This observation is particularly true in regard to Jewish-Christian history. From the separation between Jews and Christians that we see now, we assume that it was always so; we conclude that it had to be so. Yet serious consultation of the original documents, the New Testament and the ancient Jewish writings, in addition to the testimony of archaeology and the latest findings from sociology, provides us with a completely different picture. There was a time when Jews and Christians walked together; they worshipped together, they believed and hoped together.[120]

In the Book of Acts, Luke writes about the establishment and development of the Church. The reader will recall that Jesus was a Jew as were all the twelve apostles. They attended Jewish feasts in Jerusalem during Jesus' public ministry and continued to do so after the ascension. Luke underlines the importance that the temple

---

[120] Jacques B. Doukhan, *Israel and the Church: Two Voices for the Same God*, (Peabody: Hendrickson, 2002), p. 1.

played in the life of the early believers. In Luke 24:53 he writes that the apostles returned from the Mount of Olives after the ascension to "Jerusalem with great joy and were continually in the Temple praising and blessing God." In Acts 2:46 Luke writes that the new believers continued "daily with one accord in the Temple." Peter and John were going to the temple for prayer in Acts 3 when they healed the lame man. Paul was in the temple in a trance, praying when the Lord told him that the Jews of Jerusalem would not receive his testimony concerning Him (Acts 22:17,18). Finally, as late as A.D. 57, the Apostle Paul was "hurrying to be at Jerusalem, if possible, on the Day of Pentecost" (Acts 20:16). Pentecost [121] was one of the three main feasts that Jewish men were required to attend (Deut. 16:16). The feast was "the day on which the firstfruit offerings of the summer wheat crop was brought to the Temple."[122] From the day after the Sabbath associated with the Feast of Unleavened Bread, Israel was to count fifty days and then offer the firstfruits to God as an offering of appreciation. Numbers 28:26 refers to this day as the day of the firstfruits. For the Church Pentecost represents the emergence of the firstfruits as well. It was the first harvest of souls for God following Jesus as the "firstborn among many brethren" (Romans 8:29). The feast has significance for both Jews and Christians. Jesus promised the apostles, that although He was going away, a Helper would be sent to them from the Father to enable them to bear witness to Him. The Helper is the Holy Spirit and the promise was fulfilled on Pentecost. Jesus instructed His disciples to wait in Jerusalem until they had received power from the Holy Spirit. Once that power had been enabled, they were to be witnesses for Him in ever-widening circles starting at Jerusalem, spreading to the province of Judea in which Jerusalem was located, reaching Samaria, and finally saturating the entire world.

---

[121] The feast was originally referred to in Exodus 23:16 as the Feast of Harvest. In Exodus 34:22 it is referred to as the Feast of Weeks where the first fruits of the harvest were offered to the Lord. Pentecost means fifty. o and this name was used in the New Testament to identify this feast of rejoicing.

[122] Kevin Howard and Marvin Rosenthal, *The Feasts of the Lord,* (Nashville:Nelson, 1997), p. 89.

From the birth of the Church at Pentecost in the upper room at Jerusalem, the early Church did just that. Acts 1-7 describes the growth and development of the Church in Jerusalem. The stoning of Stephen in chapter 7 marks a turning point for the Jerusalem church. As a result of his stoning, a great persecution broke out against the Church and all but the apostles were scattered throughout the region of Judea and Samaria. In Romans 10:2 Paul writes concerning his countrymen, "For I bear them witness that they have a zeal for God, but not according to knowledge." This zeal in actuality was made manifest outwardly in strict obedience to the law and a tenacious opposition to any and all opponents. From a political perspective, the sect of the Zealots was constantly seeking to supplant Roman rule of Israel in favor of self-rule. Ultimately, Rome dealt harshly with Israel as a result of the two uprisings led by the zealots. The First Jewish War of A.D. 66-73 resulted in the destruction of the Temple in A.D. 70. The Second Jewish War of A.D. 132-135 resulted in the Jews being expelled from Jerusalem and the country renamed.

From a religious perspective, Saul led an intense effort to rid Judaism from the heresy associated with the emergence of the Church. In Philippians 3:6, Paul retrospectively writes that he was a "Hebrew of the Hebrews; concerning the law a Pharisee; concerning zeal, persecuting the Church." Making his defense before the angry mob at the Temple in Jerusalem, Paul says,

> I am indeed a Jew, born in Tarsus of Cilicia, but brought up in this city at the feet of Gamaliel, taught according to the strictness of our fathers law, and was zealous toward God as you all are today. I persecuted this Way to the death, binding and delivering into prisons both men and women (Acts 22:3,4).

Testifying before King Agrippa, Paul states,

> Indeed, I myself thought I must do many things contrary to the name of Jesus of Nazareth. This I also did in Jerusalem, and many of the saints I shut up in prison, having received authority from the chief priests; and when they were put to

death, I cast my vote against them. And I punished them often in every synagogue and compelled them to blaspheme; and being exceedingly enraged against them, I persecuted them even to foreign cities (Acts 26:9-11).

The Romans allowed the Jews to police their own religion according to their belief. The authority Paul received from the chief priests was in fact authority that Rome allowed the Jews to exercise in keeping with their religion.

Paul's zeal was demonstrated as he led the fight to preserve Judaism from the heresy of this new sect that was springing up amidst the synagogue. Going door to door in Jerusalem, he demanded that these new believers recant their belief in Jesus as Messiah. If they recanted, they would not face punishment. However, if they remained faithful to their belief, they were beaten or imprisoned or even stoned as Stephen had been. Paul's zeal is best described in his own words, "I persecuted the Church of God beyond measure and tried to destroy it" (Gal 1:13). But just as he now writes about his countrymen being ignorant of God's righteousness, he tells Timothy that "Although I was formerly a blasphemer, a persecutor, and an insolent man; but I obtained mercy because I did it ignorantly in unbelief" (1 Tim 1:13). Paul could easily bear witness to the zealousness of his countrymen for he had once been the leading persecutor of the early believers.

Philip the evangelist, one of the seven early deacons of chapter 6, preached in Samaria and Luke records that "there was great joy in that city" as a result of his message (Acts 8:8). The Jerusalem church heard about these things and dispatched Peter and John to investigate these claims. When they arrived in the area, they prayed for the people that they might receive the Holy Spirit just as the original group had received at Pentecost. Peter and John preached the word in many Samaritan villages on their return trip to Jerusalem. Acts 8 describes those events along with Philip's adventure with the Ethiopian eunuch and his subsequent march to Caesarea preaching in all the cities as he went. Acts 9 describes Peter as going to Lydda, then to Joppa where the men sent by

Cornelius, the Roman centurion, met him and escorted him to Caesarea where Cornelius was stationed.

Cornelius observed Jewish customs regarding prayer and giving but fell short of being a full proselyte. According to Bruce, such Gentiles were commonly called "God-fearers."[123] Men were generally identified by this name since the only requirement of becoming a full Jewish proselyte that they didn't fulfill was that of circumcision. Their status was still questioned. Bruce writes "even a moderately orthodox Jew would not willingly enter the dwelling of a Gentile, God-fearer though he might be."[124] Peter entered Cornelius' house and ate with him. This news preceded Peter to Jerusalem and upon his return, "those of the circumcision" confronted him as to why he ate with him (11:3). Peter explained to them that God had also granted to the Gentiles "repentance to life" (11:18).

The ever-widening circle had now encompassed Jerusalem, Judea, and Samaria including both Jew and Gentile. What was left was to take the Gospel message to the end of the earth. That process began in chapter 11 as those who had been scattered by the stoning of Stephen traveled to Phoenicia, Cyprus, and Antioch preaching the good news to the Jews only. Barnabas was commissioned by the leaders at Jerusalem to go as far as Antioch to investigate the progress of the message and to report his findings. Upon visiting Antioch he witnessed the grace of God in the lives of the people there and encouraged them to serve the Lord with all their heart. The church at Antioch grew and Barnabas left there in search of Saul who was living at Tarsus. When he found Saul, he convinced him to return with him to Antioch and help teach the new church. Saul came and taught there for a year.

After a trip to Jerusalem to deliver aid as a result of a famine, Barnabas and Paul were commissioned by the Holy Spirit to missionary service. Acts 13:9 tells us that Saul was the Hebrew name and Paul was the Roman name of the man that would be used by God to effectuate the spread of the gospel message

---

[123] F. F. Bruce, "The Book of Acts," (Grand Rapids: Eerdmans, 1988), p. 203.
[124] Ibid., p.205.

throughout the Roman Empire. The two missionaries had previously been referred to as Barnabas and Saul. However, from this point forward Paul would assume the leadership position.

This missionary endeavor would be the first of at least three missionary trips that spread the Gospel message to Cyprus, Asia Minor, Greece, Illyricum, and Rome. This first journey occurred in the time frame of A.D. 46-48 approximately twelve years after Paul's Damascus Road experience. The circle would widen again for the fulfillment of Jesus' words spoken to the apostles on the Mount of Olives just prior to His ascension into heaven.

It was Paul's custom to go first to the synagogue as he entered a new town. This practice was in keeping with his philosophy that the "gospel of Christ . . . is the power of God to salvation for everyone who believes, for the Jew first and also for the Greek" (Romans 1:16). The remainder of the Book of Acts details Paul's journeys finally consummating with his discussion with the Jews of Rome whom he beckoned to his place of lodging as he "testified of the kingdom of God, persuading them concerning Jesus from the Law of Moses and the Prophets from morning till evening" (Acts 28:23).

The Book of Acts concludes with Paul's Roman imprisonment which occurred from A.D. 60-62. By this time the Church would have had approximately thirty years to develop. As Paul talked with the Jews at Rome, they were anxious for him to speak to them about what he thought, especially "concerning this sect [because] we know that it is spoken against everywhere" (Acts 28:22). The sect that they were referring to was known as the sect of the Nazarenes (Acts 24:5) and The Way (Acts 19:9, 23; 22:4; 24:14, 22). The sect of the Nazarenes was so named because Jesus was from Nazareth and known as the Nazarene. Regarding the use of the Way to describe followers of Jesus, Bruce writes, "The Way is a designation for the new movement used several times in Acts. It was evidently a term used by the early followers of Jesus to denote their movement as the way of life or the way of salvation."[125] This sect was known by the Roman Jews as being spoken against everywhere.

---

[125] Ibid., p. 181.

The word *sect* used six times in Acts (5:17; 15:5; 24:5, 14; 26:5; 28:22) is translated from the Greek word *hairesis* which means heresy.[126] Early church fathers including Origen, Justin Martyr, Hegesippus, Irenaeus, and Basil are among the numerous patristic authors who use *hairesis* to refer to heresy or to heretical factions.[127] But *hairesis* also served to refer—positively, negatively, and neutrally— to any group of people perceived to have a clear doctrinal identity.[128] Josephus corroborates this more neutral usage in the Life of Flavius Josephus. He states,

> When I was about sixteen years old, I had a mind to make trial of the several sects [*hairesis*] that were among us. These sects [*hairesis*] are three: The first is that of the Pharisees, the second that of the Sadducees, and the third that of the Essenes, as we have frequently told you; for I thought that by this means, I might choose the best, if I were acquainted with them all.[129]

Verbrugge writes, "In Acts, where six of the nine examples [of the word *hairesis*] are found, it refers to parties of the Pharisees and Sadducees as groups within the Jewish community (5:17; 15:5; 26:5). From the Jewish point of view Christians too are described as belonging to a sect, that of the Nazarenes" (24:5; 24:14; 28:22).[130] Thus it seems probable that the usage in Acts "does not necessarily imply heresy, sectarian defection, heterodoxy or apostasy; rather, it refers without pejorative overtones to sects or schools of thought, including one's own."[131]

---

[126] Zodhiates, p. 882.
[127] Heinrich Von Staden. "*Hairesis* and Heresy: The Case of the *haireseis iatrikai*," in *Jewish and Christian Self-Definition*, vol. 3. eds. Ben F. Meyer and E. P. Sanders. (Philadelphia: Fortress Press, 1982), p. 97.
[128] Ibid., p. 76.
[129] Flavius Josephus, *The Complete Works of Josephus*, trans. William Whitson. (Grand Rapids: Kregel, 1981), p.1
[130] Verbrugge, p. 62.
[131] Von Staden, p. 97.

The New Oxford Dictionary of English, Online Edition defines sect as, "A group of people with somewhat different religious beliefs [typically regarded as heretical] from those of a larger group to which they belong. The word literally means following—faction—party." Jews therefore were composed of several sects or factions. There were the Pharisees, the Sadducees, the Zealots, the Hellenists, the God-fearers, and the Nazarenes. All of the sects had a different perspective on the Jewish faith but all fell under the same classification, they were Jews. As a means of illustration, we can look at the Church today. There are Baptists, Methodists, and Presbyterians to name a few. All would be considered as being Christian. Yet all would have a slightly different perspective on various theological issues.

The messianic movement was viewed as another Jewish heresy.[132] Why else would Peter and John be taken into custody and forced to appear before the Sanhedrin in Acts 3 if that body had no authority over them? Why would the Jews want to stop this body of believers who followed a carpenter from Nazareth? Why would Saul have been allowed by Roman authorities to go from house to house "dragging men and women, committing them to prison," if the early Church was completely divorced from Judaism? Why would the Jews even care about this new "religion"? The reason is that they saw in this new movement a threat to their established religion. If this new movement were in no way associated with them, they would not have cared what they believed or taught. But since this new movement was identified with them and worshipped side by side in the synagogue, they felt compelled to try and repress it. The difference in the belief of the early Church and Judaism of that day was that the early Church, which will now be referred to as Jewish believers, believed their Messiah had come in the person of Jesus of Nazareth while the Jews were yet waiting for the arrival of their Messiah.

---

[132] Marvin R. Wilson, "Our Father Abraham," (Grand Rapids: Eerdmans, 1989), p.59.

Sometimes heated debates ensued in the synagogue. Acts 18:2 mentions the fact that Aquila and Priscilla came from Italy to Corinth as a result of the Emperor Claudius' decree commanding all the Jews to depart from Rome. This occurred in A.D. 49. About this incident Suetonius writes, "He [Claudius] banished from Rome all the Jews, who were continually making disturbances at the instigation of one Chrestus."[133] The reason for the expulsion was the agitation or arguing over one Chrestus. The presumption is, although debated, that the commotion was a result of heated debates over Jesus as the Messiah. The disturbance they created was sufficient cause for Claudius to expel all of them from Rome. However, in other places in the empire, the rights of the Jews were still defended and the privileges originally given them were kept intact.

The persecution described in Acts was primarily Jews persecuting Jewish believers. The apostle Paul considered himself a Jew. In Acts 22, which occurred circa A.D. 57, Paul defends himself by addressing the Jewish mob. He states, "I am indeed a Jew" (v.3). In Romans 2:28, 29 written circa A.D. 56 he states,

> "For he is not a Jew who is one outwardly, nor is circumcision that which is outward in the flesh; but he is a Jew who is one inwardly; and circumcision is that of the heart, in the Spirit, not in the letter, whose praise is not from man but from God."

Warren Wiersbe writes, "A true Jew is one who has had an inward spiritual experience in the heart and not merely an outward physical operation."[134] Both groups considered themselves as true Jews. Neither faction wanted to be separated from the synagogue. Heated debates ended in Paul being chased out of town in Pisidian

---

[133] C. Tranqullus Suetonius, *The Lives of the Caesars*. trans. Alexander Thompson, R. Worthington, (New York, 1983), 25.2. *www.princeton.edu/-champlin/cla219/csuet.html.* 5/02.2003.

[134] Wiersbe, p. 29.

Antioch, Iconium, Philippi, Thessalonica, and Berea. He was stoned at Lystra and once received forty lashes minus one from the Jews (2 Corinthians 11:24). All this was done at the hands of the Jews. Yet, Paul continued to take the message of the Messiah to the synagogue. The first-century Jewish believers did not want to separate from the synagogue. But to the Jews they were heretics and an annoyance. Jewish authorities were concerned that further heresies would enter the discussions at the synagogue and have an even greater impact on the religion. Ben-Sasson writes,

> Decisive steps were also taken to cut off Christianity from Judaism. The various Judeo-Christian sects had generally remained within the Jewish nation, and after the fall of the Temple they even increased their missionary efforts on behalf of conversion, for the destruction of the Temple confirmed them in their faith. Judaism, however, defended itself vigorously against inroads on the part of Christians by refraining from all contact with them and by measures designed to strengthen belief in the eternal Torah and its commandments. One such measure was the insertion into the Amidah prayer of an additional, nineteenth benediction, *Birkat Haminim* (benediction against heretics), which, in its earliest Palestinian formula, was directed primarily against Jewish Christians, who shall have no hope in their belief that the Messiah has already appeared on earth.[135]

The benediction reads,

> For apostates let there be no hope, and the dominion of arrogance do thou speedily root out in our days; and let Christians and *minim* [heretics] perish in a moment, let them be blotted out of the book of the living and let them not be written with the righteous.[136]

---

[135] H. H. Ben-Sasson, ed. *A History of the Jewish People*, (Cambridge: Harvard University Press, 1976), p. 325.

[136] As quoted in Wilson, p. 65.

The benediction was composed by Rabbi Shmuel hu-Katan at the request of Rabban Gamaliel of Jamnia. David Flusser suggests that the benediction as written is found in only two fragments of the old Palestinian rite and is possibly an adaptation of a much earlier composition. He concludes however, that:

> Even without any special change in the benediction on the part of the synagogue in the period after the destruction of the Temple, Jews understood the word "heretics" as directed mainly against Jewish Christians, and the Christians themselves could assume that the benediction was directed against them.[137]

Prior to A.D. 70 and the destruction of Jerusalem, the Jewish believers left Jerusalem and took refuge in Pella, a city in what is now Jordan. The Jewish believers were not supportive of the rebellion against Rome and chose to abandon Jerusalem rather than fight for a cause in which they did not believe. The Jews felt that these Jewish believers were being disloyal and even treasonous. The split grew even wider as the Jewish believers saw in the destruction of Jerusalem God's judgment falling on the Jews for their refusal to accept Christ as Messiah. The split was exacerbated as the Jewish believers began to forsake Sabbath worship in favor of Sunday worship. In approximately A.D. 110 Ignatius of Antioch addressed this conflict between the Sabbath and the Lord's Day. He writes,

> If then, those who walked in ancient customs came to a new hope, no longer sabbathing but living by the Lord's Day, on which we came to life through Him and through His death—which some deny—through which mystery we received faith, through which we suffer in order to be found to be disciples of Jesus Christ, our only Teacher.[138]

---

[137] David Flusser, *Jerusalem and the Origins of Christianity*, (Jerusalem: The Magnes Press, 1988), p. 643. Also see p. 639-643 for a more detailed understanding of Flusser's position.

[138] William A. Jurgens, The Faith of the Early Fathers, (Collegeville: The Liturgical Press, 1970), p. 19.

This shift in worship from the Sabbath to the Lord's Day was viewed as a "rejection of the very heart of Jewish experience—rejection of the Law."[139]

> Only two of the Jewish sects survived after A.D. 70, the Pharisees and the Jewish believers in Jesus . . . Step by step they [Jewish believers in Jesus] were transformed from a competing Jewish group to the independent opponents of the Pharisees, who now represented orthodox Judaism. From A.D. 70 on, Jewish Christians saw their own way of faith as something distinct from that of the synagogue in the Jewish community.[140]

By A.D. 90 Jewish Christians were being exposed as defectors and excommunicated from the synagogue. The Roman government no longer perceived them as being under the umbrella of Judasim. They faced the dilemma of forsaking Christ as a condition of being allowed back into the synagogue or worshipping Caesar. The Jews exacerbated their problem by providing a list to the Romans of known Christians who were no longer associated with the synagogue.[141]

In A.D. 132 the Jews in Israel again plotted against Rome. Property that had previously been confiscated by Rome was targeted and reclaimed in the name of the leader of the revolt, Simon Bar Kokhba. His name means Son of the Star because the Jews thought of him as the promised Messiah. The Jewish Christians who still comprised part of the synagogue naturally refused to fight for the cause because their Messiah was Jesus. They weren't looking for a Messiah, they already had One. Their refusal to help in the rebellion was severely punished.

---

[139] Wilson, p. 80.
[140] Verbrugge, p.618, 619.
[141] C. Marvin Pate, "A Progressive Dispensationalist View of Revelation," in *Four Views on the Book of Revelation*, ed. C. Marvin Pate, (Grand Rapids: Zondervan, 1998), p. 140.

The revolt lasted three and one-half years with many Judean towns destroyed. Jerusalem suffered destruction again and was rebuilt as a Roman city and renamed Aelia Capitolina.

> "Aelia" reflected the second name of Hadrian (Publius Aelius Hadrianus), indicating the city's dedication to imperial worship. "Capitolina" was a reminder that the city was also dedicated to the worship of the Roman gods of the Capiltoline hill (Jupiter, Minerva, and Juno).[142]

> Jews were forbidden to live in the city and were allowed to visit it only once a year, on the Ninth of AB, to mourn on the ruins of their holy Temple. In an effort to wipe out all memory of the bond between the Jews and the land, Hadrian changed the name of the province from Judea to Syria-Palestina, a name that became common in non-Jewish literature.[143]

According to Bernard Lewis,

> The official adoption of the name Palestine in Roman usage to designate the suppression of the great Jewish revolt of Bar Kokhba in the year 135 C.E.[144] . . . it would seem that the name Judea was abolished . . . and the country renamed Palestine or Syria-Palestina, with the intention of obliterating the historic Jewish identity.[145]

---

[142] Howard, p. 94.
[143] Ben-Sasson, p. 334.
[144] The term CE means Common Era and is used in writings rather than the familiar A.D. (Anno Domini, i.e., the Latin designation meaning in the Year of the Lord). The term BCE means Before the Common Era and is used rather than the familiar term *B.C.* (Before Christ).
[145] As quoted in Joan Peters, *From Time Immemorial: The Origins of the Arab Jewish Conflict Over Palestine,* (Chicago: JKAP Publications, 1988), p. 139.

The First Jewish revolt of A.D. 66-70 was a decisive turning point in the schism between the Jewish Christians and the Jews. Bruce writes,

> The common view is that it was not until the final decade of the first century that the conclusive breach between Jewish Christians and other Jews took place, when the addition of the *birkat hamminim* effectively debarred Jewish Christians from participation in synagogue worship.[146]

The Jewish Christians still desired, as had been their custom, to remain in the synagogue with the hope that their fellow Jews would accept Christ as their Messiah. Jewish Christian converts would usually have stayed within the synagogue system until forced out.[147] However, the Bar Kokhba revolt of A.D. 132-135 settled the matter. The Jews looked to Bar Kokhba as the Messiah and followed him as such. The Jewish Christians could not accept such a notion. They were finally forced to separate. It was this bitter separation that evolved in acrimony between the Jewish Christians and the Jews. Early Christian apologist Justin Martyr wrote,

> Count us foes and enemies; and like yourselves, they kill and punish us whenever they have the power, as you can well believe. For in the Jewish War which lately raged, Barchochebas,[148] the leader of the revolt of the Jews, gave orders that Christians alone should be led to cruel punishments unless they would deny Jesus Christ and utter blasphemy.[149]

---

[146] Bruce, n. 20, p. 428.

[147] Max M. B. Turner, "The Sabbath, Sunday, and the Law in Luke/Acts," in *From Sabbath to the Lord's Day: A Biblical, Historical, and Theological Investigation*, ed. D. A. Carson (Grand Rapids: Zondervan, 1982), p. 125.

[148] Or Simon Bar Kohkba

[149] Justin Martyr, *First Apology*. www.earlychristianwritings.com/text/justinmartyr-firstapology.html 6/21/03.

In A.D. 155 Justin wrote a series of letters to a Jew named Trypho. In the letter he stakes claim to the Old Testament Scriptures. He talks about the words of David, Isaiah, Zechariah, and Moses regarding Christ. He asks, "Are you acquainted with them, Trypho? They are contained in your Scriptures, or rather not yours, but ours. For we believe them; but you, though you read them, do not catch the spirit that is in them."[150] With such a history of hostility, it is not hard to understand the persecution each group foisted on the other.

The final split between what we now know as Judaism and Christianity caused some theologians to conclude that Israel had rebelled against God and thereby forfeited her place as the chosen people. Since the Church had accepted Jesus as Messiah it was concluded that the Church had taken the place of Israel and thereby granted all the promises given to Israel in the Old Testament. This belief has been identified as Replacement Theology or Supersessionism because it is held that the Church superseded Israel. However, in Romans 9-11 Paul argues forcibly that there always was and always will be a plan for Israel. In 11:25 he writes, "For I do not desire, brethren, that you should be ignorant of this mystery, lest you should be wise in your own opinion, that blindness in part has happened to Israel until the fullness of the Gentiles has come in. And so all Israel will be saved." What did Paul mean by all Israel? Did he mean every Jew individually? No! In 11: 1-6 he argued that at the time of his writing there was a remnant of Israel alive of which he was a part. A remnant is a part of a whole. In the days of Elijah there were seven thousand people who had not bent the knee to Baal (1 Kings 19:18). There were certainly more than seven thousand Jews in Israel at that time. However, only a portion, a remnant, took God for His word and followed Him. The remainder followed someone else.

The purpose of this chapter is to point out to the reader just how close the early Church was to its Judaistic roots and how it was seen as a sect of Judaism. It was this experience that shaped the

---

[150] Justin Martyr, *Dialogue with Trypho* 29.8,9. www.earlychristianwritings.com/text/justinmartyr-dialoguetrypho.html 5/5/2003.

understanding of the churches of the Revelation and that eventually led to the acrimony that saw the Jews lead the way in the persecution of the early Church. That acrimony would reverse itself as the Church of the early second century began to distance itself from Judaism and ultimately practice an anti-Semitism that rivaled the early Jewish persecution. "By the middle of the second century the writings of the Church Fathers reveal considerable antagonism between gentile Christians and Jews . . . The posture of the Church was decisively set against the Synagogue."[151]

---

[151] Wilson, p. 92.

CHAPTER THREE

A Matter of Interpretation

The letters to the seven churches have often been said to represent seven periods of Church history. This theory is known as the *historico-prophetical interpretation*.
Walvoord writes,

> This point of view is postulated upon a providential arrangement of these churches not only in a geographical order but by divine purpose, presenting also a progress of Christian experiences corresponding to church history.[152]

Epp writes,

> Each letter to a specific church describes dominant characteristics of a particular period of history. We have the advantage of looking back over these things today and can readily see how these various periods correspond with what is presented in these letters.[153]

Henry Morris strikes a more moderate tone when he states,

> Although it is by no means the dominant theme, there is a sense also in which the seven churches seem to depict

---

[152] Walvoord, p. 52.
[153] Theodore H. Epp, *Practical Studies in Revelation*, vol 1. (Lincoln: Back to the Bible 1969), p. 69.

the respective stages of development and change of Christ's churches during the ensuing centuries. History has, indeed, shown such a general development through the years, and it is reasonable that the sequential development of the respective exhortations in these messages should be arranged by the Lord in the same sequence. He is not capricious in His selection. There is bound to be some significance in the sequence of the seven, as well as in the total. The Book of Revelation— all of it—is said to be prophecy, and if there is any prophecy in it concerning the Church Age, it must be here in these two chapters.[154]

The idea behind the historico-prophetical interpretation is the downward course of church history beginning with the zeal of the first love at Ephesus and ending with the lukewarmness of Laodicea. About this downward progression Walvoord writes,

> What is claimed is that there does seem to be a remarkable progression in the messages. It would seem almost incredible that such a progression should be a pure accident, and the order of the messages to the churches seems to be divinely selected to give prophetically the main movement of church history.[155]

H. A. Ironside believed that this interpretation is the key to the mystery of the seven stars and the seven golden lampstands in Revelation 1:20. He writes,

> For myself, I have no question that this was in very truth the mind of the Lord in sending these letters to the seven churches. Seven churches were chosen because seven in Scripture is the number of perfection; and you have only to read these seven letters, then take away good, reliable Church

---

[154] Henry M. Morris, *The Revelation Record*, (Wheaton: Tyndale 1983), p. 48.
[155] Walvoord, p. 52.

history and see for yourself how perfectly the key fits the lock.[156]

Ironside carried this idea even further by writing about the significance of the meaning of the name of each church. The following is the name of each church and the meaning that he gave it.

Ephesus means "desirable"
Smyrna means "myrrh"
Pergamum means "marriage" and "elevation"
Thyatira means "continual sacrifice"
Sardis means "remnant"
Philadelphia means "brotherly love"
Laodicea means "the rights of the people"[157]

Tim LaHaye assigned dates to the various church ages. Below are the ages and dates as LaHaye views them.

Church	*Period*	*Dates*
Ephesus	Apostolic	A.D. 30-100
Smyrna	Persecution	A.D. 100-312
Pergamum	Indulged	A.D. 312-606
Thyatira	Dark Ages	A.D. 606—Tribulation
Sardis	Dead Church	1520—Tribulation
Philadelphia	Philadelphia	1750—Rapture
Laodicea	Apostate	1900—Tribulation[158]

LaHaye points out that "the first three church ages differ from the last four in that each of the former stopped at the beginning of the next church. Ephesus was replaced by Smyrna, Smyrna by Pergamum, and Pergamum by Thyatira . . . Thyatira,

---

[156] H. A. Ironside, *Lectures on the Revelation*, (New York: Bible Truth Press, 1930), p. 36-37.
[157] Ibid, p. 37-74.
[158] LaHaye, p. 22-60.

Sardis, Philadelphia, and Laodicea [are] with us at the present time."[159]

This viewpoint of seven successive church ages, as elaborate as it is explained, runs afoul with the issue of the imminent return of Christ. Robert Thomas writes,

> The historic-prophetical view cannot make such a claim (emphasis on the imminency of Christ's return) because a consistent application of its interpretation would mean that Christ's coming is imminent for only one of the churches, the last. This would be the only one pictured prophetically for which Christ's coming was an any-moment expectation. On the contrary, however, there are definite references to His imminent return in the fourth and sixth letters, and possible reference in the first, third, and fifth message. If the historico-prophetical be the correct viewpoint, Christ would be guilty of deceiving these other churches, for His coming could not possibly take place within their periods of church history. Philadelphia, for example, was given a false hope of deliverance as an encouragement in persecution, since Christ's coming could not occur until the Laodicean Period. The folly of accusing Christ of such moral conduct is apparent, and consequently the inability of the historico-prophetical approach in allowing for the doctrine of imminence throughout the church age must be admitted.[160]

Another shortcoming of the historico-prophetical interpretation is the idea of the progression of evil as an indicator of the prophetic character of the letters. The argument says that evil gets progressively worse until it culminates in the apostate church. Thomas points out that

> "one cannot fully agree with this trend when he finds, for example, in Sardis one of the two worst spiritual states and

---

[159] Ibid, p. 61.

[160] Robert L. Thomas, "The Chronological Interpretation of Revelation 2-3," Bibliotheca Sacra vol. 124 Oct, 1967.

in Philadelphia one of the two best spiritual states. To describe accurately the growing failure in the church, Philadelphia should have been placed early in chapter 2, certainly before Sardis and not vice versa if declining spiritual states were a mark of these two chapters."[161]

An alternative viewpoint to the interpretation of the seven churches is known as the *historical viewpoint*. This theory sees the seven churches as real churches that were in existence in the first century in Asia Minor. These seven churches represent all churches of all time and all ages. There is no specific spiritual state, i.e., cold, faithful, lukewarm, more prevalent during one era than in another era. Just as the first-century church contained each type of church represented in the seven messages, so too, the Church in every age contains each type of church represented in the seven messages. Furthermore, every member of the Ephesian church had not left his or her first love. Every member of the church at Smyrna was not martyred. Every Pergamean was not compromising. Every Thyatirian was not corrupt. Every Sardian was not spiritually dead. Every Philadelphian was not faithful. Every Laodicean was not lukewarm. The features described in each church were dominant in that church and needed correction or strengthening. Those same characteristics are prevalent in every church in every age, including today. The notion that these seven churches represent seven successive periods of church history is not explicitly taught in Scripture. Walvoord writes,

> The prophetic interpretation of the messages to the seven churches, to be sure, should not be pressed beyond bounds, as it is a deduction from the content, not from the explicit statement of the passage.[162]

Based on the strengths and weaknesses of the two theories, the historical method appears the more viable means of interpretation and the one utilized in this commentary.

---

[161] Ibid.
[162] Walvoord, p. 52.

CHAPTER FOUR

Ephesus:

The Church That Left Their First Love

Background

Ephesus has been continually inhabited as a city for more than three thousand years, according to Selahattin Erdemgil, director of the Ephesus Museum.[163] Between 1300-1100 B.C. colonies were formed due to a migration to the western coastland of Asia Minor also known as Anatolia. The security of settling on islands and coastlands seemed to appeal to the new colonists. One such colonist was Androklus, the son of Kodros, the king of Athens. Androklus and his supporters wanted to leave Athens and form a new colony in Asia Minor, which the Greeks called "Anatole" meaning country of the sunrise. They were uncertain about where to settle and decided to consult the oracle of Apollo for advice. The communication they received from the oracle was to establish a city "at a location, which would be indicated by a fish and a boar."[164] The legend says that Androklus was preparing fish to eat in the new land when a fire broke out from the campfire. The flames scattered from the dry brush to become a large field fire. Out of the flames ran a wild boar. Androklus caught the boar and killed

---

[163] Peter Scherrer, ed. "Ephesus, The New Guide", (Turkey: Graphics Ltd, 2000), p. 5.

[164] Selahattin Erdemgil, "Ephesus Ruins and Museum," (Istanbul: Net Turistic Yayinlar A. S., 1986), p. 9.

it. He was convinced that the advice from the oracle had come to pass thus he established his city on that spot, ultimately driving out the Carians and the Leleges who at the time inhabited the area.¹⁶⁵ To commemorate his founding of the city, he built a temple to Athena. Ephesus existed in that vicinity for four hundred years ruled by the descendants of Androklus known as the Basilids.¹⁶⁶

The most famous citizen of Ephesus was the philosopher, Heraclitus (540-480 B.C.). He was an Ephesian noble and one of the last surviving descendants of Androklus. Heraclitus disdained the masses and offered this opinion of his fellow citizens, "They ought to go out and hang themselves and turn over the city to the juveniles." He considered himself above the average citizenry and severely criticized their idolatry and base thinking.¹⁶⁷ Barclay contends that he was called the "weeping philosopher" and explained his tears to be the result of the immorality of the city.¹⁶⁸ Heraclitus felt that no one could live in Ephesus without weeping at the immorality which he must see on every side.

The Greek colonists in their new land naturally worshiped their own deity but also being polytheistic worshipped the deity who presided over the land, who in this instance was Artemis. Gradually they came to pay more respect to her than to their own patroness and guardian deity, Athena, who had led them across the sea from Athens.¹⁶⁹ But the goddess though worshipped by the Greeks, was not transformed into a Greek deity. She remained an Anatolian deity in character and in ritual.¹⁷⁰

Ephesus was in a unique location for a city. The harbor allowed it to become a center for trade and the place of disembarkation to Greece and the rest of Europe. The city was often engaged in war.

---

¹⁶⁵ Strabo 14.1.21
¹⁶⁶ Scherrer, p. 15.
¹⁶⁷ Dagobert D. Runes, "Pictorial History of Philosophy," (New York: Philosphical Library, 1959), p. 92.
¹⁶⁸ Barclay, p. 60.
¹⁶⁹ Ramsey, p. 158.
¹⁷⁰ Ibid, p. 159.

Not because the citizens weren't peace-loving people, but because the city's geographic location was enviable.

In the seventh century B.C. Ephesus withstood an attack by the Cimmerians,

> an Asiatic tribe of horsemen related to the Scythians (and driven by them out of their homeland in south Russia), who spread like a whirlwind over Asia Minor . . . leaving behind them death and destruction.[171]

The allure of the city spread everywhere. Croesus, king of Lydia, was inordinately rich and powerful. He coveted the coastline and successfully surrounded the city and placed it under his control in 560 B.C. According to Herodotus, Ephesus was the first city that Croesus attacked.[172] During this time the Ephesians were attempting to rebuild the Temple of Artemis which had been destroyed. Croesus engaged the services of Kersifron, an architect from Crete, to rebuild the temple.[173] Croesus himself made considerable donations in an attempt to please the reigning deity. The temple became one of the Seven Wonders of the Ancient World.

Croesus ruled the western part of Asia Minor until his defeat in 546 B.C. by Cyrus the Great of Persia. This battle will be explained more fully when the history of Sardis is discussed.

The Temple of Artemis was destroyed and rebuilt several times. On June 21, 356 B.C. a man named Herostratos, characterized as a madman, wanting to have his name etched in history, set fire to the temple. The temple was burned on the night that Alexander the Great was born. The legend surrounding this incident says that a question was asked concerning the whereabouts of Artemis on that night and why was she not protecting her temple. The answer given was that she was in Greece attending the birth of Alexander. The possibility exists that the whole ordeal with

---

[171] Scherrer, p. 15.
[172] Naci Keskin,. "Ephesus." (Istanbul: Keskin, 2000), p. 20.
[173] Herodotus Histories 1.26

Herostratos was instigated by the temple priests who feared that the rising water table of the area was causing the temple to slowly sink into the ground.

After the fire, the Ephesians embarked on an ambitious plan to erect a new temple. When Alexander the Great came to Ephesus for the first time in 334 B.C. he saw that the project was still incomplete. He offered to donate all the funds, "both past and future, on condition that he should have the credit therefore on the inscription."[174] The Ephesians did not want to accept the offer nor did they want to offend Alexander. They diplomatically informed him that "it would be unseemly for one god to donate a temple to another god."[175]

The new temple was an imposing structure. Thirteen steps led from ground level to the floor of the temple. It was rectangular in shape measuring 425 feet long and 220 feet wide. The roof and capital sat on 120 columns which rose in height 60 feet.

Having defeated the Persians who controlled Asia Minor, Alexander ruled until his death in 323 B.C. Upon his death

> Alexander's generals fought each other for possession of his territories and by 300 B.C. four distinct victors emerged. (1) Cassander held Greece and Macedonia. (2) Lysimachus controlled Thrace and the western part of Asia Minor, but later forfeited those territories to the Seleucids. (3) Seleucus I took northern Palestine and as much of Persia as he could control. (4) Ptolemy ruled over Egypt and southern Palestine.[176]

Ephesus was under the rule of Lysimachus until 281 B.C. when control was wrested from him by the Ptolemies and then the Seleucids. In 188 B.C. the Pergamene kingdom took control. More

---

[174] Strabo 14.1.22
[175] Scherrer, p. 17.
[176] James A. Borland, "A General Introduction to the New Testament." rev. (Lynchburg: University Book House, 1989), p. 24.

about the Pergamene Kingdom will be discussed in the background of the church at Pergamum. In 133 B.C. Ephesus came under Roman rule.

In Roman times Ephesus was the gateway to the province of Asia. Barclay writes,

> Ephesus was by far its greatest city. It claimed as its title "The first and the greatest metropolis of Asia." A Roman writer called it *Lumen Asiae*, the light of Asia . . . It was the greatest harbour in Asia . . . One of its distinctions, laid down by statute, was that when the Roman proconsul came to take up office as governor of Asia, he must disembark at Ephesus and enter his province there. For all the travelers and the trade, from the Cayster and Meander valleys, from Mesopotamia, Ephesus was the highway to Rome . . . Its position made Ephesus the wealthiest and greatest city in all Asia.[177]

The religious life of Ephesus was centered around Artemis and the famous temple that was located there. People from all over the world sailed into the harbour of Ephesus just to visit and worship the goddess at the temple. The statue of Artemis in the Ephesus Museum depicts her as follows according to Erdemgil.

---

[177] Barclay vol 1, p. 58, 59.

> The legs of the statue are motionless as though fused. Although the nodes on her chest were thought to be breasts, it has become apparent that they represent the testes of bulls sacrificed for her. Testes symbolize fertility since they produce "seeds." The bulls, lions, and sphinxes that are on her skirt, indicate that she was the protectress of animals. The lion depicted on both sides of Cybele in her reliefs are seen on her arms in these statues.[178]

The temple served not only as a religious purpose but it also gave asylum to those lawbreakers who could make it safely to the confines of its precincts. Prostitutes operated there and were considered as priestesses.

Magic, sorcery, and superstition were a large part of everyday life. The term *Ephesian Letters* came to represent amulets and charms which people bought from all over the world thinking them remedies for sickness, childlessness, and a precursor of success.

It was into this setting that the Apostle Paul arrived on his third missionary journey in A.D. 53. He had visited Ephesus previously having arrived there on his way from Greece to Jerusalem. Accompanying him were Aquila and Priscilla. As was his custom, Paul went to the synagogue and reasoned with the Jews. They asked Paul to stay with them longer but he declined saying, "I must by all means keep the coming feast in Jerusalem; but I will return again to you, God willing" (Acts 18:21).

In fact, God was willing and Paul returned to Ephesus. This time Paul stayed in Ephesus for three years (Acts 20:31). His first strategy was to enter the synagogue where he spoke boldly regarding the gospel of Christ for three months. But when dissension broke out among the synagogue attendees, Paul left there and spoke at the school of Tyrannus for the next two years. Luke records that during this time, "All who dwelt in Asia heard the word of the Lord Jesus" (Acts 19:10). Regarding this Wood writes,

---

[178] Erdemgil, p. 28.

The impact of Paul's mission was felt far beyond the boundary of Ephesus itself. The entire area was affected and there were converts everywhere. Those who came into the capital on business or pleasure could not fail to hear of what was happening. Some apparently became Christians and then went back to their own towns to communicate the gospel. It seems like evangelists like Epaphras, were sent out from Ephesus to the outlying districts. It is important to realize that Paul's Ephesian mission was by no means limited to the city itself but influenced the whole province. The places in proconsular Asia explicitly named in the NT include the seven churches referred to in Revelation 2 and 3, together with Troas, Assos, Adramyttium, Miletus, Trogyllium, and Heiroplois.[179]

The province of which Ephesus was the principal city became and remained the leading center of Christianity for many centuries.[180]

Wherever the Church flourishes, Satan makes himself known in powerful ways to attempt an overthrow. Just such an event occurred in Ephesus in Acts 19:25-41 when the silversmiths led by Demetrius feared that their trade was in jeopardy because many people were turning to Christ and away from Artemis. The silversmiths made replicas of Artemis for the people to buy. Today we see images of religious figures on the dashboard of cars, worn as a necklace, or featured in a prominent place in the home. The more people are influenced for Christ, the less they will purchase the replicas of Artemis and the more tenuous the silversmith's economic situation becomes. It was only natural for them to react to what was happening.

If Paul was allowed to continue to preach, he might convince everyone to follow Jesus. They argued that if this happened, the Temple of Artemis may become less and less of a destination and the economy of the city would be in jeopardy. Notice how he was able to engage the interest of the other merchants who eventually

---

[179] A. Skevington Wood, "Ephesians." The Expositor's Bible Commentary Frank Gaebelein, ed. Vol. 11. (Grand Rapids: Zondervan, 1978), p. 13.

[180] Bruce, p. 366.

joined him in the uprising. With the cry of "Great is Diana[181] of the Ephesians" Demetrius led a public disturbance which took place in the theater of Ephesus that lasted at least two hours until the city clerk was able to quell the highly charged emotions. This event caused Paul to leave Ephesus never to return to the city again.

Although Paul did not return to Ephesus, he did speak one last time with the elders of the church. On his return to Jerusalem in A.D. 57, Paul stopped at Miletus and beckoned the Ephesian elders to come to meet with him there. Among the things Paul discussed with them was their future as a church. He said to them,

> For I know this, that after my departure savage wolves will come in among you, not sparing the flock. Also, from among yourselves, men will rise up, speaking perverse things, to draw away the disciples after themselves (Acts 20:29, 30).

Paul's warning included a threat from within and from outside the Church. Satan would attack on both fronts.

After Paul's departure from Ephesus, Timothy was appointed bishop.[182] Paul alludes to this in the first letter to Timothy (1:3) written ca A.D. 62-64. Fox reports that he

> zealously governed the church until A.D. 97. At this period, as pagans were about to celebrate a feast called Catagogion, Timothy, meeting the procession, severely reproved them for their ridiculous idolatry, which so exasperated the people that they fell upon him with their clubs, and beat him in so dreadful a manner that he expired of the bruises two days later.[183]

John returned to Ephesus upon being released from his exile on Patmos. Eusebius writes,

> After fifteen years of Domitian's rule, Nerva succeeded to the throne. By vote of the Roman Senate Domitian's honors

---

[181] The Roman counterpart for the Greek goddess Artemis.
[182] Eusebius 3.4
[183] *http://www.ccel.org/f/foxe-j/martyrs/fox102.htm* 10/26/2002

were removed, and those unjustly banished returned to their homes and had their property restored to them. This is noted by the chroniclers of the period. At that time the Apostle John, after his exile on the island, resumed residence at Ephesus, as early Christian tradition records.[184]

Exposition

The letters to the churches have a similar format. Some commentators break the structure of the letters down into seven categories generally using some type of alliteration to tie them all together. Whereas this technique is a valuable tool, all the churches do not fit all the categories. It seems best to break down the letters into two specific categories: (1) encouragement, and (2) exhortation. These two categories will be used in each of the messages to the churches.

For the sake of clarity, definitions for the two terms are offered below.

Encouragement—The act of encouraging. To encourage means to inspire with courage, spirit, or hope according to the Merriam Webster Online Dictionary. It means to hearten or an infusion of fresh courage. It means to spur or to stimulate. It means to give help or patronage, to foster. Finally, it means to embolden. Surely given the circumstances that they were experiencing the seven churches needed to be inspired, heartened, stimulated, fostered, and emboldened.

Exhortation—The act of exhorting. To exhort means to incite by argument or advice. It means to give warning or advice. It means to make urgent appeals. Just as the churches needed encouragement, they also needed to be convinced by reason that changes needed to be made in their thought process ultimately affecting their actions. They needed to be made aware that their behavior needed to match their belief. They needed to live their lives as though they truly believed what God had to say to them.

---

[184] Eusebius 3.20.4.

To the angel of the church at Ephesus write, these things says He who holds the seven stars in His right hand, who walks in the midst of the seven golden lampstands.

Encouragement comes immediately to the church at Ephesus. John is instructed to write to the messenger of the church a correspondence from "He who holds the seven stars in His right hand, who walks in the midst of the seven lampstands."

John had just finished explaining that the seven stars were the messengers of the seven churches. They are firmly held in the right hand of Christ who walks in the midst of all the churches ministering to every need that each church might have. After the Israelites had crossed the Red Sea, Moses led the children of Israel to sing a song of thanksgiving and praise. Exodus 15:6 records this part of the song, "Your right hand, O Lord, has become glorious in power; Your right hand, O Lord, has dashed the enemy in pieces." Concerning this verse Walter Kaiser writes, With repeated use of "Your right hand, O Lord" the song announces the beginning of the second strophe using a descriptive metaphor for the omnipotence of God."[185]

Not only does Jesus walk in the midst of the seven churches ministering to them, but He has the power (omnipotence) to care for their every need. He holds them securely in His right hand such that "neither shall anyone snatch them out of My hand" (John 10:28). How encouraging it must have been for a people persecuted from within by people claiming to be apostles and from without by those who are evil to know that they are firmly held in the right hand of One who can keep them in His care. The One who holds them is powerful enough to keep them for Himself.

I know your works, your labor, your patience, and that you cannot bear those who are evil. And you have tested those who say they are apostles and are not, and have found them liars; and you have persevered and have patience and have labored for My name's sake and have not become weary ... But this you have, that you hate the deeds of the Nicolaitans, which I also hate.

---

[185] Kaiser, p. 394.

Next He informed them that He knows all about them, their works, their labor, their patience. He not only knows these things about them but He also knows the intensity of their deeds and labor. Nothing that has happened to them or ever will happen to them goes unnoticed. He is the omniscient (all knowing) One as well as the omnipotent (all powerful) One. They have persevered because He has granted it to be so.

The Risen Lord gives them positive examples of what He knows about them. He says that He knows: (1) that they cannot bear those who are evil. Not being able to bear evil implies that the Ephesians are in a state of anxiety about the anti-God attitude that was pervasive in their society. It would be similar to the feeling a Christian gets when he hears God's name used on the front end of a curse or that helpless feeling when a young pregnant teenager chooses abortion saying that she is too young to have a baby. The evil that is perpetrated on society in the form of humanism, philosophy, or relativism should cause the Christian to cringe in a feeling of unbearable loss. It is open rebellion against the holiness of God.

He tells them (2) that He knows they have tested those who say they are apostles and are not, and have found them liars. People who came into the church were not merely accepted as authentic. They were tested perhaps in the same way the Bereans tested Paul by "searching the Scriptures daily to find out whether these things are so" (Acts 17: 11b). The Ephesians had a history of good leadership starting with Paul, they had astute teachers in Apollos, Aquila and Priscilla, Tychicus, Timothy, and of course, John. They not only tested their leaders they found some to be liars which implies that they made their feelings known about some who claimed to be apostles. They were a doctrinally sound group of people. They believed the right things.

Paul had warned the Ephesian elders saying, "Also from among yourselves men will rise up, speaking perverse things, to draw the disciples after themselves." Eusebius reports just such an incident that occurred in Ephesus between the Apostle John and Cerinthus.

> And there are people who heard him (Polycarp) describe how John, the Lord's disciple, when at Ephesus went to

take a bath, but seeing Cerinthus inside rushed out of the building without taking a bath, crying, "Let's get out of here, for fear the place falls in, now that Cerinthus, the enemy of truth is inside."[186]

He tells them (3) they have persevered and have labored and not become weary. The motive for their perseverance and tireless labor was for "My names sake." They labored and endured for the sake of the Risen Lord. They had a history of right motives.

He tells them (4) they hate the deeds of the Nicolaitans which He also hates. In the case of Ephesus, the Nicolaitans were doing things that the Christians there hated. Who were these Nicolaitans and what were they doing that roused the Ephesians' and the Lord's ire?

Tenney writes concerning this sect,

> Aside from the record in Revelation, little is known of them. Irenaus, who wrote late in the second century, nearly a hundred years after Revelation, said that they were founded by Nicolaus the proselyte of Antioch mentioned in Acts 6:5, and that they lived lives of unrestrained indulgence.[187]

Eusebius quotes Clement of Alexandria who wrote ca A.D. 202 saying "and by following example and precept crudely and unquestioningly the members of this sect do in fact practice utter promiscuity."[188]

The Nicolaitans were members of the church at Ephesus who had been desensitized to the immoral environment surrounding them. They saw nothing wrong with immoral and unrestrained indulgence, practicing utter promiscuity. They apparently rationalized their behavior by thinking that everyone else in Ephesus was doing it and certainly everyone else cannot be wrong. It was all done as MacArthur writes "in the name of Christian liberty."[189]

---

[186] Eusebius 4.14.1.
[187] Tenney, p. 62, 63.
[188] Eusebius 3.29.
[189] MacArthur, p. 61.

Their theory could be summarized by saying, "yes, you can have God and everything else you want."

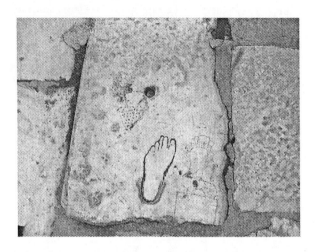

The pervasiveness of the immorality in Ephesus can be demonstrated by two interesting features found today by a visitor to the ruins of the city. While walking on Marble Street in Ephesus, the tour guide will point out to the pilgrim a part of the street that has been imprinted to form a message to those second century visitors who were unfamiliar with the city.

The picture above depicts the head of a woman along with an

imprint of her left foot pointing. Also included is a heart with stars on the inside. Below the head of the woman is a rectangular box. Taken as a whole, these images constitute what today we would call in advertising, a billboard. The woman is saying, "You can find me on the left side of the street. If you give me money (depicted by the rectangular box), I will give you love (depicted by the heart full of stars)." Located just ahead on the left hand side of Marble Street was a brothel.

In addition to this second century advertisement, there was a passageway underneath Marble Street leading from the library to the brothel for those upstanding citizens who did not want people to see them entering the brothel directly. The picture above was taken from in front of the Celsus Library. The top portion of the picture is at the street level of Marble Street.

At first blush this may seem like just an interesting tour guide story. But in the city of Pompeii, Italy, there is further evidence that this type of advertising existed in the 1st century A.D.. Pompeii was destroyed by the eruption of Mount Vesuvius in 79 A.D.. The city has been excavated and one of the buildings found in the city was a brothel. There are frescoes in the brothel located at a height that would be over the doorways to the individual rooms and continue along the wall on both sides of the hall. The frescoes depict several rather explicit sexual positions. Leaving the brothel, a visitor would walk down the street to the next intersecting street which was a main street leading to the city gate. On the main street a phallic symbol has been chiseled into the road indicating that the brothel is located left at the next intersection. Visitors would have no trouble finding the brothel. The similarity between the Pompeii street markings and the Ephesus street markings seem to corroborate that some form of advertising for sexual pleasure existed as early as 79 A.D..

These are the encouragements the Risen Lord gave to the church at Ephesus:

1) He knows their hard work.
2) He knows how they have tested their leaders.
3) He knows that they have tirelessly persevered.
4) He knows they hate the deeds of the Nicolaitans.

Nevertheless, I have this against you, that you have left your first love.

However, as good as these positive tendencies may be, He needs to exhort them. He says, "I have this against you, that you have left your first love." What does it mean to leave your first love? First of all if you have left your first love, then you must have at one time possessed love. Having left their first love implies a choice that was made along the way to depart from one position to another. In A.D. 60-62 Paul commends the Ephesians for their love. He writes to them from prison in Rome saying, "Therefore, I also, after I heard of your faith in the Lord Jesus, and your love for all the saints do not cease to give thanks for you" (Ephesians 1:15). The love they have for the saints is indicative of the saving faith they have in the Lord. When someone genuinely accepts Christ as their savior, there is a change in that person. They become as Paul tells us in 2 Corinthians 5:17 "a new creation, old things pass away; all things become new." As that change is made, an appreciation for what Christ has done in the life of the new believer becomes very real causing the believer to want to share this newness of life. With time, however, that first zeal begins to wear off and the believer has a tendency to let the things of this world take more precedence than the appreciation for what Christ has done for the believer. Apathy sets in and unless checked it will cause the heart to grow cold and lethargic. The NIV uses the word *forsaken* rather than *left*. To forsake means to renounce or give up something. Something that has been left is something from which one departs, abandons. Although it may seem harsh to say, the implication is that the Ephesians made a conscious choice to yield their love for Christ by merging into the wiles of Satan. If you are driving your car and see a recognizable triangular sign that says "Yield," it means that you must enter into the flow of traffic when it is safe to do so. You must relinquish your right of way and merge into another lane. This is similar to what the believers in Ephesus had done. They were moving along with the Lord doing the things Paul that had taught them. Their love was evident. Paul did not say that he saw their love. He wrote in Ephesians 1:15 that he heard of their love. If he heard of their love, other people had witnessed that love being expressed and reported it to Paul. Unfortunately, they yielded that love and merged into another lane. They maintained their belief but not out of love. Rather, habit or some other motive replaced love and as a result their actions became mechanical.

In marriage it is not uncommon for one spouse to feel that their mate takes them for granted. Simply put that means that one party to the marriage presumes on the other party making little effort to foster a deeper relationship. The offending party is normally unaware that they are doing anything different. But over time they have failed to appreciate their spouse. They have been ensnared by a condition of indifference. If you asked the offending spouse if they loved their mate, they would respond affirmatively. Yet they have done little if anything to engender a deeper relationship.

That is precisely what the Risen Lord is saying to the church at Ephesus. When confronted with this allegation they might be taken aback. After all didn't He commend them for their tireless effort, their doctrinal purity, and their perseverance for His name's sake? How then could such an allegation be made?

Love turned cold by apathy reflects itself in a mechanical manner. They still attended church but did so out of habit not devotion. They continued doing good deeds because it was expected not out of concern for the recipient. The motive for their behavior was introspective rather than other oriented. They were holding on to tradition as opposed to holding on to the vibrant ever-increasing love of Christ.

Remember therefore from where you have fallen; repent and do the first works or else I will come to you quickly and remove your lampstand from its place—unless you repent.

Jesus exhorts them further by telling them to remember from where they have fallen. Go back He says and revisit the circumstances of your conversion. Recall that you were once dead in your trespasses. And even though you were a sinner and unworthy of Jesus dying on the cross in your place, He redeemed you with His blood. You may have received salvation at no cost to you, but it cost Jesus dearly. By calling them to remembrance, Jesus is helping them focus on what they have obviously forgotten. The human condition makes it easy to forget from where we came. The moment is seemingly more important and attracts our attention like a magnet attracts metal. Focusing on what we were rather than what we are has a tendency to bring us back to reality so that we appreciate what we have.

But remembering is still not enough. Jesus tells them to repent and do the first works. *Repent* means to turn from the direction in which you are going and reverse course. It is a verb that demands action asking the question, "What are you going to do about what you profess to believe?" When belief does not match behavior, a change in course is mandatory.

If a change is not made certain consequences are sure to ensue. Jesus tells them that the resultant action of their failure to heed His exhortation is the removal of their lampstand. Ephesus was the *Lumen Asiae*, the Light of Asia in the secular world. At the time of Paul's stay there they were the light that allowed Christ to shine so that "all who dwelt in Asia heard the word of the Lord Jesus, both Jews and Greeks" (Acts 19:10). To have their lampstand removed was no small consequence. Yet over time this is precisely what happened to this church and this city. Even though church councils were held there, a time came when the Muslim influence so permeated the area that what was once a seat of Christianity is now ninety-eight percent Muslim. Leaving your first love has devastating results with long-lasting consequences.

He who has an ear, let him hear what the Spirit says to the churches. To him who overcomes I will give to eat from the tree of life, which is in the midst of the Paradise of God.

Jesus completes the message with a warning and a promise. The warning is "He who has an ear, let him hear what the Spirit says to the Churches." This warning is issued in each of the messages and is intended to get readers' attention. Everyone has ears, but everyone doesn't pay attention to what is said. This warning is directed to those who will hear and respond positively, those who will respond negatively, and those who will hear and not respond at all. Not responding is decision by indecision but clearly a decision. A person does not have to reject the Lord. They simply chose to do nothing about Him.

The overcomer is mentioned in each of the messages. In 1 John 5:5 the overcomer is identified as "he who believes that Jesus is the Son of God." This belief does not simply believe in Jesus; Satan and the demons believe in Jesus. They believe that He exists. The overcomer believes in Jesus enough to voluntarily submit themselves to all that Jesus is, i.e., Savior and Lord. These overcomers are the ones called, sanctified by God the Father, and preserved in Jesus Christ" (Jude 1). By Him who is able to keep you from stumbling, and to present you faultless before the presence of His glory with exceeding joy" (Jude 24).

To the overcomer at Ephesus, the Risen Lord promises to allow them to eat from the tree of life, which is in the midst of the Paradise of God. The tree of life was in the midst of the Garden of Eden. God provided the tree and its fruit to sustain life. Adam freely ate of the tree according to Genesis 2:16. However, when Adam and Eve ate from the tree of the knowledge of good and evil in intentional rebellion to what God had commanded, they were exiled from the garden. The exile was presumably for the purpose of keeping them from eating from the tree of life and sustaining their life. James Montgomery Boice writes, "If Adam and Eve had been allowed to live forever, they would have lived as sinners. They were to be set free only by literal death and resurrection,"[190] MacArthur writes that "driving the man and his wife out of the garden was an act of merciful grace to prevent them from being sustained forever [in their sin] by the tree of life."[191]

Once again the mercifulness of God shows forth. The overcomer will be allowed eternal access to the tree of life, which provides life-sustaining fruit. Adam and Eve may have been exiled from the tree due to sin but the overcomer will be continually and perpetually sustained because of the righteousness imputed to them by Jesus.

---

[190] James Montgomery Boice, "Genesis" vol. 1.(Grand Rapids: Baker, 1998), p. 242.

[191] MacArthur Study Bible note on Genesis 3:22, 23.

The tree of life was God's original gift to sustain life and will continue to be for the overcomer. Jesus said, "I have come that they may have life, and have it more abundantly" (John 10:10). The abundant life sustained by the tree of life contrasts sharply with the second death that is mentioned in 2:11 and described in 20:11-15.

Application

You have left/forsaken your first love. How does this happen?

1. Behavior doesn't match belief.

The church at Ephesus was commended for having a knowledge of doctrine. They tested those who claimed to be apostles and found some to be liars. However, their knowledge did not issue in behavior that matched what they claimed to believe. This condition didn't occur overnight. It crept in insidiously leading them to believe that all was still well; that their personal relationship with the Lord was still okay. Unfortunately, their condition deteriorated to the point of Jesus exhorting them that they had at one point made a conscientious decision to allow this to happen. They left their first love. Those Ephesian believers were no different than believers today. Many claim to have sound doctrine and if asked to expound on that doctrine could ably do so. However, as is so often the case, lives are lived in ways that an outsider would never guess that the person is a Christian. It's simply a case of one not living life as though one truly believed what one claimed. The old saying, "Your actions speak so loud I can hardly hear what you are saying," becomes increasingly more relevant. The cure for this spiritual malady is the same today as it was in the first century.

Remember from where you have fallen.
Repent.
Return to the first works of making your relationship
with Christ paramount in your life.

Saying you believe something and living your life as though that were true is sometimes very different. Jesus was very specific to His disciples when He said, "If you love Me, keep My commandments" (John 14:15) and "You did not choose Me, I chose you and appointed you that you should go and bear fruit" (John 15:16). It is expected that a follower of Christ is to be obedient and bear fruit commensurate with their belief. If there is no obedience and no fruit then a question must be asked about the person's belief. Behavior follows naturally after belief.

2) Moral purity becomes relative.

The Ephesians despised the deeds of the Nicolaitans. However, not everyone in that society found those deeds reprehensible. Society at large found nothing wrong with what they did. As a matter of fact, they joined them in moral decay. The church at Ephesus was clearly a minority of the population of the city, which at that time was around two hundred fifty thousand. In despising the deeds of the Nicolaitans, the Ephesians were going headlong against what the rest of society found acceptable.

Over time, society has a tendency to wear the believer down until the deeds that once seemed reprehensible no longer appear to be that bad. In the late 60s and 70s when the sexual revolution kicked into high gear, people were aghast at the behavior of the free love generation. Almost forty years later the same behavior that caused those gasps is viewed every night on television. Sexual behavior whether it be heterosexual, homosexual, or bi-sexual is so commonplace that many simply tolerate what they see or hear. The Apostle Paul writing in Romans 1:28-32 describes the debased mind that consents "to do those things, which are not fitting." He presents a list of those activities and concludes by saying that those who do these things knowing of the righteous judgment of God are deserving of death. Not only the ones that commit these acts, but also those who "approve of those who practice them." Approving of those who practice them does not necessarily mean giving tacit approval of someone's evil activities. It also means supporting those activities by looking the other way or watching the glorification of those activities on television or at the movies laughing at jokes that make you feel uncomfortable or even tolerating the use of God's name as part of a curse.

3) Zeal for the truth diminishes.

In a society that scoffs at truth as being relative, it becomes easier and easier to go along for the ride. Not leaving your first love means holding on to what you know of the truth of God. It means placing God's truth above all else even when it seems to go against human logic or philosophy.

Jesus was before Pilate on the day of His crucifixion. Pilate asked Him if He was a king as He had been accused. Jesus answered by telling him that not only was He a king but that He had come into the world specifically to bear witness to the truth. "Everyone who is of the truth hears My voice," He told him. To which Pilate sardonically replied, "What is truth?" (John 18:38)

Truth is earnest enthusiasm to know God. Just before he was to die, Moses spoke these words in the hearing of all the assembly of Israel,

> For I proclaim the name of the LORD: Ascribe greatness to our God. He is the Rock, His word is perfect; for all His ways are justice, a God of Truth and without injustice; righteous and upright is He (Deut 32:3, 4).

In John 14:6 Jesus tells His disciples, "I am the way, the truth, and the life." And in John 14:16,17 Jesus says, "And I will pray the Father, and He will give you another Helper, that He may abide with you forever—the Spirit of Truth."

Finally, in His high priestly prayer of John 17, Jesus prays to the Father and asks Him to sanctify the disciples by "Your truth." He follows that with, "Your word is truth" (v 17).

The answer to Pilate's question is that truth is God the Father, God the Son, God the Holy Spirit and the word that proceeds from them. Zeal for the truth is earnestly seeking to know God and His word. When that zeal diminishes, love grows cold.

4) Service issues from wrong motives.

When Paul wrote to the Ephesians they were commended for their love of their fellow believers. At the time of John's writing, Jesus was still commending them for their works. They were still doing good deeds. However, when love grows cold the motive for performing those deeds begins to take on a different look. Many good works are done out of habit, guilt, self-satisfaction or for an ego boost. None of these are proper motives for being fruitful. Proper motives are the ones expressed by Jesus in the Sermon on the Mount. In Matthew 6:3, 4, Jesus said "But when you do a charitable deed, do not let your left hand know what your right hand is doing, that your charitable deed may be in secret; and your Father who sees in secret will Himself reward you openly."

Over time the relevance of these four factors weigh heavily on a once-vibrant love, causing it to slowly fade away. Songwriter Paul Simon puts it this way:

> April come she will
> When streams are ripe and swelled with rain;
> May she will stay,
> Resting in my arms again.
>
> June she'll change her tune,
> In restless walks she'll prowl the night;
> July she will fly
> And give no warning to her flight.
>
> August, die she must
> Autumn winds blow chilly and cold;
> September I'll remember.
> A love once new has now grown old.[192]

---

[192] April Come She Will. Simon and Garfunkel Collected Works. CBS Records, Inc, 1990

CHAPTER FIVE

Smyrna:

The Fragrant Church

Background

The city of Smyrna was located approximately thirty-five miles north of Ephesus. It was a harbor city with important trade routes to the north and south adding to its geographic desirability. The first settlement established in Smyrna was by Greek colonists who located the city directly on the harbor. The city was settled ca 1000 B.C. by the Aeolians who originated in the central part of Greece but later migrated to the islands of the Aegean, specifically Lesbos, then on to the northwest of Asia Minor establishing twelve cities along the coast. One of those cities was Smyrna.

While the Aeolians were settling in the city, the Ionians, who occupied the northern Peloponnesus of Greece, were being invaded by the Dorians, who originated in Northern Greece. The Peloponnesus is the southern peninsula of Greece connected to the mainland by an isthmus between Athens and Corinth. The Ionians migrated to Asia Minor and established a powerful presence there. Just prior to 688 B.C. Smyrna was captured by the Ionians.[193]

Heredotus described the manner in which Smyrna was captured.

> The following is the way in which the loss of Smyrna happened. Certain men from Colophon had been engaged

---

[193] Knight, Kevin, *The Catholic Encyclopedia*, vol, XIV Online edition, 2002.

in a sedition there, and being the weaker party, were driven out by the others into banishment. The Smyrnaeans received the fugitives, who after a time, watching their opportunity, while the inhabitants were celebrating a feast to Dionysus outside the walls, shut to the gates, and so got possession of the town. The Aeolians of the other states came to their aid and terms were agreed on between the parties, the Ionians consenting to give up all the moveables, and the Aeolians making a surrender of the place. The expelled Smyrnaeans were distributed among the other states of the Aeolians, and were everywhere admitted to citizenship.[194]

Over the next one hundred years the Ionians extended their borders and battled the Lydian Kingdom to the east. But the Lydian power, with its center at Sardis, was increasing during that period; Smyrna gradually fell before it, until finally about 600 B.C., the city was captured and destroyed by King Alyattes. In one sense, Smyrna was now dead; the Greek city ceased to exist.[195]

Strabo writes,

> After Smyrna had been razed by the Lydians, its inhabitants continued for about 400 years to live in villages. Then they were reassembled into a city by Antigonus, and afterward by Lysimachus, and their city is now the most beautiful of all.[196]

The imagery of the city being rebuilt four hundred years later became a source of pride for the people of Smyrna. Hemer suggests that the residents were "prone to dwell upon the splendid rebirth of the city,"[197] as opposed to dwelling on the difficulties associated with its destruction.

---

[194] Herodotus 1.150.
[195] Ramsey, p.182.
[196] Strabo, 14.1.37.
[197] Hemer, p. 63.

The new city was engineered by Alexander the Great who allegedly received his vision of the city from two Smyrrnaean goddesses, Nemesis and Fates.[198] The new city would be located approximately two miles on the opposite side of the harbor from the original city. From the harbor the land slopes gradually to an elevation of approximately five hundred feet.[199] The picture below is taken from the acropolis of Mt. Pagos where a sixth-century-A.D. castle was built over the ruins of the previous city.

The beauty of the city was a great source of pride for the inhabitants. On the coins they minted the phrase "First of Asia." Ramsey elaborates on this attribute of the city.

> Strabo says its beauty was due to the handsomeness of the streets, the excellence of the paving, and the regular arrangement in rectangular blocks. The picturesque element, which he does not mention, was contributed by the hills and the sea, to which in modern times the groves of cypress trees in the large Turkish cemeteries must be added. Groves of trees in the suburbs are mentioned by Aristides as one of the beauties of the ancient city. On the west the city included a hill which overhangs the sea and runs back southward till it nearly joins

---

[198] Ramsey, p. 183.
[199] Mounce, p. 73.

the western end of Pagus. In the angle the road to the south issued through the Ephesian Gate. The outer edge of the western hill afforded a strong line of defense, which the wall of Lysimachus took advantage of, and Pagus constituted an ideal acropolis, as well as a striking ornament to crown the beauty of the city.[200]

Rising gradually until it overlooked the harbor, Mt. Pagus was adorned with the street of gold which transverses the foothills beginning with the temple of Zeus then crisscrossing to reach the top. There the temple of Cybele stood.[201]

The citizens of the rebuilt Smyrna greatly prized loyalty and early in their existence aligned themselves with Rome. The Roman philosopher Cicero (106-43 B.C.) in his writings described Smyrna as one of "our most faithful and most ancient allies."[202] Barclay relates that:

During the campaign against Mithiradates in the far east things had gone badly with Rome. And when the soldiers of Rome were suffering from hunger and cold, the people of Smyrna stripped off their own clothes to send to them.[203]

Smyrna was steadfast in its loyalty to Rome and was rewarded by Rome for that continuing loyalty. It became the first city to build a temple to the goddess Roma from which Rome got its name. In 23 B.C. eleven cities including Smyrna competed to be the select location for a temple built to the Emperor Tiberius. In view of its long devotion to Rome, the senate chose to grant the honor of erecting the temple to Smyrna.[204]

The Roman province of Asia had a large Jewish population the beginning of which can be traced at least to Seleucus Nicator who

---

[200] Ramsey, p. 185, 186.
[201] Barclay, Vol. 1, p.74.
[202] *http://www.perseus.tufts.edu/cgi-bin/ptext?lookup=Cic.+phil.+11.4.*
[203] Barclay Vol. 1, p. 74.
[204] International Dictionary of the Bible Vol. 4, p. 393.

reigned over Syria and part of Asia Minor from 312-280 B.C. According to Josephus,

> The Jews also obtained honor from the kings of Asia, when they became their auxiliaries; for Seleucus Nicator made them citizens of those cities which he built in Asia, and in lower Syria, and in the metropolis itself, Antioch; and gave them privileges equal to those of the inhabitants, insomuch as these privileges continue to this day.[205]

Antiochus III was also responsible for populating the provinces of Lydia and Phrygia with two thousand families of Jews who were then residing in Mesopotamia and Babylon. His reasoning

> was that they will be well-disposed guardians of our possessions, because of their piety towards God, and because I know that my predecessors have borne witness to them that they are faithful, and with alacrity do what they are desired to do.[206]

The Book of Acts attests to the fact that pockets of Jews existed in cities of both Asia Minor and Greece. Paul contended with the Jews in Pisidian Antioch, Lystra, and Ephesus in Asia Minor. In Greece he contended with the Jews in Philippi, Thessalonica and Berea.

The presence of the Jews is particularly important in Smyrna and Philadelphia where the phrase *synagogue of Satan* is used. Apparently the Jews were more hostile to the churches in those cities than they were in the other five churches of the Revelation. One means the Jews may have used to inflict their will on the Christians would have been through delation.

> The Romans had no prosecuting officer; it was left to the interest or public spirit of individuals to bring criminals to justice, and the private prosecutors were rewarded for their

---

[205] Joshepus, *Antiquities* 3.1.
[206] Ibid., p 3.4.

services by a share of the property of their victims. Hence it became a trade, and a very lucrative one, to hunt up offences and bring them to justice. This was called delation, and the prosecutors delatores.[207]

Today we might call such a person a bounty hunter.

The major crime with which a believer would have been charged was failure to worship the emperor.

> During the reign of Domitian (A.D. 81-96) emperor worship became compulsory for every Roman citizen on threat of death. Once a year a citizen had to burn incense on the altar to the godhead of Caesar, after which he was issued a certificate. Such an act was probably considered more as an expression of political loyalty than religious worship and all a citizen had to do was burn a pinch of incense and say "Caesar is Lord."[208]

An example of this crime and the subsequent punishment can be illustrated in the city of Smyrna in A.D. 156 less than sixty years after the writing of the Book of Revelation. An 86-year-old man by the name of Polycarp was asked to publicly declare "Caesar is Lord." It was Saturday, classified by Eusebius as a Great Sabbath. The residents of Smyrna were gathered at the stadium to witness the torture and death of those Christians who had refused to bend the knee to Caesar. It was a sporting event that attracted a large crowd. Wild animals were brought into the stadium and those Christians who had been convicted of the crime of failure to comply with Caesar worship were forced to defend themselves against the animals. The odds favored the beasts. While the activities were proceeding, Polycarp was arrested and taken into the custody of the chief of police. The chief gave Polycarp an opportunity to recant his position of refusing to pay homage to Caesar. Polycarp informed him that he had no intention of so doing, whereupon the chief

---

[207] William F. Allen, *A Short History of the Roman People*, (New York: Ginn & Company, 1890), P.246.

[208] Johnson, p. 437.

delivered Polycarp to the proconsul at the stadium. Polycarp was well known by the people of Smyrna. When he entered the stadium, a shout went up from the crowd. As he stood before the proconsul, he was given yet another opportunity to recant and pay homage to Caesar. When he again refused, the proconsul attempted to reason with him to save his life. For Polycarp, to say Caesar is Lord would have been tantamount to denying Christ. Polycarp replied,

> For eighty-six years I have been His servant, and He has never done me wrong: how can I blaspheme my King who saved me? . . . If you imagine that I will swear by Caesar's fortune, as you put it, pretending not to know who I am, I will tell you plainly, I am a Christian. If you wish to study the Christian doctrine, choose a day and you shall hear it.

The proconsul was so astounded by Polycarp's reply that he had an announcement made to the people in the stadium that Polycarp had confessed to be a Christian. The crowd composed of Gentiles and Jews alike were so incensed that they called for his immediate execution. Since the time for the beasts had already expired, Polycarp was to be burned alive at the stake.

The crowds rushed to collect logs and material to start the fire. It was reported that the Jews were joining in with more enthusiasm than anyone and applying persistent pressure to see to it that Polycarp was executed. Polycarp was burned, his bones were collected by his followers and taken to a proper place. He was not the only martyr that day but due to his life and age he is specially remembered.[209]

An interesting aspect of the name Smyrna is its meaning. The Greek word *smurna*, used in Revelation 2:8 to identify the city, has a root meaning of bitter. The word is translated as *myrrh*. Concerning myrrh, Vine's states, "the taste is bitter, and the substance astringent, acting as an antiseptic and a stimulant."[210]

---

[209] The account of Polycarp taken from Eusebius 4.14-16.
[210] Vine's, p.423.

Myrrh was highly prized in antiquity. It is a gumlike resin obtained from a shrublike tree that grows in South Arabia, Ethiopia, and Somalia. Arab merchants explored the trade of myrrh by transporting the product beginning in the southeastern part of Arabia, known today as Yemen, and ending in the port cities of Gaza. Yemen was one of the major trade centers of the ancient world, especially strong in the transport of myrrh.

> Around 2000 B.C., thanks to the domestication of the camel, a complex trade network evolved to transport the priceless resins from the remote valleys where the trees grew to the markets where kings and emperors vied for the finest grades. From the beginning of the first millennium B.C. to the fourth century A.D., the incense trade was as vital to the civilization of the West as the silk trade was to that of the East. Today the Silk Road, which links such legendary cities as Kashgar and Somarkand, is well traveled. But the Incense Road has been lost to history.[211]

From the tree to the resin, myrrh can be described as follows:

> The bushes yielding the resin do not grow more than 9 feet in height. There are ducts in the bark and the tissue between them breaks down, forming large cavities, which with the remaining ducts, becomes filled with a granular secretion which is freely discharged when the bark is wounded, or from natural fissures. It flows as a pale yellow liquid, but hardens to a reddish brown mass, being found in commerce in tears of many sizes, the average being that of a walnut. The surface is rough and powdered, and the pieces are brittle, with a granular fracture, semi-transparent, oily, and often show whitish marks. The odour and taste are aromatic, with the latter also acrid and bitter.[212]

---

[211] David Roberts, "On the Frankincense Trail," *Smithsonian Magazine*, (October 1998), p. 121.
[212] *http://www.botanical.com/botanical/mgmh/m/myrrh-66.html* 12/26/02

In the Bible, myrrh was used as a perfume (Esther 2:12; Ps 45:8; Pro 7:17), as an ingredient in the holy ointment (Ex 30:23), as a means of embalming (John 19:39), and as an anesthesia (Mk 15:23). Herodotus reports of the Persians finding a wounded comrade and "being anxious to save his life, since he had behaved so valiantly, dressed his wounds with myrrh and bound them up with bandages of cotton."[213] Myrrh was used as an astringent, in mouthwash, in toothpowder, and as an ingredient in incense.

The city was a proud city. Its very name evoked images of beauty and treasure. The appropriateness of the name compared with the situation in which the church finds itself will be explored more fully in the exposition of the passage.

Exposition

And to the angel of the church in Smyrna write, these things says the First and the Last, who was dead and came to life.

The message to Ephesus began with the phrase, "To the angel of the church of Ephesus write." The message to Smyrna and the next five churches begins with "And to the angel of the church write." The word *and* does not appear in the NIV. The implication is that the message written to Ephesus is also intended to be read by the churches that follow. These were collective messages that didn't simply apply to one church only. The words of the Risen Lord had particular meaning to each church as it was written. However, the collective message was to be heard and understood by all of the churches. People leaving their first love were not exclusive to Ephesus nor were those persecuted for their faith restricted to Smyrna and Philadelphia. Antipas was from Pergamum, yet he was martyred for his faith. The messages to the churches were to be read and heeded by all the churches to which the Book of Revelation was written. The Word of God is

> living and powerful, and sharper than any two-edged sword,
> piercing even to the division of soul and spirit, and joints

---

[213] Herodotus, 7.181.

and marrow, and is a discerner of the thoughts and intents of the heart (Heb 4:12).

Therefore, that same word issued to the first recipients is equally true of the Church in every age including today. There are Ephesian members of the church as well as Smyrna members, etc.

John has already used the description of the sender of this message in 1:17, 18. There the First and the Last was tenderly reassuring John that he had nothing to fear even though John saw a sight so terrifying that he fell as if dead.

The title First and Last was used twice in the Old Testament by the prophet Isaiah. In Isaiah 41:4 the prophet seeks to assure Israel of God's help. He calls their attention to the eternality of God when he writes, "Who has done it, calling the generations from the beginning? I, the LORD, am the first; and with the last I am He." "God existed before history and will exist after it."[214]

In 44:6 the prophet writes,

> Thus says the LORD, the King of Israel, and his Redeemer, the LORD of hosts: I am the First and I am the Last; besides Me there is no God. And who can proclaim as I do? Then let him declare it and set it in order for Me, since I appointed the ancient people. And the things that are coming and shall come, let them show these to them. Do not fear nor be afraid; have I not told you that time and declared it? You are My witnesses. Is there a God besides Me? Indeed there is no other Rock; I know not one.

In 43:10, Isaiah writes,

> You are My witnesses, says the LORD, and My servant whom I have chosen, that you may know and believe Me, and understand that I am He. Before Me there was no God formed, nor shall there be after Me.

---

[214] MacArthur Study Bible note on 41:4.

Just as John needed reassurance from the Risen Lord regarding his circumstance, so did the people of Smyrna. They were already undergoing persecution but more was on the way. Jesus tells them in verse 10 not to fear the suffering that was to come. There was to be continuing tests and tribulation. Even though this was to be true, they could be assured that the One who was there from the beginning and the One who will be there at the end was in charge of their circumstance. Even though tribulation is certain, the First and the Last has the keys to the seen and the unseen. No matter what the god of this age might do to them, the God of the universe was assuring them that when all is done, He will still be there to fulfill every promise that He ever made. In the face of earthly tribulation was the encouragement of heavenly triumph.

Not only was sender the First and the Last, but He was also the One who was dead and came to life. Death could have no power over the Risen Lord; in fact, the Risen Lord had power over death. The people of Smyrna could relate to one who was dead and came to life. Their city's history was an example of being discovered and destroyed, laying dormant as a city for four hundred years then coming alive as a city of beauty and renown. They were aware and proud of this rebirth. As the messenger began reading the portion of the letter that related directly to them, their attention would have been riveted to what would be said next because they had already been faithful and needed a word of encouragement to continue on in their struggle.

I know your works, tribulation, and poverty (but you are rich); and I know the blasphemy of those who say they are Jews and are not, but are a synagogue of Satan. In every message the Risen Lord tells the reader that He knows their works. In the case of Ephesus, Pergamum, Thyatira, Sardis, and Laodicea, He sees their works, commends some and demands others be changed. God's knowledge of their works becomes an exhortation for these churches. In Smyrna, His knowledge of their works takes the form of encouragement. He knows the difficulty of their circumstance and offers them solace. It is as though the merciful, compassionate God lovingly looks at this Church and says, "I know how difficult your circumstances are. I am not unaware of your trials. I fully understand how hard your life has been in detail. And because I have been in your place and know first hand the heartache of fighting the daily battle against Satan, I can encourage you by letting you know that I care and I am in your midst. Victory is mine and you share in that victory because you belong to Me. Remember, I overcame death that you might have life."

In 33:13-15 the Psalmist writes,

> The LORD looks from heaven; He sees all the sons of men. From the place of His dwelling He looks on all the inhabitants of the earth; He fashions their hearts individually; He considers all their works.

He also knows their poverty. The word used for poverty carries the meaning that they were destitute.[215] The poverty spoken of here is abject poverty. What could have caused a class of people living in a wealthy harbor community to be destitute? The text does not say specifically. However, there may be hints in what it does say. It does say that they were afflicted and suffered from slander. Clearly the environment in which they lived was antagonistic. The implication seems to be that they were destitute as a direct result of their belief and their failure to conform to the society around them. Perhaps their goods had been plundered. Maybe they lost their earning potential due to their belief in one God rather than in a plurality of gods. The possibility also exists that the Jews of the city, influential in government and in the community, had incited action sufficient to cause economic destitution.

All of the preceding is speculation. What is certain is that the Christians of Smyrna were living in abject poverty and the Lord takes time in this letter to exhort them by reminding them that treasure is not measured by the standards of this world. They are not destitute as they think despite their situation. They are rich. The Greek word used means abounding with wealth.[216] Just as their poverty is abject, their riches are abundant. Their riches are heavenly treasures sent on ahead for deposit into their eternal account. These treasures will not tarnish or fade but will remain of eternal value.

---

[215] Vine's, p. 478.
[216] Zodhaites, p. 62.

As alluded to earlier, they are forced to deal with the blasphemy of those who say they are Jews and are not, but are a synagogue of Satan. Blasphemy is generally directed toward God. To revile the Church that bears Christ's name can be to mock Christ and thus indirectly to blaspheme against God.[217]

This blasphemy more than likely took the form of slanderous accusations against the Christians at Smyrna. The perpetrators of the accusations were those who claim to be Jews but in actuality are instruments of Satan. As stated earlier, there was a significant population of Jews living in Smyrna. They proudly claimed to be Jews because of (1) their ancestry or (2) their belief in the faith of Abraham.

In the early days Christianity was considered a sect of Judaism. You will recall that Paul was anxious to keep the coming feast in Jerusalem in Acts 19:20. In Acts 22:3 Paul says, "I am indeed a Jew." And Philippians 3:4, 5 states, "If anyone else thinks he may have confidence in the flesh, I have more so; circumcised the eighth day, of the stock of Israel, of the tribe of Benjamin, a Hebrew of the Hebrews." Paul's common practice was to go to the synagogue upon entering a new city to teach there. The Jews were granted privilege to practice their monotheistic faith without fear of reprisal from the government. As long as Christianity was considered a sect of Judaism, Christians also enjoyed that protection. Perhaps part of the slander the Jews were directing toward the Christians was intended to make sure everyone saw a clear separation between the two beliefs.

The claim to be true Jews was in direct opposition to what Paul had written to the Romans. In 2:28 he writes, "For he is not a Jew who is one outwardly, nor is circumcision that which is outward in the flesh; but he is a Jew who is one inwardly; and circumcision is that of the heart, in the Spirit not in the letter; whose praise is not from men but from God." The Jews of Smyrna were claiming to be Jews but the First and the Last did not claim them as His. He calls them a synagogue of Satan due to their

---

[217] Verbrugge, p. 226.

alliance with pagans for the purpose of persecuting the very people He ransomed with His own blood. When Saul was breathing out threats against the Church and going door to door dragging people to prison, Christ appeared to him on the road to Damascus and said to him, "Saul, Saul, why are you persecuting Me?" Saul's persecution of the Church was considered by Jesus a direct persecution of Him. So too, the persecution of the Christians at Smyrna was seen by the Risen Lord as persecuting Him. Christ's admonition in Matthew 12:30, "He who is not with Me is against Me," sums up the attitude against those who would persecute the Church. These Jews of Smyrna had become tools of Satan and thus adversaries of God.

Do not fear any of those things which you are about to suffer. Indeed, the devil is about to throw some of you into prison, that you may be tested, and you will have tribulation ten days.

The Risen Lord lets His people know in advance that suffering is part of the life to which they have been called. He does not leave them unaware of the cost of following Him. Even from the beginning, Christ told the disciples that they needed to count the cost of being His followers. In John 15:20 Jesus tells them, "If they persecuted Me, they will also persecute you." Then in John 16:33 He states, "In the world you will have tribulation: but be of good cheer, I have overcome the world."

Not only does He let them know that persecution is on the way, but He lets them know from whom the persecution is coming. He says the devil is about to throw some of them in prison. Naturally, Satan himself will not be doing the persecution personally. Nonetheless, those doing the persecution are pawns used by Satan to carry out his work.

The mention of ten days of tribulation may be a literal ten-day period or more likely it is an expression to indicate that the persecution will be for a limited duration. Some commentators see in this expression ten specific periods of persecution from Roman Emperors ranging from Nero (A.D. 54) to Diocletian (A.D. 305).

Be faithful until death, and I will give you the crown of life.

The exhortation is to be faithful. He has told them previously that He is the First and the Last indicating that He is in control of all things. Now He tells them to appropriate that benefit by holding on as tightly as they can to that belief as they proceed through the tribulations that await. Their success has been guaranteed if only they persevere.

This exhortation would have been especially meaningful to them in light of their historical preference to Rome. The loyalty of their forefathers to Rome was a historical reality always mindful to Smyrna. They were proud of their "stick-to-it-tiveness." Jesus subtly reminds them that their civic pride and the resultant reward are minuscule in comparison to the reward that lies ahead for those who persevere in Christ. The apostle Paul writes, "For I consider that the sufferings of this present time are not worthy to be compared with the glory which shall be revealed to us" (Romans 8:18).

The faithfulness to Christ will result in a reward called the *crown of life*. Some commentators suggest that the correct reading should be "the crown which is life." This phrase is used here and in James 1:12. The word for crown used in both of these passages refers to the victor's crown which would have been awarded an athlete for performance in athletic competition. The Ionian Games were held in Smyrna.[218] On many occasions the citizens would have witnessed the winner of an event at the games receive the garland of victory. The crown would be awarded because the athlete competed and won the race in which he ran. All the efforts and rigors of his training were worth the time and energy he utilized as he stood there on the victory stand to receive his reward, a reward that will perish.

How much more valuable and lasting the crown of life will be for those who earn it through their faithfulness, obedience, and labor for the Lord? Both James and John speak of this crown as being awarded as a result of the believer's perseverance in times of trial and temptation. It is an imperishable crown. This crown is

---

[218] Pausanias, 6.14.3

not awarded because of the martyrdom of the people of Smyrna. Not all the Christians at Smyrna were martyred. Yet all were promised the crown if they persevered. If they remain faithful, they receive the crown. If they do not remain faithful, they do not receive the crown. The issue is not the believer's position in Christ but rather the believer's rewarding.[219]

The believers at Smyrna could look forward with eagerness to that time when the First and the Last place the garland of victory on their heads proclaiming, "Well done, good and faithful servant."

He who has an ear, let him hear what the Spirit says to the churches. He who overcomes shall not be hurt by the second death.

The phrase "let him hear what the Spirit says to the churches," emphasizes the collective nature of these messages. Each message has this admonition thereby making all the messages applicable to all the churches.

To the church at Smyrna the promise is that they will not be hurt by the second death. The first death is physical. Hebrews 9:27 says, "And as it is appointed for men to die once, but after this the judgment." The term *second death* appears four times in Revelation (here and in 20:6, 14; 21:8). In each case the second death refers to the final spiritual judgment of unsaved mankind in the Lake of Fire. The church at Smyrna will be unharmed by the second death because they were faithful while on earth; thus instead of a second death, they will be rewarded with eternal life.

The church at Smyrna lived up to its name, myrrh. The bitter taste of the resin is associated with the bitterness of the persecution the church underwent. The fragrant aroma accords with the sweet smell that the lives of the martyrs at Smyrna offered. The smoke of the incense of their lives wafted heavenward as a pleasing offering. Finally, the antiseptic that binds their wounds finds its fulfillment in the faithful endurance until death.

---

[219] Paul N. Benware *The Believer's Payday*, (Chattanooga: AMG, 2002), p. 123.

CHAPTER SIX

Pergamum:

The Church Where Satan's Throne Is

Background

The city of Pergamum was situated approximately twenty miles inland from the Aegean Sea and about fifty-five miles north of Smyrna. Unlike Smyrna and Ephesus, Pergamum was not a commercial center. It was, however, an administrative center and capital city of the Kingdom of Pergamum.

Although it is an ancient city, its prominence in Asia began in 282 B.C. The city was in the charge of the Greek general, Lysimachus, who placed Philetaertus as custodian. Lysimachus was beset with domestic problems as well as battling an invasion by the Seleucids. Philetaerus, who had been slandered by Lysimachus' wife, took the opportunity to successfully lead Pergamum in a revolt against Lysimachus to gain the city's freedom. He ruled the city and expanded the kingdom until 263 B.C. Philetaerus had two brothers: Eumenes, the older brother and Attalus, the younger brother. Their descendants ruled Pergamum until 133 B.C.

During the reign of the Eumenes and the Attalids, Rome became an important ally. When the Seluecid king, Antiochus the Great invaded Pergamum, Rome came to their aid. In 190 B.C. Antiochus was defeated and the Pergamene Kingdom reached its greatest extent including all the country west of the Taurus Mountains that had previously been under the rule of Antiochus. The loyalty between Rome and Pergamum was strong.

Control of the Pergamene Kingdom passed from one descendant to the next. The ruler was sovereign and such control passed to succeeding generations, as did the dominion over the kingdom. In 138 B.C. Attalus Philometer became king. He ruled for five years before dying of disease. As his descendants before him, Attalus passed as his inheritance the sovereignty of the kingdom. However, instead of passing control to a son or other family member whom he distrusted to keep Pergamum free, Attalus bequeathed his dominion to Rome. Plutarch writes, "About this time King Attalus, surnamed Philometer, died and Eudemus, a Pergamenian, brought his last will to Rome, by which he made the Roman people his heirs."[220] The Romans proclaimed the kingdom a province and named it Asia.[221] In 29 B.C. in honor of Augustus and their long association with Rome, Pergamum erected a temple for the emperor worship.

Geographically, Pergamum was picturesque.

---

[220] Plutarch, *The Lives of the Noble Gecians and Romans*, Trans. John Dryden (New York: Random House).

[221] Adapted from information contained in Strabo, *Geographies* 13.4.1,2 http://perseus.tufts.edu/cgi-bin/ptext?doc=Perseus%3Atext%3A1999.01.0198&layout=& 4/8/02; Harry Thurston Peck, *Harpers Dictionary of Classical Antiquities* (1898) http://perseus.tufts.edu/cgi-bin/ptext?doc=Perseus%3Atext%3A1999.04.0062&layout=&4/8/02; Will Durant, *The Life of Greece*, (New York: Simon & Shuster, 1939), p. 578.

On the side of the city stood a mountain rising one thousand feet. The mountain was somewhat terraced with plateaus readily visible. At the base of the mountain on the south side were built the residences of the inhabitants. From the acropolis the residents and visitors traveled south on a twenty-four-foot wide columned road paved with large rectangular stones. Known as the Via Tecta,

this road led travelers to the temple of Asklepios where people from all over the known world were treated for light illnesses and mental health.

Culturally, the city strove for excellence by rivaling Alexandria as center for cultural growth.[222] Evidence of this is the library, which at one time contained more than two hundred thousand parchments. The library was founded during the reign of Eumenes II (197-159). In his zeal for cultural significance, Eumenes contacted Aristophanes of Byzantium, the librarian of the Alexandria, Egypt library. The Alexandrian library was the largest and best known library in the world at the time. Aristophanes agreed to come to Pergamum to establish a library there.

---

[222] Durant, p. 578.

Unfortunately, the king of Egypt, Ptolemy VI, took a dim view of Eumenes' enticement of his librarian and put Aristophanes in jail. Additionally, to punish Eumenes for his blatant recruitment, the king refused to provide papyrus to Pergamum any longer. Papyrus was made from the reeds that grew along the Nile River. Without papyrus writing was made very difficult. Due to the inventive nature of the Pergamenes, this obstacle was overcome through the development of parchment which was the treated skins of sheep and calves.

> The library became the centre of a school of great importance in the history of ancient learning; among its leaders were such distinguished men as Crates of Mallos, who introduced philological studies into Rome. The Pergamum library was afterwards presented by Antony to Cleopatra and united with the Alexandrian.[223]

Surpassing its geographical aura, its administrative importance, and its cultural quest was the aspect of its religious significance. The city honored many gods and goddesses including Zeus, Athena, Dionysus, and the emperor. The altar dedicated to Zeus was on one of the plateaus on the mountain. Residents and visitors alike would see the smoke rising daily from the altar where sacrifices were offered. Regarding the altar Durant writes,

> At Pergamum Eumenes II made his capital the talk of Greece by building, among many noble structions, that famous Altar to Zeus which the Germans exhumed in 1878, and having skillfully reconstructed in the Pergamum Museum in Berlin. A majestic flight of steps mounted between two porticoes to a spacious colonnaded court; and around one hundred and thirty feet of the base ran a frieze as supreme in its period as that of the

---

[223] Harry Thurston Peck, *Harpers Dictionary of Classical Antiquities* (1898).

Mausoleum in the fourth century, or the Parthenon in the fifth.[224]

Alber Trever further describes the altar,

> A striking example of Hellenistic architecture was the great Altar of Zeus erected by Eumenes II (197-159 B.C.) of Pergamum to commemorate the Pergameme victories over the Galatians. On a massive foundation 15 feet high rose beautiful Ionic colonnades on three sides, crowned with a marble coffered ceiling. On the front, a grand staircase led to the summit. A continuous frieze of almost colossal figures surrounded the base . . . the titanic 7 foot figurines of gods and giants in the high relief, symbolizing the struggle of Greeks with Gauls, is one of the most remarkable products of ancient sculpture.[225]

The city was full of statues, altars, and sacred groves.[226]

Perhaps the most famous aspect of the city was a center for healing. The temple to Asklepios Soter, known as the Asclepieion, was established ca 400 B.C. Its fame as a center of health was second only to the original Asklepieion at Epidauros in Greece. The temple was located at a spring, which was said to have healing power in its water. The building consisted of a two-story circular treatment center, a complex of luxurious public latrines, a library, a stoa, and a gymnasium, A vaulted subterranean passage led from the treatment center to the center of the plaza where there were other small temples, fountains, and mud baths.

---

[224] Durant, p. 618.
[225] Albert A. Trever, *The Ancient Near East and Greece*, vol. 1, (New York: Harcourt Brace, 1936), p. 502.
[226] Walvoord, p. 65.

Asklepios, the god of healing, was depicted by a snake.

Columns excavated from the area have snakes sculpted on them. These columns were apparently erected at the entrance to the temple area. The symbol of Asklepios, as found on ancient coinage, was a snake coiled around a staff. Today that same symbol is used as the logo for the American Medical Society and can be seen on ambulances and emergency medical vehicles. So vast was the reputation of the healing of Asklepios that it has been referred to as "the Lourdes of the ancient world."[227]

Healing at the temple of Asklepios took several forms. The waters from the spring were used as a treatment. Another aspect involved the use of non-poisonous snakes. The sick often spent the night in darkness in the temple where these snakes were allowed to roam.

---

[227] As quoted by Barclay, p. 89.

If a person was touched by one of these snakes (i.e., by the god himself), he was cured of his illness.[228] Another method of cure involved the priests at the temple. At various intervals over the subterranean passageways through which the patients passed to get to the central courtyard, were open rectangular grates

(see picture above where the man kneeling is looking through one of the grates). The priests would whisper through those grates

---

[228] William Barclay, *Letters to the Seven Churches*, (New York: Abingdon, 1957), p. 43.

positive-thinking messages as a means of healing the psychological illnesses of the patients. This power of suggestion served as a catharsis in the healing process. One unusual method they used could be classified by today's standards as shock therapy. As the patients walked through the passageway tuned into the power of suggestion, the priests would drop through the grates a handful of snakes on top of the unsuspecting patient.[229] The methods, however unorthodox by today's standards, must have been acceptable for the number of people coming to the Asklepieion did not diminish. As a matter of fact, the fame of Pergamum and the Asklepieion reached its peak in the second century A.D. about the time of the writing of the Book of Revelation.[230]

Whereas this information on Pergamum may seem strange, one should always keep in mind the desire people have for wholeness and well-being. The people visited Pergamum not necessarily for physical debilities, but for a variety of reasons. Perhaps a person needed a getaway from the demands of normal activities. Stress knows no time period; it transcends time. Maybe there was a problem with alcohol or depression. Maybe the relaxation of the mud baths or the swirling of the spring waters was enough to bring refreshment for which people searched. One should not lose perspective that people have not changed. In contemporary society, people seek the same relief in spas and resorts all over the world; a place to go to escape the pressure of life and to be pampered by attendants. Not much has really changed.

Pergamum's fixation on gods and goddesses may seem strange today. But one need only look at modern history to see that the thought process that links gods to healing have not been eliminated. The Hippocratic Oath to which each medical student is asked to adhere begins,

---

[229] Information obtained from Turkish tour guide in November 2000 and 2002.
[230] Information on the Asklepieion adapted from Perseus Site Catalog, http://www.perseus.tufts.edu/cgi-bin/pText?doc=Perseus%3Atext%3A1999.04.0042%3Ahead%4/8/02

> I swear by Apollo Physician and Asclepius and Hygenieia and Panaceia and all the gods and goddesses, making them my witnesses, that I will fulfill according to my ability and judgment this oath and this covenant.[231]

Whereas each medical graduate is asked to adhere to the Hippocratic Oath, some do not. Up until 1964 when Louis Lasagna revised the oath the above rendition was used. Today that oath has been modified to read, "I swear to fulfill, to the best of my ability and judgment, this covenant."[232]

The oath is still administered; however, medical professionals do not distinguish to whom they are calling on to be their witnesses. One thing is for certain. In neither oath do the oath takers call on God Almighty as their witness.

Today there exists an association of medical professionals associated with The Church of Jesus Christ of Latter-Day Saints, alumni of Brigham Young University, and other interested parties called Collegium Aesculapium Foundation, Inc. *Collegium* is the general Latin term for an association. The word was applied to express the mutual relation of its members. The Collegium's website says,

> College Aesculapium extends a hand of fellowship to physicians, health professionals, and students who approach medical service with high ethical and moral values and with open hearts . . . Because the temples of Aesclapius were sanctuaries of healing in ancient Greece, the name Aesculapius became synonymous with physician/healer. Anciently, healing encompassed more than physical stability; the closest word for "health" in Biblical Hebrew is shalom meaning peace, wholeness, and well being. Today, health is defined by the Health Organization as "a state of complete physical, mental, and social well being, not just the absence of disease."

---

[231] Nova website, *http://www.pbs.org/wgbh/nova/doctors/oath-classical.html* 4/15/02.

[232] Nova website, *http://www*.pbs.org/wgbh/nova/doctors/oath-modern.html. 4/15/02

This attitude toward healing, reflecting not only that of the medical profession but also the teaching of Jesus Christ, permeates the spirit of Collegium Aesculapuim. To physically restore is a primary part of the greater effort to make whole and to save the soul as well as the body. As the gospel spreads increasingly throughout the world, many opportunities to improve human health arise.[233]

As holistic and positive as this statement may sound, it can't escape the connection of the ancient Greek gods with the teachings of Jesus Christ. This is precisely the type of compromise that was going on in Pergamum. They found it acceptable to mix the spiritual with the secular and tolerated those things in their midst.

Exposition

And to the angel of the church in Pergamos write, these things says He who has the sharp two-edged sword.

The message delivered to Pergamum comes from "He who has the sharp two-edged sword." The listeners would already be familiar with the description of the sender for John described Him in 1:16 as the One out of whose mouth went a sharp two-edged sword. This coupled with the admonition given in 2:16 about "fighting against them with the sword of My mouth," leaves little room for any other possibility other than judgment. Further in Revelation 19:15 John describes Jesus coming in judgment using these words; "Now out of His mouth goes a sharp sword, that with it He should strike the nations. And He Himself will rule them with a rod of iron. He Himself treads the winepress of the fierceness and wrath of Almighty God." Finally, in 19:21 those who were gathered against the rider on the white horse "were killed with the sword which proceeded from the mouth of Him who sat on the horse."

In Isaiah 34:5, 6, the prophet speaks of the sword of the Lord as being bathed in heaven and filled with blood. The passage concerns the judgment that is to come upon Edom. In Jeremiah 47:6, the prophet writing about the judgment of Philistia asks,

---

[233] *http://www.collegiumaesclapium.org/about.html* 4/12/02.

"O you sword of the Lord, how long until you are quiet?" Gideon's battle cry in Judges in the battle against the Midianites was, "The sword of the Lord and Gideon." The sword represented God's judgment in battle. Jeremiah 12:12 says, "For the sword of the Lord shall devour from one end of the land to the other end of the land."

The Servant Song of Isaiah 49 describes the Servant's mission as partly being a "light to the Gentiles." In verse 2 the prophet says of the Servant, "And He Himself has made My mouth like a sharp sword." The Servant will be given power to conquer His enemies through the power of His words. Hosea 6 calls for Israel to repent. In 6:5 as a result of their failure in this area, the prophet writes, "Therefore, I have hewn them by the prophets, I have slain them by the words of My mouth; and your judgments are like light that goes forth."

The writer of Hebrews follows up on this idea when he writes,

> For the word of the Lord is living and powerful, and sharper than any two-edged sword, piercing even to the division of soul and spirit, and of joints and marrow, and is a discerner of the thoughts and intents of the heart. And there is no creature hidden from His sight, but all things are naked and open to the eyes of Him to whom we must give an account (4:12, 13).

I know your works, and where you dwell, where Satan's throne is. And you hold fast to My name, and did not deny My faith even in the days in which Antipas was My faithful martyr, who was killed among you, where Satan dwells.

It is this image of the depiction of Christ that is burned into the minds of the church at Pergamum. Because of this ominous beginning portending disaster, the Risen Lord encourages His people. He assures them that He knows their works. On the whole, the church has continued to hold fast to the name of the Lord despite the emperor worship that demanded citizens to annually proclaim "Caesar is Lord." Failure to do so meant imprisonment and likely death. They had continued to battle the forces of Satan who were very much alive and well in the city so much so that the city is referred to as "Satan's throne" and where "Satan dwells." The combination of polytheistic worship, temples, altars, and the seat of emperor worship constituted more than temptation that was common to man. It was a satanic stronghold. Persecution had taken the lives of many but one, Antipas, is singled out as "My faithful martyr." Tradition says that Antipas was roasted alive in the time of Domitian. Interestingly enough, Antipas is said to be a faithful martyr in the English translation. However, the Greek word used for martyr in English is the same word used in Revelation 1:5 to describe Christ as the faithful witness. Additionally, the same word is used in Acts 1:8 where Christ instructs His apostles that they will be His witnesses. Antipas was His witness to the point of being martyred. None of these things have escaped the attention of the Risen Lord.

But I have a few things against you, because you have there those who hold to the doctrine of Balaam, who taught Balak to put a stumbling block before the children of Israel, to eat things sacrificed to idols, and to commit sexual immorality.

The fact that the church at Pergamum counted among its members those who hold the doctrine of Balaam and the doctrine of the Nicolaitans had also not escaped the Risen Lord's attention. In their own right, either of these doctrines are plagues. The combination of the two is so repulsive to the Lord that He warns in strong language that it not only needs to stop, but it must be eradicated. The consequence of continuing along this path means that the church will face the Lord's judgment and face it quickly.

Balak and Balaam

Balak was king of the Moabites who were descendants of Lot through the incestuous activity of his daughter (Gen 19:30-38). The Israelites were camped in the plains of Moab having just come through the land of the Amorites defeating Sihon, the Amorite king and his troops. Balak knew that Israel had defeated Sihon and was fearful of what Israel might do to the Moabites. He was not just afraid. Numbers 22:3 tells us that "Moab was exceedingly afraid of the people because they were so many, and Moab was sick with dread because of the children of Israel."

In order to strengthen his position, Balak entered into an agreement with the Midianites who occupied the area south of Moab extended along the eastern shore of the Gulf of Aqaba to the Red Sea. Balak and the elders of Midian made a decision to contact a prophet from Mesopatamia to curse the Israelites so that they could not defeat Moab. The elders of Moab and Midian set out on a journey of more than five hundred miles to seek out Balaam, the prophet, who lived in Pethor.

Balaam must have been a well-known prophet in Mesopatamia. Why else would Balak send for him so far away? The trip to Mesopatamia would have taken approximately three weeks. When the elders arrived and spoke to Balaam, he informed them that God had instructed him not to accompany them back to Moab and not to curse Israel. The elders took that information back to Balak.

Upon hearing the news, Balak sent another delegation whose standing was even higher than the first elders to entice Balaam to come to Moab. The first delegation had taken a fee to pay to Balaam but this delegation was authorized to offer much more. Even though God had already told Balaam not to go, the prospect of the riches to be paid to him was more than he could resist. So he asked the delegation to spend the night so that he could inquire of God one more time. This time, God allowed him to accompany the delegation back to Moab but adjured him to speak only what God spoke to him.

At this point it should be noted that Balaam was not a prophet of God. Numbers 22:7 tells us that the fee the first group of elders took to Balaam was the diviner's fee. Numbers 24:1 tells us that Balaam used sorcery or enchantments when he sought God prior to his first and second oracles. Balaam was essentially what we would consider today as a New Age prophet, one that represents many gods.

God made Himself clear to Balaam. He even caused Balaam's

donkey upon which he was riding to speak to him. Carrying on a conversation with a donkey is certainly out of the ordinary. But having to defend your actions to a donkey surely would give a person pause. Additionally, God allows Balaam to see the pre-incarnate Lord with His sword drawn in judgment telling him, "I have come to stand against you, because your way is perverse before Me. The donkey saw Me and turned aside from Me three times."

Balaam was affected by what he experienced. Balak offered him many riches to curse the Israelites, but Balaam refused, and four times blesses Israel rather than curse him. Whereas Balaam was unable to curse the Israelites, he was able to do something worse. He advised the Moabites and the Midianites how to get Israel to bring down God's judgment on themselves. Numbers 25 details how the Midianite women enticed the Israelite men into sexual immorality and to offering sacrifices to their god, Baal. God could not tolerate such idolatry and dealt harshly with His people causing twenty-four thousand to die. Not only did God take vengeance on His people, but He instructed Moses to take vengeance on the Midianites for their part in the blasphemy. Numbers 31 details this battle. Moses, speaking to the Israelites, links the activity of the Israelites with the Midianites with the counsel of Balaam. Second Peter 2:15 speaks concerning Balaam, "They have forsaken the right way and have gone astray, following the way of Balaam the son of Beor, who loved the wages of unrighteousness." As a result of his unrighteousness, Balaam was killed with the sword by the Israelites along with the rest of the kings of Midian.

What benefit is it to know this much detail about Balak and Balaam in regard to the Book of Revelation? The Risen Lord sent a message to His church at Pergamum. In it He exhorts them that He has something against them. That something is that some in this congregation hold to the doctrine of Balaam who taught Balak to put a stumbling block before His people. That same condition existed in the church at Pergamum.

Just as Balaam was a prophet who served many gods, the attitude of some in the church at Pergamum was the same.

Pergamum had temples or altars to the emperor, Bacchus, Zeus, Asclepius, and Athena. Today we would consider that a pluralistic society tolerant of many beliefs. For the world that is acceptable, for the Christian it is not! The Risen Lord holds such belief on toleration within the Church in derision and condemnation.

A Christian businessman tells a true story. One day the businessman was calling on a client whose office the businessman had not visited in some time. The businessman noticed that the client had rearranged the office since the last visit and saw some papers taped to the wall that had not been there previously. Being curious, the businessman walked over to read the papers. To his surprise there was on the wall a small article written by a prominent Christian writer along with a prayer that ended "in the name of Jesus."

This intrigued the businessman since he was certain that the client was not a Christian. When the client came to greet the businessman in the waiting area of the office, the businessman immediately walked with the client to the area where the papers were attached to the wall and asked the client to explain why he had placed them there. The client explained that over the past several months he had experienced a spiritual renewal due to the influence of a longtime friend. The businessman asked the client if he had accepted Jesus Christ as his savior. "Oh yes," replied the client. "I read various spiritual writers and I follow the spiritual direction of four of them." The businessman pressed further to find out that the client worships not only the Lord Jesus, but also three other deities taking the best spiritual nourishment from each.

This attitude of a pluralistic spirituality did not just occur in the church at Pergamum. It is alive and well in our society, our families, our churches today. Of that attitude and thought process, the Living Lord says, "I will come to you quickly and will fight against you with the sword of My mouth." Just as God instructed Moses to take vengeance on His chosen people for being enticed by the doctrine of Balaam, so too, the Risen Lord warns the Church that He will come quickly and take vengeance on His body of believers for the same mistake.

What connections can be made between the message of Pergamum and the story of Balaam? The Apostle Paul writing to the Corinthians says, "Now these things become our examples" (1 Corinthians 10:6). He was speaking of the activities of the Israelites in the Old Testament and how we should learn from their experience. The following are the representative of the similarities of both passages.

The Israelites are enticed into unrighteous activity through the influence of the Midian women. The men apparently saw no harm in attending the sacrifices the Midians were making to Baal. Before long some Israelites had gone beyond being spectators to become active participants both in the sacrificing as well as the sexual immorality that accompanied it.

The church at Pergamum had some who didn't see a distinction in the participation of the temple sacrifices and their mandate to be loyal to God and Him alone. It appears that the participation, or at least the sanction of it, by those church members in the sacrifices and the indulgence in sexual activity with temple prostitutes did not sound an alarm. Perhaps they were so accustomed to seeing this type of activity that they had become desensitized to its abhorrence.

God warns Balaam through the actions of a donkey. The Angel of the Lord appears to him with a sword in His hand as an adversary warning him that his way is perverse.

He who has the sharp two-edged sword speaks to the church at Pergamum. The purpose of the message is to exhort the church to repent or turn away from their current practice of participating in or condoning the advocacy of the doctrine of Balaam. The result of their failure to comply will be the quick appearance of the Lord to fight against them with the sword of His mouth.

Thus you also have those who hold the doctrine of the Nicolaitans, which thing I hate.

Nicolaitans

Aside from those who held to the doctrine of Balaam, the church at Pergamum also had those in their midst who held to the doctrine of the Nicolaitans. The group has been mentioned in the message to Ephesus; however, the deeds of the Nicolaitans were hated by the Ephesians as well as by Christ. In Pergamum these same deeds were either carried out or tolerated to the point that Christ threatened to come quickly and fight against them if they continued.

Some say the Nicolaitans were followers of Nicholas, one of the seven men selected to help with the problem of the Hellenist widows in Acts 6.[234] Nicholas allegedly went astray. His followers formed a cult and lead lives of "unrestrained indulgence teaching that it is a matter of indifference to practice adultery, and to eat things sacrificed to idols."[235]

Clement of Alexandria exonerates Nicholas attributing this doctrine of promiscuity, which the sect claimed to have derived from him, to a malicious distortion of works harmless in themselves.[236]

Those who understand the Nicolaitans as representing "unrestrained indulgence" argue that this sect participated in the pagan practices and festivals under the banner of religious liberty. Tenney writes, "that the teaching of the Nicolaitans was an exaggeration of the doctrine of Christian liberty which attempted an ethical compromise with heathenism."[237] As members of the Pergamum church they did not necessarily profess belief in the pagan deity but saw no harm in celebrating with their fellow citizens the festivities of the day perhaps citing Paul's letter to the Romans: "But now we have been delivered from the law, having died to what we were held by, so that we should serve in the newness of the Spirit and not in the oldness of the letter" (Romans 7:6). Unfortunately, they failed to consider the whole of his teaching which further states, "For you brethren, have been called to liberty; only do not use liberty as an opportunity for the flesh, but through love serve one another" (Galatians 5:13).

---

[234] Eusebius, 3.29.1

[235] Irenaus, *Against Heresies* 1.25.3

[236] Kevin Knight, *The Catholic Encyclopedia*, vol XI OnLine Edition, 1999.

[237] Tenney, p. 61.

Another theory involving the Nicolaitans centers around the Greek derivation of the name. The term is from *nikao* meaning to conquer and *laos* meaning people; thus, the Nicolaitans were conquerors of the people. The heresy of this sect according to this view is to subject the people of God to a hierarchical structure.

Just what the Nicolaitans taught or thought is uncertain. What is certain is that the sect was short-lived[238] and that the Risen Lord was against them. The exhortations to repent of the things the Risen Lord held against Pergamum meant that those within the Church must recognize that the doctrines of the world cannot and will not be tolerated in the Church. Perhaps Pergamum was desensitized to the behavior that surrounded them. The Risen Lord calls them to a higher plain of understanding that doesn't compromise with the world but runs counter to it. He is so strong in His admonition that He threatens to fight against the very Church that He formed.

Repent, or else I will come to you quickly and will fight against them with the sword of My mouth.

Christ calls the church at Pergamum to repent. He has encouraged them and exhorted them. As good as some of their deeds were, there needed to be an understanding that there were things that needed desperate attention. To those who were taking religious license with their behavior, He writes to shock them into reality. To those who tolerate the behavior that is going on in the Church, He chastises. To those who are placing stumbling blocks in the way of the people as Balaam did, He promises judgment. To those who pay no attention to what He says, He comes quickly to fight. In all cases, there was a need in the Church to repent.

He who has an ear, let him hear what the Spirit says to the churches. To him who overcomes I will give some of the hidden manna to eat. And I will give him a white stone, and on the stone a new name written which no one knows except him who receives it.

The overcomers in the church at Pergamum are promised hidden manna. Manna was given to the children of Israel for

---

[238] Eusebius, 3.29.1.

sustenance as they wandered in the desert. It was available to them each morning with the admonition to gather only what they needed for the day. Tomorrow's provision would appear tomorrow. Any manna that was over what a family needed would spoil before the next day (except the Sabbath). This manna was for physical needs. As a means of causing Israel to remember what the Lord had done for them, God instructed Moses to take manna and place it in a pot to be put in the ark as a memorial so that when succeeding generations came to worship they would be able to see that God had provided for His people. This manna was readily apparent to the people of the Old Testament. Because of the manna, Israel did not perish physically.

To the overcomer, Jesus promises hidden manna. Just as the manna of the Old Testament was for physical sustenance, the hidden manna is for spiritual sustenance. It is hidden in the sense that it may not seem readily available but by faith it is always there. The overcomer succeeds because the manna is there. The church at Pergamum will prevail because of the spiritual sustenance symbolized by the hidden manna.

A white stone is also promised. Barclay speaks of at least six possible explanations of the white stone. The most viable option explained the manner in which juries decided on the innocence or guilt of a defendant in a court case. Each juror was given a white and a black stone. If the juror decided to acquit the defendant, they would select a white stone. If they decided to condemn the defendant, they would select a black stone. Just as the white stone acquitted the defendant, so too the Risen Lord would acquit the overcomer.[239]

To be an overcomer required a radical change in a person. When Abram obeyed God he was given an assignment and a new name, Abraham. The same can be said for Jacob whose name was changed to Israel. Simon became Peter. The overcomer will be given a new name to go along with the hidden manna and the white stone.

---

[239] Barclay (Revelation), p. 95-97.

Application

What applications can be derived from the message to Pergamum?

- One must realize that the faith and name Pergamum held on to belonged to Christ. In verse 13 He says, "And you hold fast to My name, and did not deny My faith." Regardless of the circumstances the name and faith belong to Christ. His job is to preserve the Christian. The Christian's job is to hold on to what He has given.
- Christians are bombarded with philosophies, movements, and intellectual and theological theories that scoff at Scripture as being outdated and culturally insignificant, where values are decided by circumstance and truth is relative. It is tempting to compromise Scriptural values for that which the world deems acceptable. David Jeremiah writes, "Modern counterparts to the Church at Pergamum have muddied their Christain commitment with compromise. So much of the world is in the Church and so many of the Church is in the world that there is no difference between the two."[240] Theodore Epp writes, "He [Satan] tries to get God's people wrapped up in fleshly things . . . it was because of this that many in Pergamos sought popularity through alliances with worldly groups and individuals."[241] The Risen Lord calls us to abandon compromise with the world and invites us to an enhanced commitment with Him.
- Just as those in Pergamum lived where Satan dwells, so too does the Christian. Satan is described as the prince of this world (John 12:31). Manford George Gutzke writes, "There is one thing about Satan that we do well to keep in mind: he is not in hell now. We would be much better off if he

---

[240] David Jeremiah, *Escape the Coming Night*, (Dallas: Word, 1990), p. 46.
[241] Theodore H. Epp, *Revelation*, vol. 1, (Lincoln: Back to the Bible, 1969), p. 107.

were, but that is not where he is."[242] Satan is among us and subtly works his schemes. In the life of our Church and individually, Satan seeks to carry out his devious plans by subterfuge, by lulling Christians into a false sense of security often camouflaging his deception to make it appear as truth. David Jeremiah makes this observation about Satan in Pergamum. "Satan did not make a frontal attack by coming in as a roaring lion [1 Peter 5:8]. He slithered in the back door and led them astray as a deceiving serpent."[243] So too he operates today on a seek and destroy mission to corrupt the Church from within making incredibly evil doctrines seem culturally correct. Beware, danger lies ahead.

- Whereas God's people cannot be permanently lost, they can be temporally missing in action and ineffective witnesses.
- Doctrine is a bad word in many churches today. Doctrinal correctness is avoided as divisive and in some cases opposed. Epp writes, "A church that tolerates evil teaching and evil people in its midst must expect to receive discipline from God."[244]

---

[242] Manford George Gutzke, *Plain Talk on Revelation*, (Grand Rapids: Zondervan, 1979), p. 48.
[243] Jeremiah, p. 44.
[244] Epp, p. 115.

CHAPTER SEVEN

Thyatira:

The Tolerant Church

Background

Thyatira was located on the main trade route that connected Constantinople with the southwestern regions of Asia Minor including the port cities of Smyrna and Ephesus. That same route also included Pergamum, the capital of the province during Roman times, approximately forty miles to the north-northwest. This designation alone made the route one of the most important roads in the province. The city was situated in a fertile alluvial plain between the Caicus and Hermus rivers. The topography is relatively flat lacking an acropolis like Smyrna or Pergamum. This topographical feature played a significant role in the city's ability to defend itself.

Not much is known about the early history of the city. After Alexander the Great's death in 323 B.C., Lysimachus, one of Alexander's generals, controlled the area of the Caicus valley which included Pergamum. Seleucus, another of Alexander's generals, controlled the Hermus valley and the land west to Syria. Lysimachus established a colony of Macedonian soldiers at his eastern border in order to fortify his position. During the revolt of 282 B.C. led by Philetaerus, both Pergamum and the military outpost that protected it fell from Lysimachus' control to the influence of Seleucus. The military outpost was named Thyatira by Seleucus and was populated by importing large numbers of people including a body of Jewish believers. Ramsay writes,

> Seleucus I, the founder of Thyatira, is mentioned by Josephus as having shown special favor to the Jews and made them citizens in the cities which he founded in Asia. The probability that he settled a body of Jews in Thyatira must therefore be admitted, for he knew well that soldiers alone could not make a city[245].

Control of Thyatira frequently changed hands between the Pergamene and Seleucid rule. The relationship between Pergamum and Thyatira became close due to the military dependence of one to the other. Due to its lack of natural defenses, Thyatira could never hope to stave off hostile forces. The best the outpost could hope for was to delay forces trying to advance against Pergamum which was naturally fortified. Whether forces were trying to defend Pergamum or advance from Pergamum, Thyatira was the middle ground of defense to delay advancing forces until reinforcements could be deployed.

As part of the Pergamene Kingdom, around 190 B.C., Thyatira came under the influence of Rome and in 133 B.C. it became part of the province of Asia under Roman dominion. An era of peace and prosperity ensued.

The city grew and became a commercial center under Roman control. Industry and trade developed through the efforts of coppersmiths, tanners, leatherworkers, dyers, woolworkers, and linen workers. These crafts formed associations called *collegia*. Some commentators refer to these associations as guilds and categorize them as the forerunners of modern trade unions. However, historians take a somewhat different perspective.

> Guilds were not unions in the modern sense, but associations of specialists in the same trade that offered their members financial benefits such as assistance with funerals and the construction of tombs. The variety of guilds demonstrates

---

[245] Ramsay, p. 236

the high degree of specialization that characterized the workforce.²⁴⁶

Although many collegia were composed of men practicing the same craft or trade, there is no evidence that their object was to maintain or improve their economic conditions. In most cases they were burial clubs, while their real purpose was to foster friendliness and social life among their members.²⁴⁷

The following information regarding collegia or guilds helps give perspective to a more informed understanding of those organizations and the impact they had on their culture.

We should no doubt consider separately the skilled workers, such as bakers, whose service to the community merited and attracted special attention. They and analogous workers such as masons, silversmiths, wool-workers, undertakers belonged to trade associations, or collegia, which possessed social, religious, and sometimes quasi-political functions, as well as providing an organization for the businesses with which they were concerned.²⁴⁸

The trade guilds were active in the ceremonial and pageantry of their cities. When Constantine entered Autun in 311, he was received by the usual crowds, and by the statues of the gods, music, and the emblems of the collegia; the emblems were evidently not devised for this particular occasion, but indicate the regular part played by the trade guilds in the cities public lives.²⁴⁹

---

²⁴⁶ Michael Grant and Rachel Kitzinger, *Civilization of the Ancient Mediterrean: Greece and Rome*, vol 1, (New York: Charles Scribner's Sons, 1988), p. 307.
²⁴⁷ Simon Hornblower and Anthony Spawforth, *The Oxford Classical Dictionary*, 3rd ed. (Oxford: Oxford University Press, 1996), p.352.
²⁴⁸ John Broadman, Jasper Griffin, Oswyn Murray, *The Oxford History of the Classical World*, (Oxford: Oxford University Press, 1986), p. 766.
²⁴⁹ Ibid., p. 766.

> Few, if any collegia, were completely secular. Some took their name from a deity or deities, e.g., *Aesculapius et Hygia*, and their members were styled *cultores*. Even when their name was not associated with a god, collegia often held their meetings in temples and their clubhouse might bear the name of a divinity. The collegia illustrate the rule that all ancient societies from the family upwards had a religious basis. Collegia are associated with trades and professions (merchants, scribes, workers in wool and metal).[250]

> Although the collegia had religious functions, they were above all concerned with status, solidarity, sociability, and aspects of social security.[251]

> All collegia seem to have had a religious character and they aimed at giving members a framework for social activity . . . the collegia had their own officials and constitutions, and their members paid fees.[252]

From the information above, the following points can be made about the collegia.

- They were associations of specialists.
- They were concerned with benefits to members.
- They paid dues to be a member.
- They had a religious basis and generally their own deity.
- They existed to foster friendliness and social life among members.
- They had their own rules and hierarchy.
- They were active in the civic life of their community
- Their members were referred to as *cultores* (Latin for worshiper or supporter).[253]

---

[250] Hornblower and Spawforth, p. 352.
[251] Grant and Kitzinger, vol II, p. 1222-23.
[252] Michael Avi Yonah and Israel Shatzman, *Illustrated Encyclopedia of the Classical World*, (New York: Harper & Row, 1975), p.132.
[253] Words by William Whitaker, *http://lysy2.archives.nd.edu/cgi-bin/words.exe?cultores* 4/17/02.

- They held their meetings in temples.
- They named their meeting places after their patron deity.

According to Ramsay, there were more trade guilds in Thyatira than in any other Asian city.²⁵⁴ Membership in the guild was compulsory.²⁵⁵ Failure to be a member would mean severely restricting the opportunity to ply one's trade. Furthermore, the socialization that went along with guild membership would be non-existent for a non-member. Success in the world of commerce and society was intertwined with guild membership.

Social activities of the guild included a communal meal at which guild members were expected to attend. The meals would ofttimes be held in a temple and included sacrifices to the patron deity. The meat sacrificed to the god of the temple would then be eaten by the guild members who acknowledged the meat as a gift from the patron deity.²⁵⁶ The meetings were occasions for excessive drinking and immoral activity including ritual sexual behavior with priestesses and temple prostitutes.

The principle deity of Thyatira was Apollo. Barclay refers to a local hero-god named Tyrimnus who appeared on coinage struck by Thyatira. Tyrimnus' temple was located prior to the entrance to the city. There was also a shrine to Sambathe, a female fortune telling oracle.²⁵⁷

Exposition

The message to Thyatira is the longest of the seven. In the NKJV there are 11 verses containing 281 words. The city was termed insignificant by Pliny in the early part of the second century but the Risen Lord addresses more words to this church than to any of the others. Perhaps by earthly values the city was

---

[254] Ramsay, p. 238.
[255] Thomas, p. 207.
[256] Ibid., p. 208.
[257] Barclay, p. 101.

merely a stopgap, but Christ exhorts this church to rise from their perceived human insignificance to true spiritual power.

The description of the sender is given in three phrases. The first phrase defines the sender, the Son of God, while the next two phrases describe abilities attributed to Him. The term *Son of God* appears forty-seven times in the New Testament but only here in Revelation. In Revelation 1:5,6 John describes Jesus as "Him who loved us and washed us from our sins in His own blood, and has made us kings and priests to His God and Father." Obviously if God is His Father, then He is the Son of God. In 1:13 the title Son of Man is used to emphasize Christ's identification with believers as an encouragement to persecuted Christians. By identifying Himself as the Son of God to Thyatira, Christ is emphasizing His deity and judgment in contradistinction to His earthly humiliation.

The resident Christians at Thyatira may often be in the presence of the gods and patron deities as they attend the guild banquets, but this message is being sent to them from the only Deity. This message is coming directly from the Divine Judge in front of whom these Christians will appear at the Bema judgment described by Paul in 2 Corinthians 5:10 and Romans 14:10.

The Son of God is described as having "eyes like a flame of fire." That gaze from Christ is like a laser penetrating to the very soul, the essence of the being of every Thyatiran. Nothing is beyond the gaze, nothing is disguised, nothing is hidden so deep within that it escapes that piercing stare. In describing Christ's Second Coming in triumph, John describes the eyes of the rider on the white horse as being "like a flame of fire." In Daniel's vision of chapter 10, the prophet described the person he saw as having "eyes like torches of fire" (v 6). These eyes see things as they truly are and not how the people of Thyatira would like them to appear. There is no place to hide from this penetrating stare. The One who sees through these eyes is omniscient. Nothing escapes His attention.

The Son of God is described as having "feet like fine brass." Once again in Daniel 10:6 the vision Daniel saw had feet described as like "burnished bronze." This description matches the description John used in Revelation 1:15 where he says the image which he turned to see had "feet like fine brass as if refined in a furnace." Because of the metalworking that was done in Thyatira, this description would have been particularly meaningful. Ramsay makes this point in his description of coinage found from Thyatira. He writes,

> A special interest attaches to figure 29 [the coin is pictured]. The divine smith Hephaestus, dressed as a workman, is here seated at an anvil (represented only by a small pillar), holding in his left hand a pair of forceps and giving the finishing blow with his hammer to a helmet, for which the goddess of war, Pallas Athena, is holding out her hand. Considering that the guild of bronzesmiths is mentioned at Thyatira, we cannot doubt that this coin commemorates the peculiar importance for the welfare of Thyatira of the bronze workers handicraft, and we must infer that bronze work was carried to a high state of perfection in the city.[258]

Not only would the image be important to the people at Thyatira, but the imagery of the feet like fine brass could be linked to the bronze work done in the city.[259] Poythress writes,

> The Greek word for burnished bronze in v.18 is unique: it occurs only here, in 1:15, and in later commentaries, but nowhere else in all of Greek literature. It may well have been the trade name for the special kind of bronze produced in Thyatira. The Thyatiran guild carefully guarded a secret process for making this prized kind of bronze, so that no one could get it except from Thyatira—no one that is, except Christ.[260]

---

[258] Ramsay, p. 239.
[259] Wall, p. 77.
[260] Poythress, p. 88.

The brass could simply refer to the irresistible strength in which Christ will trample the wicked unless they repent. Whichever idea as to the significance one places on the "feet like fine brass," one thing is certain, the church at Thyatira knew what the speaker was trying to convey. Barclay writes, "A message which begins like that will certainly be no soothing tranquilizer."[261]

The Omniscient One identified in verse 18 encourages the readers by letting them know that He is aware of the positive things they are doing. Just as in every message thus far and in every message hereafter, the Lord knows the works of the churches. He knows what they are doing and what they are not doing. He doesn't need to be reminded. He is acutely aware. Even if their works were done for the right reasons with the right motives, it is nevertheless encouraging to know that someone is paying attention and recognizes and appreciates that which is done. Thyatira is not only encouraged that the Lord knows their works but He compliments them that unlike Ephesus where the church had regressed, these Christians were doing greater things now than they had done in the past. This is a forward moving congregation. Their love and faith by which they are commended are directed toward God while their service and patience are directed toward each other.[262] The word for patience means enduring difficult circumstances. Despite these difficult circumstances which they find themselves in, they continue to serve.

As commendable as their sacrificial service toward them might be, there is ample reason to exhort this church. No amount of loving and sacrificial works can compensate for tolerance of evil.[263] For the Risen Lord has this against them, "because you allow that woman Jezebel, who calls herself a prophetess, to teach and seduce My servants to commit sexual immorality and eat things sacrificed to idols."

Who is this Jezebel? Morris suggests that the name is symbolic. "Certainly no Jew would have borne it in view of the evils done by Ahab's wife. Jezebel had become proverbial for wickedness."[264]

---

[261] Barclay, p. 103.

[262] Wall p. 78.

[263] Warren W. Weirsbe, *Be Victorious*, (Colorado Springs: Chariot Victor Publishing, 1985), p. 33.

[264] Morris p. 70.

Thomas writes, "Another meaning attached to Jezebel is that she is a personification of heresy"[265] or "that Jezebel is a symbolic name for some prominent woman in the church of Thyatira."[266] Henry Morris says simply that Jezebel may have been a graphic appellation given her by Christ.[267]

The Risen Lord tells Thyatira at least eight things about this person.

- That woman
- Her name is Jezebel
- She calls herself a prophetess (self-proclaimed)
- She is teaching in the church
- She seduces the members
- She has been given warning but fails to heed it
- She will be cast into a sickbed
- Her children will be killed

The designation *that woman* in the majority text is translated as *thy wife*. (The majority text is determined by a consensus of all the existing Greek manuscripts. Where there is a difference in translation form the traditional text of the Greek-speaking churches, called the Received Text or Authorized Version, the designation variant is used. This translation of thy wife is a variant reading from the Authorized Version). If this translation is accurate, then there must be a husband. Some commentators believe that the husband was the angel of the church at Thyatira where angel refers to pastor or leader of the church. If this woman were the wife of the pastor that could explain the position of authority she seemingly had as a teacher in that church. Mounce writes,

> As the variant is improbable, so also is the identification. The Thyatiran Jezebel is probably some prominent woman within the church who, like her OT counterpart, was influencing the people of God to forsake loyalty to God by promoting a

---

[265] Thomas, p. 213.
[266] Ibid., p. 214.
[267] Henry Morris, *The Revelation Record*. (Wheaton: Tyndale, 1983), p. 60.

tolerance toward the involvement in pagan practices. This extended to sexual immorality and participation in the religious feasts connected with membership in trade guilds.[268]

It is more probable that the phrase *that woman* was identifying Jezebel as the person about whom the Risen Lord was referring. That woman's name was Jezebel.

She is a self-proclaimed prophetess. This is a stinging indictment. In the Old Testament Book of Jeremiah there were people claiming to be prophets that spoke against God's prophet Jeremiah. One such self-proclaimed prophet was named Pashur. Pashur heard the words that Jeremiah uttered at the command of God, struck him, and placed him in stocks. The next day Jeremiah prophesied about Pashur,

> And you, Pashur, and all who dwell in your house, shall go into captivity. You shall go to Babylon, and there you shall die and be buried there, you and all your friends, to whom you have prophesied lies (Jer 20:6).

God takes a dim view of those people claiming to speak for Him that He has not appointed or called for that purpose.

Her teaching in the church is obviously done with the approval of the church leaders. Otherwise, the church leadership would not be called to account for tolerating her behavior. Mounce writes,

> It is questionable whether her teaching was in any sense formal. It may only have taken the form of popular persuasion built upon unexamined assumptions. In any case, it had seduced a considerable number of believers into a fatal compromise with paganism.[269]

She has been given ample warning and time to repent, yet she refuses. The grace of God and His longsuffering is clearly

---

[268] Mounce, p. 87.
[269] Mounce, p. 87.

demonstrated here. God has every right to bring His judgment upon Jezebel. However, as Peter writes,

> The Lord is not slack concerning His promises, as some count slackness, but is longsuffering toward us, not willing that any should perish but that all should come to repentance (2 Peter 3: 9).

She will be cast into a sickbed. Jezebel had run out of time. The words used here to describe Jezebel's punishment stress the imminence and certainty of the act.[270] On the other hand, it appears that those who follow her still had opportunity to repent. They may suffer great tribulation, but there is still time for them.

Her children will be killed. These children are not literal offspring, but are composed of those who unabashedly follow what Jezebel teaches. As followers, they will be judged harshly and their judgment will result in their death.

Taking the information from the text it appears that Jezebel was a real person, living at a real time, with a real name, headed for real trouble. Regardless of the interpretation one applies, the connection to the Jezebel of the Old Testament is inescapable. At this point it will serve well to review what the Old Testament says about this woman and her enduring influence on Israel.

Jezebel was the daughter of Ethbaal, king of the Sidonians. His name means "Baal is alive." First Kings 16:31 tells us that Ahab, king of Israel, married Jezebel and "he went and served Baal and worshipped him." Ahab also built a temple and an altar to Baal in Samaria. The 450 prophets of Baal and the four hundred prophets of Asherah were provided for by Jezebel. They ate at her table. Although Baal was not new to Israel, Ahab's position as king of Israel gave Baal official sanction for the first time. Jezebel's influence on an already evil Ahab induced the king to give legitimacy to this false god. Her fame caused Jehu to say to her son, Jehoram, "What peace as long as the harlotries of your mother Jezebel and

---

[270] Ibid., Footnote 17, p. 88.

her witchcraft are so many" (2 Kings 9: 22b). She had Naboth killed under false pretense (1 Kings 21) and she killed all the prophets of the Lord except those hidden in the cave by Obadiah (1 Kings 18:13). Jezebel was killed by Jehu, being trampled to death by his horses and her remains eaten by dogs.

Her impact went much deeper than her sway over Ahab. It extended to Judah and almost extinguished the Davidic line. Ahab and Jezebel had three children of note, Ahaziah, Athalia, and Jehoram. When Ahab died, Ahaziah became king and ruled Israel for two years. He continued in the way of his father by serving Baal and did evil in the sight of the Lord. Ahaziah had no sons so his brother, Jehoram became king of Israel. Jehoram ruled for twelve years before being killed by Jehu at God's instruction.

Athalia married Jehoram, king of Judah (not to be confused with Jehoram king of Israel). He reigned in Jerusalem for eight years and went the way of the kings of Israel for he had married the daughter of Ahab and Jezebel. Jehoram caused the people of Judah to commit harlotry and led them astray (2 Chron 21:11). Of Jehoram it is written, "He reigned in Jerusalem eight years, and to no one's sorrow departed" (2 Chron 21:20b). Upon his death his son, Ahaziah (not to be confused with Ahaziah of Israel) became king but reigned only one year. "He walked in the ways of the house of Ahab, for his mother advised him to act wickedly" (2 Chron 22:3).

Upon the death of Ahaziah, Athalia, his mother, had all the royal heirs killed so that she could rule. All but one of Ahaziah's sons were killed. One, Joash, was hidden away by Ahaziah's sister, Jehosheba, for six years. During these six years Athalia reigned as queen of Judah. However, when Joash was seven years old he was brought out of hiding and crowned king of Judah and Athalia was put to death. Had it not been for the bravery of Jehosheba, the line of David would have ended with Ahaziah.

It was Jezebel's intent to establish Baal as the god of Israel. Her husband and children were equally committed to this task. She murdered the prophets and through the influence of her offspring nearly caused the end of the Davidic line. Her devotion to Baal permeated the highest levels of Israeli leadership. Like leaven, her treachery spread until it formed a cancer that God extricated from the land.

The influence of Jezebel of Thyatira was beginning to permeate the highest level of the church. This malignancy must be terminated before it spread like leaven to affect the entire church. No wonder the Risen Lord gave more attention to this church than to the other six. This cancer from within would only grow larger and larger until the only option left would be death.

Just as the children of the Old Testament Jezebel carried out her treachery, this New Testament Jezebel obviously desired to repeat their deeds. Some might argue that this is stretching the text. However, Christ immediately follows the promise to Jezebel with one to her children. Only when the followers of Jezebel are eradicated will the church be free of this false teaching from within.

Not all of the people of Thyatira had been seduced by Jezebel. The Risen Lord exhorts them to hold on to what they have until He comes. These people were already under several burdens. First of all they were burdened by the economic and social constraints of the guilds. Secondly, they were burdened by the excessive sin that was in their midst. Thirdly, they were burdened by the false teaching that was being promulgated in their own assembly. A Sunday school teacher related a story of how one of the members of the Sunday school class held a very strong belief to the point of fanaticism in a particular teaching. As the Sunday school teacher taught each week, the class member would encounter the teacher after class and sometimes in class, with objections. At first the teacher tried patiently to answer the objections. However, the disruptions in class and the disruptions in the thought process of the teacher in the midst of a lesson began to wear thin. The student wrote a rather scathing letter to the teacher relating how painful it was to sit in the class each week being forced to hear explanations with which the student vehemently disagreed. The teacher wrote a letter back to the student urging them to find a class where they felt more comfortable with the teaching. Not only was it difficult for the student, but each week as the topic would arise, the teacher was equally uncomfortable knowing that a member of the class was cringing with each word. The student left the class and presumably found another one more to their liking in another church.

The people of Thyatira who did not tolerate the teaching of Jezebel would be given no other burden except that which they were already bearing. They had been burdened enough by living in a community that compromises with the world, a community that tolerates wickedness in its midst and pretends that it is normal behavior. To these people the Risen Lord says "hold fast what you have until I come." The promise of His coming and the exhortation to hold on is what the believers need to hear. In the face of seemingly overwhelming difficulty it is good to hear the voice of One who knows the unknown and sees the unseen speaking encouragement that touches the very being of the listener. Those in Thyatira who had not succumbed to the teaching of Jezebel were willing listeners. They hear what the Risen Lord says and they are holding on perhaps because that is all they can do. Their options are limited. Everyone else is marching to the beat of a different drummer. They are out of sync not just with the community around them, but even within their own body of believers, they are suffering serious opposition. In John 6: 60-70, the apostle relates a story about a hard teaching of Jesus about which His followers were confused. Many began to leave Jesus rejecting His teaching and "walking with Him no more" (v 66). Jesus asked the disciples, "Do you also want to go away?" Peter speaking for the group says, "Lord, to whom shall we go? You have the words of eternal life. Also, we have come to believe and know that You are the Christ, the Son of the living God" (v 68,69). Peter and the disciples may not have understood the teaching that Jesus was trying to convey at that point, but they did understand that their only option was to trust in the One who had the answers. The disciple's options were to trust in Christ or trust in their own understanding. It didn't take long to figure out there was only one choice to make. The people of Thyatira who had not held to the teaching of Jezebel had this same option. They could try to battle the odds or they could hold on to what they had with the hope that Christ would come and justify their faith. When one sees life from this perspective, there is only one choice that makes sense.

To the overcomer at Thyatira, it is promised that power will be given over the nations. The true believers of Thyatira were powerless to affect their community. Their past history was a story in powerlessness. They were the garrison city whose sole purpose it was to fight until they could fight no more, until the provincial capital at Pergamum could be fortified. Their defeat was always inevitable. They could not win but they could and did fight. As overcomers their historical powerlessness would one day be exchanged for power given them by the Risen Lord.

They are promised the morning star. Second Peter 1:19 speaks of that day "when the morning star rises in your hearts." He is referring to that day that will dawn and Christ will come again and those experiencing that day in hopeful anticipation will be internally transformed. In Rev 22:16, Jesus identifies Himself as the morning star. It is this star promised to those who hold fast until He comes who will "shatter the darkness of man's night and herald the dawn of God's glorious day."[271] Those who have accepted Jesus Christ as Savior and Lord have that very morning star rising in their heart at this moment.

Application

In enduring difficult circumstances, some of the people at Thyatira succumbed to compromise in order to get along. They thought it would be okay to do things every one else was doing. Perhaps they said, "God will understand." God does understand our situations. He tells Thyatira as well as us today that He knows all and sees all. He fully understands and fully expects us to seek His enabling in every situation. We have been given the power of the Holy Spirit so that there is no excuse acceptable to God for our serving Satan and ignoring God's empowerment in our lives.

Tolerating false teaching only allows Satan to obtain a stronger foothold in the life of our Church. *Tolerance* is a fashionable term in our society. Daniel Taylor writes,

---
[271] MacArthur Study Bible footnote Rev 22:16, p. 2025.

> A challenge for those who prize tolerance as one of the highest public goods is to distinguish between healthy tolerance and a diseased moral passivity or indifference. What is the difference between a genuinely tolerant society and a morally bankrupt one, incapable of calling evil what it is? Is Chesterton on to something when he says tolerance is the virtue of those who don't believe in anything? Too much of what passes as tolerance in America is not the result of principled judgment but is simple moral indifference. Invoking "it's not my business" may keep us from becoming a nation of prudish snoops, but historically it also has led nations into collaboration with great evil.[272]

Tolerance today masks itself with terms like relativism. Society tells us that truth is relative so that what is true for one person may or may not be true for someone else. Relativism becomes the only nonnegotiable truth where everyone is right unless they claim to be.[273]

> Because relativism has become increasingly popular in our culture, the absolute necessity of faith in Christ for salvation has become a more uncomfortable position for many to hold. Over nineteen centuries of Christian missionary activity hinged on this belief alone, but studies reveal that this remains the single most socially offensive aspect of Christian theology, and that this has been the most prominent impact of theological liberalism.[274]

Thyatira is not, was not, and will not be the only example of tolerance taken to the point of exhortation by the Risen Lord. The question is not whether Christians will experience this insidious disease, rather how will they respond to what is clearly repulsive in the eyes of the Lord.

---

[272] Daniel Taylor, *Deconstructing the gospel of tolerance*, Christianity Today (January 1999), p.42-52.
[273] Keener, p. 139.
[274] Ibid., p. 140.

CHAPTER EIGHT

Sardis:

The Attention-Deficit Church

Background

Sardis was the capital city of the province of Lydia. The *World Book Encyclopedia* reports that the origin of the city goes back to 1300 B.C. and perhaps beyond. The main thrust of recent archaeological activity in the area has been under the jurisdiction of the Archaeological Exploration of Sardis jointly sponsored by The Harvard University Art Museum and Cornell University.[275]

The Kingdom of Lydia was ruled by Gyges who established the Mermnad Dynasty circa 685 B.C. Gyges reigned until 652 B.C. when he was killed by the Cimmerians, invaders from southern Russia who overtook Sardis, the capital of Lydia. It is reported that in the reign of Gyges gold was discovered initiating an age of industrialization in Lydia specifically effecting Sardis.

The city was situated in the Hermus Valley. The plain of the Hermus is fertile, dotted by small hill ranges with the Tmolus Mountain range at the southern end of the valley. The Tmolus range rises to a height of seven hundred feet. The Hermus river flows through the plain ultimately emptying into the Aegean

---

[275] More information regarding Sardis and the Archaeological Exploration of Sardis can be found at *www.museums.harvard.edu/sardis/sardis.html; www.harvard-magazine.com/issues/may98/sardis.html; www.bsu.edu/alumni/alumnus/jan99/onscene.html.*

Sea. A tributary of the Hermus, the Pactolus River, runs through the city. Pausanias writes,

> This stream which comes down from Mount Tmolus, and brings the Sardians a quantity of gold dust, runs directly through the market place of Sardis, and joins the Hermus, before that river reaches the sea.[276]

Concerning the Pactolus River and its impact on the city of Sardis, William Young writes,

> Considerable quantities of gold were extracted from the alluvial sands of the Pactolus in about 700 B.C. and were collected by the founder of the Lydian Empire, Gyges. By means of his gold and his successful trading ventures, he gained in wealth and power, and he became the first despotic ruler from the point of view of this study. Gyges realized the importance of establishing a sound currency. During his rule the first stamped, authenticated gold coinage of the western world was produced.[277]

> The coins of Lydia were made of electrum, a Greek word meaning "amber" for the color of the metal that was carried down from Mount Tmolus along the Pactolus River toward Sardis, the capital of Lydia.[278]

The Mermnad Dynasty reigned in Lydia from the time of Gyges to the fall of Sardis in the time of Croesus (546 B.C.). Though the rulers before him were certainly men of renown, Croesus must be considered the most famous. He was by far the wealthiest of all known rulers (Solomon excluded) and acted as

---

[276] Pausanias, 5.101.
[277] William J. Young, "The Fabulous Gold of the Pactolus Valley," Bulletin: Museum of Fine Arts, Boston, 1972, p. 9-10.
[278] Robert A. Mundell, "The Birth of Coinage," Columbia University Department of Economics Discussion Paper 0102-08. *www.columbia.edu/cu/economics/discpapr/DP01o1-08.pdf.*

co-regent to his father, Alyattes, before assuming the throne in 560 B.C. Under Croesus, the Lydian Kingdom reached the height of its renown.

Croesus implemented a policy to make himself the sovereign of the cities along the western coast of Asia Minor known as Ionia. Among these cities were Ephesus and Smyrna. He allowed them to keep their governmental structure and culture as long as they formerly recognized their allegiance to Lydia by continuing to pay the tribute imposed upon them. With the natural resources of Lydia at his disposal and the access of the Ionian port cities for the Lydian trade, Croesus became notorious for his wealth.[279] The term "as rich as Croesus" survives as a simile for legendary wealth. The phrase was first recorded in English in A.D. 1577, more than 2,100 years after the end of his rule in Lydia.[280]

> Croesus can be credited with a remarkable monetary innovation, one that was to have a profound impact on the future of the international monetary system. He replaced the electrum coinage by a currency system of gold and silver, probably struck at Sardis . . . It has been claimed that this is the first known example of bimetallism, commonly defined as a monetary system in which the government fixes the exchange rate between gold and silver . . . The new system adopted by the Lydians represented an innovation of world-shaking importance. It set a monetary pattern based on a fixed bimetallic ratio, with one metal overvalued, that is convenient to term "assymetric bimetallism." It was widely imitated throughout the Mediterranean world and the Near East. It would find its echoes in the Persian, Greek, Macedonian, and Roman Empires and endure until the breakdown of the international monetary system that followed the sack of Constantinople in A.D. 1024.[281]

---

[279] Henry Sayce Archibald, *Ancient Empires of the East*, vol. 1. (New York; P.F. Collier & Son, 1932), p. 146.

[280] Christine Ammer, *The American Heritage Dictionary of Idioms*, (Houghton Mifflin Company, 1997), *www.xrefer.com/entry636168* 1/23/03.

[281] Mundell, p. 20.

Businessmen, bankers, philosophers, and engineers came to Sardis to visit Croesus. Sardis became the financial capital of the near-Eastern world. Additionally, the men of Lydia were known as the earliest retailers with permanent shops to display and sell their wares of textile, patterned fabric, rugs, and hats. All of this commercial activity earned the Lydians a reputation for enervating luxury.[282]

The city of Sardis was attacked and captured on several occasions. The first attack came under the rule of Gyges with the agora (marketplace) being destroyed. Ten years later the city was again besieged, Gyges was killed, and the marketplace destroyed. During the reign of Ardys (651-625 B.C.) the city was attacked and completely occupied by the Cimmerians who looted the city, taking away all that they could carry.

Two attacks on Sardis are worth mentioning in detail since they seemingly impact the recipients of John's letter. Hemer points out that "to capture the acropolis of Sardis" was proverbially to "do the impossible."[283]

The first attack occurred as a result of the ongoing animosity between the Lydians and the Medes. Croesus inquired of the Delphi Oracle whether or not he should attack Cyrus the Great of Persia. Cyrus combined the empire of the Medes with his own to form the Medo-Persian Empire. The oracle replied that if Croesus attacked the Persians, he would destroy a mighty empire.[284] Croesus attacked the Persians fully expecting to defeat them and fulfill the prophecy of the oracle. He had initial success until Cyrus gathered his troops and went on the offensive. Croesus retreated to the Plain of Sardis where the two armies met. Cyrus took all the camels which he had brought in caravan from Syria, removed their loads, and assigned riders

---

[282] Michael Grant, *The Rise of the Greeks*, (New York; Charles Scribner's Sons, 1987), p. 291.
[283] Hemer, p. 133.
[284] Herodotus, 1.53.

to them. He commanded the riders to guide the camels to the front of his troops. Upon smelling the camels and having a natural dread for them, the horses of the Lydian soldiers turned and galloped in the opposite direction, having a natural dread of the camel. The Lydian soldiers dismounted and engaged the Persians hand to hand. The battle was fierce and the Persians finally routed the Lydians who retreated to the acropolis where they felt secure.

The citadel of Sardis was approximately 1,500 feet high with steep cliffs precluding anyone from successfully attacking the city. The picture above shows the steep acropolis with the Temple of Artemis at the foothill.

The rock was so precipitous that the walled fortress seemed impregnable. Ramsay writes that Sardis had the reputation of a "great, wealthy, impregnable city against which none could strive and prevail."[285] Herodotus writes of an attack by the Ionians,

> They walked along the course of the River Cayster and, coming over the ridge of the Tmolus, came down upon

---

[285] Ramsay, p. 262.

Sardis and took it, no man opposing them; the whole city fell into their hands, except only the citadel which Artaphernes defended in person having with him no contemptible force.[286]

It was in this walled fortress high above the Hermus Valley that Croesus took refuge, feeling safe and secure from the threat of Cyrus in the plain below. The Persians attempted to assault the city but without success. One of Cyrus' soldiers, Hyroeades, determined to resolve the problem. He watched while a Lydian soldier descended an area of the fortress to retrieve a helmet that had rolled down the hill from the hilltop fortress. He witnessed him pick up the helmet and ascend back up the hill. Later, he climbed up the hill via the same path taken by the Lydian soldier. Other Persian soldiers who easily took the city followed him. Ramsay writes,

> An attack by this path could only succeed if the assailants climbed up entirely unobserved, and they could not escape observation unless they made the attempt by night. Hence, even though this be unrecorded, a night attack must have been the way by which Cyrus entered Sardis. He came upon the great city "like a thief in the night."[287]

> By the middle of the sixth century B.C., the city attained such a high level of respect that when its downfall came at the hands of a little-known enemy the Greek cities received the news of it with disbelief.[288]

Even though Croesus was clever, had resources at his disposal and wealth that was legendary that did not preclude the fact that he left all that he had unguarded for the enemy to take at will, all the while thinking that he was secure.

---

[286] Herodotus, 5.100.
[287] Ibid., p. 264.
[288] Thomas, p. 241

History has a tendency to repeat itself. In 195 B.C. Antiochus the Great was battling over the control of Sardis with Achaeus who had sought refuge in the citadel. For a year the battle was waged day and night. In the second year of battle, Lagoras, from Crete fighting for Antiochus, determined to settle the issue by finding a way to enter the impregnable city. He concluded that cities were captured at the point of its greatest strength. He observed that a portion of the wall near a place called the Saw was left unguarded. The place was extremely steep at this point with a deep gully below. Under cover of the night he went to that spot.

Lagoras developed a plan approved by Antiochus whereby he and two other men would take ladders to climb the steep hill at night. A contingent of men would be waiting to rush the city once the three men had climbed the hill and entered the city. The mission was executed as planned. At the point of its greatest strength, the city was left unguarded, Lagoras led the Persians into the city, and Sardis once again fell because there was no guard to watch for the enemy.[289]

Six miles to the northwest of the acropolis are the burial grounds of Lydian royalty, a sight where more than one hundred berms called Bin Tepe are located. Bin Tepe means one thousand mounds.[290] The tombs of the rulers of the Mermnad Dynasty (685-560 B.C.) stand out among the rest. The tomb of Alyattes, known as Karniyark, is the largest of the three standing 160 feet high with a perimeter of more than 650 feet. Graves of the average citizenry were located to the west of the city across the Pactolus River. These tombs are simple chamber tombs which stand in stark contrast to those of Bin Tepe.

In 1959 under the direction of George Hanfman, curator of Harvard's Fogg Art Museum, a huge Roman bath-gymnasium complex

---

[289] Polybius, 5.17.15-18.
[290] Janet Tassel, "The Search for Sardis," Harvard Magazine (May 1998).

(pictured above) with a row of Roman-Byzantine retail shops was uncovered. This find was impressive enough but one year later the largest known synagogue of the ancient world was uncovered. Inscriptions dating in the second half of the third century A.D. gave credit to the Jewish donors who had paid for part of the cost of building the synagogue. Eighty Greek inscriptions were found which "point to a Jewish population of great vigor and substance, one that flourished in Sardis since the sixth century B.C.E. (Before the Common Era).[291]

Due to the road system established by the Romans, Sardis continued to be a city of wealth in the first century A.D. albeit not legendary. The breeding of sheep was a predominate occupation from Sardis to the north regions. Sardis was well known for the production of woolen goods during this time period. Weaving, dyeing, and carpetmaking became an industry. The people of Sardis claimed for itself the invention of dyeing wool. Loom weights found in structures in the lower city support the reputation.

In A.D. 17 Sardis was devastated by one of the many earthquakes to occur there throughout the city's history. Of this earthquake Pliny writes,

---

[291] Ibid.

> The greatest earthquake within the remembrance of man, was that which chaunced during the Empire of Tiberius Caesar, when 12 cities of Asia were overturned and laid flat in one night.[292]

Tacitus writing in A.D. 109 states,

> That same year twelve famous cities of Asia fell by an earthquake in the night, so that the devastation was all the more unforeseen and fearful. Nor were there the means of escape usual in such a disaster by rushing out into the open country, for these people were swallowed up by the yawning earth. Vast mountains, it is said, collapsed; what had been level ground seemed to be raised aloft, and fires blazed out amid the ruin. The calamity fell most fatally on the inhabitants of Sardis, and it attracted to them the largest share of sympathy.[293]

The Roman Emperor Tiberius emerged as a major benefactor to Ionia in general and Sardis in particular. Tiberius forgave all tribute payable to Rome for the next five years and pledged considerable sums of money to the rebuilding process.[294] Even though the earthquake decimated the city, the reconstruction fueled by the generosity of Tiberius gave Sardis a new start. So grateful was the city to Tiberius that they competed nine years later with ten other cities for the right to erect a temple to Tiberius.

Perhaps the most famous citizen of Sardis was ironically a slave. He was a storyteller whose stories had some moral thought. These stories were handed down through oral tradition from about 600 B.C. to the first century A.D. when some of the stories took written

---

[292] C. Plinius Secundus, *The History of the World*, trans. Philemon Holland (1601) Book II Chapter 84.
www.penelope.uchicago.edu/holland/Pliny2.html *2/1/03*
[293] Tacitus Book II *www.classics.mit.edu/Tacitus/annals.2.ii.html* 2/1/03
[294] Ibid., Book II

form through the work of a Roman writer. A Greek writer wrote down the remainder of the stories in the early second century A.D. These stories have been preserved for us today and are known as Aesop's Fables.

Exposition

And to the angel of the church at Sardis write,
Hemer points out that the name Sardis in the Greek is plural. Every time the name is mentioned in Scripture (Rev 1:11; 3:1, 4) it is in the plural form. Herodotus writes about a battle at Sardis in 499 B.C. whereby the Ionians attacked the city and took it, but the citadel fortress was defended by a single person, Artaphernes, until reinforcements arrived.[295] This account of the attack against Sardis appears to be describing two different locations. One location was a city on a plain which was overcome while the other, an acropolis, was easily defended. Thomas writes of the aspect of two cities, one an elevated plateau and one on the foothills. "Since it was a double city, its name was pluralized like that of Athens."[296] The citadel was a natural stronghold watching over the lower city. By Roman times the acropolis ceased functioning as a fortress but remained an important link to the past. It was re-established in the Middle Ages when Islam triumphed and eroded the Christian population. The lower city had its own civic buildings, commercial district, and residential areas.

These things says He who has the seven Spirits of God and the seven stars.
The message given to the church at Sardis is from He who has the seven Spirits of God. The seven Spirits have already been mentioned in 1:4. The allusion could be to Isaiah 11:2 where the prophet speaks of the Spirit of the Lord, the Spirit of wisdom, the Spirit of understanding, the Spirit of counsel, the Spirit of might, the Spirit of knowledge, and the Spirit of the fear of the Lord. Or

---

[295] Herodotus, 5.100.
[296] Thomas, p. 240.

it could refer to Zechariah 4:1-10 where God gives the prophet a picture to convey God's divine enablement for life and the endless supply of power available to the servant of God. The picture of the two olive trees connected to the seven-branched lampstand depicts the unending supply of oil necessary to fuel the lampstand continuously. In 4:7 the Lord tells Zechariah, "Not by might nor by power, but by My Spirit, says the LORD of hosts." The Spirit is a never-ending supply of life-giving power enabling the believer to conduct their life on earth in the assurance of God's love and control. Whether the reference is to Isaiah or Zechariah, the message is the life-giving power of the Holy Spirit.

The seven Spirits of God are not meant to convey that there are seven different spirits. The number seven in Revelation and throughout Scripture is the number of completeness. The seven Spirits of God conveys the idea of the completeness of the Spirit whereby nothing else needs to be added. The power of the Spirit is complete within Itself.

As the members of the Sardis church listened to the message being read, they would have already heard the phrase "He who has an ear, let him hear what the Spirit says to the churches." That phrase was repeated after each of the previous four churches and would be repeated to the next three churches including Sardis. The admonition is to listen and to heed the words that are spoken. As the sender of the message, Jesus is letting the members of the Sardis church know that He has the Spirit of life to give to whomever He chooses or to withhold from whomever He chooses. It is within His power and authority to do either.

In Acts 19 Paul has arrived in Ephesus circa A.D. 53, approximately forty years before this letter was written. At that time the people of Ephesus were aware of the teachings of John the Baptist but they had no concept of the Holy Spirit. When asked if they had received the Holy Spirit when they believed, they responded, "We have not so much as heard whether there is a Holy Spirit" (v2). Paul explained to them about the Lord Jesus, they believed, and the Holy Spirit came upon them in power just like He came upon the apostles at Pentecost. This news and Paul's teaching continued for two years and the Book of Acts records that "all who dwelt in Asia heard the word of the Lord Jesus, both Jews and Greeks" (v 10). All who dwelt in Asia would certainly have included the people of Sardis who resided only fifty miles away. It was from Ephesus that the rest of Asia was evangelized. Thus, Sardis would have come to know about Christianity and the power of the Holy Spirit from those in Ephesus who would have taken seriously the Great Commission.

As John wrote what the Spirit of God pressed upon his heart, he would surely have remembered Jesus' words in Matthew 10:8. As the disciples were instructed to go on their first missionary journey, Jesus told them "Freely you have received, freely give." Perhaps he would have recalled Paul's words to the Romans, "for all have sinned and fallen short of the glory of God, being justified freely by His grace" (3:23, 24). Finally, in Ephesians 1:6 Paul writes, "to the praise of His glorious grace, which He has freely given us in the One He loves" (NIV). It should be remembered that John was just as much a recipient of this letter as were the seven churches in Asia to whom the letter was sent. John did not sit down and decide to write this correspondence. He was commanded to write (Rev. 1:19). The information John received was just as new to him as it was to the original listeners. John needed to grasp what Christ had to say in order to declare it.

Along with the seven Spirits of God, the sender also has seven stars. In 1:20 Jesus identified the seven stars as the angels of the seven churches. The angels have been identified earlier as messengers and not celestial beings. Christ has the seven stars. In 1:16 the Risen Lord is depicted as having in His right hand the seven stars. He holds them tightly so that no one can snatch them from His hand (John 10:28). They are secure in Him and their security is in Him. There are at least two ways of looking at this statement. The first is to see in the stars held in Jesus' hand the security of the Church. In Matthew 16:18 Jesus said to Peter, "And I also say to you that you are Peter, and upon this rock I will build My Church and the gates of Hades shall not prevail against it." The Church belongs to Christ and He will minister to it and protect it from all harm. Nothing will be able to remove the Church from the protection of Christ. Another view is to see that Christ is in control of the Church just like He is in control of the Spirit. He has charge of both of them. In John 16:13 Jesus tells the apostles that the Holy Spirit will not speak on His own authority but "whatever He hears He will speak." He directs the Holy Spirit. Therefore, He speaks with authority that assures us that what He says is going to occur. This can be a comforting thought or it can be very uncomfortable. In any event, the Risen Lord is letting the readers know that He has the power and authority to carry out what is contained in this message.

An impregnable fortress can fall, a reputation can be lost, a life can be forfeited but the Risen Lord holds His sheep tightly in His right hand so that no one can snatch them away. Conversely, if one does not belong to the sheepfold, the security of being held in that strong right hand does not exist.

He who has the seven Spirits of God and holds securely what is His has the authority to freely give His grace or to withhold it.

I know your works, that you have a name that you are alive, but you are dead.

Interestingly enough there are no positive deeds that the Risen Lord mentions regarding Sardis. In the case of the previous churches, their positive deeds were at least enumerated, not so with Sardis. They had no works worthy of mention.

At the time of John's writing, Sardis was still a wealthy city. The reputation of the city was legendary as has already been observed. The city was living on past deeds. Jesus uses the knowledge of their past to bring them back to the reality of their present condition. They were dead spiritually. A church that heard and saw the mighty works of the Spirit in just forty years was classified by the Risen Lord as being dead. The worst part is they thought they were alive. After all, people told them that they were alive. People from all over must have been impressed with what they saw. However, what men think and what men see are only those things on the surface. Christ sees something quite different. He sees a church separated from the source of its life. He sees a church set adrift in a sea of carnality. He sees a church concerned about what men think and see. They were becoming a "church of the consumer" specializing in catering to the appetites of the public. Caring more about lifestyles than about truth. They maintain a façade of religion but their conduct denies their validity. How else would they have earned such a reputation? They thought they were alive spiritually. So did those around them. However, they were as dead as those buried at Bin Tepe and the graveyard that contained the bones of the common people nearby.

What could have caused them to enjoy this reputation for being alive? The probable cause would have been the activity in which the Church was involved. The programs must have been numerous. They were a busy church, outwardly active. However, true spiritual vitality was dying if not non-existent. It is interesting to note that this is the first church where there is no heresy from within to condemn (Acts 20:30) and no persecution from without to coerce (Acts 20:29) as has been the case in the previous messages. They have brought their spiritual condition on themselves. They have deluded themselves into thinking that everything is okay. Satan doesn't need to incite false teaching within this church nor does he need to bring outside persecution. He simply leaves the church to its own devices. The Risen Lord's words are intended to jolt the listeners into heeding the warning signs of their downward spiral.

Be watchful, and strengthen the things which remain, that are ready to die, for I have not found your works perfect before God.

For a city that puts so much stock in its history, Sardis continued making the same mistake. Jesus tells them to "be watchful." "Wake up" might be a better way of describing what Jesus had in mind for this church. Remember how Sardis was captured during the reign of Croesus? They failed to be watchful. Remember how Antiochus captured Sardis? They failed to be watchful. Their security was merely a state of mind and not a reality. Christ is telling them that their past is a picture of what is to come unless they change their outlook. They have placed their spiritual security in their own ability. Perhaps they should take some advice from their most famous citizen who told the story of the "Dog and the Shadow."

> It happened that a dog had got a piece of meat and was carrying it home in his mouth to eat it in peace. Now on his way home he had to cross a plank lying across a running brook. As he crossed, he looked down and saw his shadow reflected in the water beneath. Thinking it was another dog with another piece of meat, he made up his mind to have that also. So he made a snap at the shadow in the water, but as he opened his mouth the piece of meat fell out, dropped into the water and was never seen more.

Moral: Beware lest you lose the substance by grasping at the shadow!

If Sardis is dead spiritually, it is in that condition because the life-giving power of the Holy Spirit is not in the church. They have been lulled into a false sense of security because they are active in their works. People are impressed by their outward appearance but, just like the Scribes and Pharisees of Matthew 23:27, they were pretty and clean on the outside but full of dead men's bones on the inside.

That doesn't mean they knew they were being hypocritical. It does mean that the works being done were being done in their own ability and not the power of the Holy Spirit. For that reason the Risen Lord can say that their works are not perfect before God. In fact, they could not be perfect before God without being done in the power of the Holy Spirit. As Zechariah said, "Not by might but by My Spirit says the LORD."

Those in the church who were genuine believers needed to repent and get back in fellowship with God. Those who were pretenders needed to make a conscientious decision to accept Christ as Savior and Lord. Many aspects of the believer's relationship with God were already dead. There were some things that were still hanging on even if only minimally. Christ exhorts them that their remaining works are not complete and that they are in danger of letting them go as well. There is an urgency about strengthening those things which remain. It carries the idea of taking action now rather than waiting until it's too late.

Remember therefore how you have received and heard; hold fast and repent.

Jesus encourages Sardis to think back and call to mind how they received nothing from their own effort but were given all things by God. In 1 Corinthians 4:7 Paul writes, "what do you have that you did not receive?" Not only did God give them everything they could possibly need, but it is His power that is the only means by which we can hear spiritual matters. God chooses to reveal Himself to man. In Matthew 16:17 Jesus tells Peter, "for flesh and blood has not revealed this to you, but My Father who is in heaven." In 1 Corinthians 2: 10, 11,

> But God has revealed them to us through His Spirit. For the Spirit searches all things, yes the deep things of God. For what man knows the things of a man except the spirit of the man which is in him? Even so no one knows the things of God except the Spirit of God.

God chooses to reveal things to man in His own time. We can't understand spiritual matters unless God allows us to understand them. He opens our hearts that we may hear what the Spirit says. Christ calls the church at Sardis to remember not only what they received, i.e., salvation through the blood of Christ, but how they heard the love of God in order to receive it. This recall of the salvation experience should be a humbling experience so that the Holy Spirit can once again have a heart prepared to hear and heed the message of the Holy Spirit.

Furthermore, He tells them to hold fast and repent. One fruit of the Spirit is patience. Christ who controls the Spirit has the power and authority to give us whatever patient endurance we need to fight against the schemes of Satan that are designed to cause us to give up. If we repent of our self-absorption and become absorbed in Christ we will repent and Christ will give the patient endurance to persevere. As Jude 24, 25 says,

> Now to Him who is able to keep you from stumbling, and to present you faultless before the presence of His glory with exceeding joy, to God our Savior, who alone is wise, be glory and majesty, dominion and power, both now and forever. Amen.

The use of the word *remember* means to keep on remembering. It is a constant exhortation.

Therefore, if you will not watch, I will come upon you as a thief, and you will not know what hour I will come upon you.

Just as Sardis was overtaken because they did not watch, Christ warns them that He will come like a thief. A thief does not inform the person they are going to rob lest that person take action to be ready for the thief and thwart his plan. Christ tells them to be watchful and ready and His coming will not surprise them. Rather, they will be watching in welcome relief of His coming and be prepared for the visit. It is interesting to note that not only did the two successful invasions of the Sardis acropolis occur at night, but so did the devastating earthquake of A.D. 17. The account by Tacitus of that event showed clearly that the town was taken by surprise. The words he used to describe the event were *unforeseen* and *fearful with there being no means of escape*. The earthquake was an act of nature unable to be stopped by mankind. There would be no way to prepare for such a catastrophe. Jesus coming like a thief is a sure prophecy. There is a way to prepare for that event and He exhorts the church at Sardis to take advantage of the opportunity before the devastation occurs.

You have a few names even in Sardis who have not defiled their garments; and they shall walk with me in white, for they are worthy.

Despite the flaws of the church at Sardis, there were a few who were true to Christ. He says "you have a few names." In John chapter 10 Jesus tells of the Good Shepherd. Verse 3 says, "To him the doorkeeper opens, and the sheep hear his voice; and he calls his own sheep by name and leads them out." Just as the Good Shepherd calls His sheep by name, Jesus knows the names of the sheep in Sardis who have not soiled their garments. He will call them out by name to walk with Him. "And when he brings out his own sheep, he goes before them; and the sheep follow him for they know his voice" (John 10:4). They are worthy and follow Him not because of what they have or have not done. They are worthy because they belong to the Shepherd. They are worthy to be called Christians and followers of Christ. Their lives were an open book that had been read by Christ and honored. They walk with Christ. Their garments are white representing purity. They were not stained or soiled or smeared by the world around them. They would have been the ones who would have taken Paul for his word when he wrote, "Do not be conformed to this world but be transformed by the renewing of your mind."

He who overcomes shall be clothed in white garments, and I will not blot out his name from the Book of Life; but I will confess his name before My Father and before His angels.

The overcomer shall be clothed in white garments. The significance of being dressed in white has already been addressed from the perspective of purity. In 3:4 those who walk with the Risen Lord dressed in white not only signify purity but also ceremony and celebration. Ramsay writes,

> All Roman citizens wore the pure white toga on holidays and at religious ceremonies, whether or not they wore it on ordinary days. In fact, the great majority of them did not ordinarily wear that heavy and cumbrous garment, and hence the city of festivals and holidays is called *"candida urbs,"* the city in white. Especially on the day of triumph white was the universal color.[297]

The overcomer would surely be dressed in white for purity

---
[297] Ramsay, p. 282.

due to the righteousness of Christ purifying the repentant sinner. The white of victory represents the overcoming of death through the resurrection of Christ. But there may be further significance to the overcomer being dressed in white. Once again Ramsay offers an idea. He writes, "A dirty and dark toga, on the other hand, was the appropriate dress of sorrow and guilt. Hence it was worn by mourners and by persons accused of crimes."[298]

The overcomer will neither mourn nor sorrow. There will be no accusation leveled against them and no guilt proclaimed. The white garment of purity and victory stands in stark contrast to the garment of accusation and guilt. The promise to the overcomer of being dressed in white signifies the cleansing of the soul as well as the body. No superficiality of a misconstrued reputation; instead, genuine life. As Isaiah states, "Your iniquity is taken away, and your sin purged" (6:7).

There is a further promise made by Christ to those who overcome. He says, "I will not blot out his name from the Book of Life; but I will confess his name before My Father and His angels." The Book of Life is sometimes confusing and some commentators believe that the reference here implies that people can be blotted out of the book effectively losing their salvation. Alan Johnson writes, "A person enrolled in the book of life by faith remains in it by faithfulness and can be erased only by disloyalty."[299] This thought contradicts other Scripture and therefore should be rejected. Romans 8:38, 39 assures the believer that nothing can separate them from the love of God. Additionally, John assures the believer from the words of the Lord, "I give them eternal life, and they shall never perish; neither shall anyone snatch them out of My hand" (John 10:28).

Some commentators understand the blotting out of the book to be a literary device called a *litote* whereby an assertion is made by denying its opposite. An example of this literary device would be the phrase "no small storm." The phrase actually carries the

---

[298] Ibid., p. 283.
[299] Johnson, p. 449, 450.

idea of a violent storm. Using this argument, the name not being blotted out would be an emphatic assurance that the name of the overcomer will be retained in the book. The idea would be that there is no way in which a name could be erased. Closely associated with the idea of the litote is an idea called emphatic negation in which the speaker emphasizes by way of promise, that he will "never ever" or "certainly not" blot out the names of the overcomers. The double negative is designed to add emphasis and certainty to the promise.[300]

Those who hold to the emphatic negation view argue that Christ's words to the seventy-two in Luke 10:20 and Paul's reference to fellow laborers having their names written in heaven would ring hollow in the ears of the listener. They contend that these verses point to a contradiction and would be of no value to the listener.[301] However, one could equally argue that the promise of knowing that your name is indelibly written in heaven as a result of faith in Christ provides comfort and security for the believer. Whereas some may have their name blotted out as a result of never having accepted Christ as Savior and Lord, the genuine believer takes comfort that his/her name will never be blotted out.

Some commentators see in this blotting out a semblance to the citizen registers of the Old Testament era as well as that of the Greek and Roman world. Each citizen was placed on the register at birth and erased at death. Hemer writes, "The idea of a citizen-register was equally familiar in the Greek world. There are numerous epigraphic references to the registrars and record-offices of the cities of Asia Minor."[302] The thought process is that here in Sardis those who merely claim faith in Christ but have not actually made a genuine profession of faith are included in the book along with genuine believers. Genuine believers will remain in the book while those with empty professions will be blotted out.

---

[300] Private correspondence from Dr. Wayne Brindle, Professor of New Testament, Liberty University.

[301] Charles R. Smith, *The Book of Life*, Grace Theological Journal vol. 6 Fall, 1985.

[302] Hemer. p. 148.

Names are in fact recorded in heaven. In Luke 10:20 Jesus tells His disciples to rejoice because, "your names are written in heaven." The Book of Hebrews refers to the "general assembly and church of the firstborn who are registered in heaven" (12:23). Daniel 12:1 speaks of deliverance for "everyone found written in the book." In Philippians 4:3 Paul speaks of his fellow workers "whose names are written in the Book of Life." Revelation 20:15 and 21:27 informs us that only those written in the Book of Life will escape the second death and be allowed entrance in the New Jerusalem.

The problem is not that there is a Book of Life. Rather, the problem has to do with the blotting out or erasure from the book. When Jesus says He will not blot out the overcomers' name from the book it clearly implies the possibility that there are names that will be blotted out and there will be names that will remain in the book. In Exodus 32:31-33 Moses is interceding for the Israelites due to the golden calf incident. He speaks with God, "Oh, these people have committed a great sin, and have made for themselves a god of gold. Yet now, if you will forgive their sin—but if not, I pray, blot out my name from Your book which You have written." Moses clearly understood that there was a book and requested to be removed from that book if God would not forgive the Israelites. In verse 33, God responds by saying, "Whoever has sinned against Me, I will blot him out of My book." In Psalm 69:28 David urges God to blot out of the book of the living those who have committed iniquity. The problem of being blotted out of the book is real according to these verses.

In both the Exodus passages and Psalm 69 it is the wicked that are blotted out of the book. Wiersbe contends that the Book of Life contains the names of all the living, the wicked as well as the righteous.[303] When a person professes true saving faith in Christ their name becomes permanent in the Book of Life never to be erased. Unbelievers' names remain in the book until they die physically and there is no more opportunity for them to make a choice to believe. John 16:9 says man's sin is unbelief in Christ. The word *sin* in this instance is singular denoting specific sin, that

---
[303] Wiersbe, p. 39.

of unbelief. This is the sin that separates a sinful man from a holy God. When this sin is removed there is nothing that will separate that one from the love of God. Upon a genuine profession of faith in Christ that sin is removed. God told Moses that "Whoever has sinned against Me, I will blot out of My book." Upon death the unbeliever's name is erased from the Book of Life.

Revelation 13:8 and 21:27 refer to this book as the Lamb's Book of Life. And truly it is. For at the final judgment only those who are true believers will be recorded there.

In Matthew 10:32, 33, Jesus tells His disciples "Whoever confesses Me before men, him I will confess before My Father in heaven." The word *confess* means "to declare openly by way of speaking out freely, such confession being the effect of deep conviction of facts."[304] Jesus is saying that for those who out of a true conviction openly profess Him, He will openly profess to the Father. The promise to the overcomer is just that. Jesus will openly acknowledge as His the overcomer. However, Matthew 10:33 states, "But whoever denies Me before men, him I will also deny before My Father who is in heaven." The word *deny* here means to disown or renounce.[305] Jesus will openly disown or renounce as His those who have disowned Him in this life.

The encouragement is to the overcomer but the clear implication is that Jesus is exhorting the members of the Sardis church who have not declared openly out of deep conviction their loyalty to the Risen Lord. Although not literally stated, the erasure from the book and the failure to confess the name speaks loudly to the spiritually dead church. Just as Sardis was comprised of two cities, an upper city and a lower city, the church at Sardis was comprised of two classes of membership. There were those who were genuine and there were those who were pretenders. Jesus encourages those who are genuine through the positive reward of walking with Him in white garments, remaining in the Book of

---

[304] Vine's, p. 120.
[305] Zodhiates, p. 892.

Life, and the acknowledgement before the Father and His angels. He exhorts the pretender through the obvious absence of these same rewards.

The final exhortation is that of listening to the plea of the Holy Spirit who continues to work in the life of the Church to convict, comfort, and guide. This is the altar call, the invitation to acknowledge before God and man the utter dependence man has in a merciful and gracious God.

Application

How does a church or organization go from being alive in the Spirit to thinking they are alive but in fact are spiritually dead? In less than fifty years the church at Sardis experienced this phenomenon. There are many potential reasons that could be discussed but the following seem critical.

Comfort and contentment lull a person into a false sense of security.

The people of Sardis placed their security in an impregnable fortress that was to protect them from marauders. They became comfortable not realizing their real vulnerability. As a result the enemy captured their city.

Christians often face similar situations and that contentment with spirituality leaves one ill prepared for Satan's onslaught. If left unchecked, this contentment will lead to apathy. Satan will have no need to attack. He will simply allow the believer to continue in this spiritual stupor until the heart atrophies. That's why Jesus could warn the believer to "be watchful and strengthen the things which remain, that are ready to die." A believer who is watchful is a believer who realizes the danger of being disconnected to the power of the Holy Spirit. That disconnection has subtle beginnings that need to be recognized immediately. It might start with being too busy to have a quiet time with God each day. Or maybe it starts when a different worldview causes one to think that the Bible is in fact outdated and in need of modernization. Or perhaps it starts when one clings tightly to their belief but fails to practice that belief, effectively demonstrating that the belief they say they hold is merely a shadow and not reality.

Does this suggest that the believer can lose their salvation? No! But what does it say about future generations reared in this environment? Believers who are in spiritual malaise can't be fruitful in their faith. Succeeding generations don't witness a vibrancy in the spirituality of this debilitated believer. Therefore, the faith that once burned brightly becomes lackluster until it finally burns out. Asia Minor was once alive with the Spirit. Now it is 98 percent Muslim. Once it believed that Jesus was the Son of God and one with the Father. Today it believes that the same Jesus was merely a prophet less important than Mohammed. Over time comfort and contentment eats away at the core of faith much like rust destroys metal. After a while there is only rust.

Reputation, rules, requirements become more important than ministry.

Sardis had a reputation for being alive when in fact it was dead. They conducted themselves as though they believed they were doing the right things for the right reasons. They were deluded.

Churches, ministries, and individual believers fall into this same trap. Appearance becomes important. What others think about the church, organization, or individual becomes important. They grasp at the shadow and lose the substance of what they truly are about. Scripture may be held in high esteem and even taught earnestly but not practiced. Instead of doctrine, rules and regulations become more important. Individuals become expendable and their needs unimportant as long as the rules and regulations are kept sacred. The problem is not new. Jesus accused the Pharisees of the same thing. In Matthew 15:6 He asked them, "Why do you transgress the commandment of God because of your tradition?" Then in verse 7-9 He tells them,

> Hypocrites! Well did Isaiah prophesy about you saying:
> These people draw near to Me with their mouth, and honor

Me with their lips, but their heart is far from Me. And in vain they worship Me, teaching as doctrine the commandments of men.

In the parallel passage of Mark 7:8, Jesus makes their intentions even more apparent when He says, "For laying aside the commandment of God, you hold the tradition of men—the washing of pitchers and cups, and many other such things you do."

Make no mistake about it, the Pharisees thought themselves to be very spiritual. The people thought the Pharisees to be their spiritual leaders. They followed them in practice. But Jesus called them hypocrites because they added rules and regulations to God's word. They cared more for their own rules and regulations, called tradition because it had been handed down from generation to generation as truth, than they did for people. Nowhere is this more evident than the man with the withered hand in Matthew 12:9-14. Jesus was in the synagogue on the Sabbath. Present in the congregation was a man suffering from an affliction in his hand. Jesus asked, "Is it lawful to heal on the Sabbath?" There was no answer. He then asked two more rhetorical questions. (1) "What man among you who has one sheep, and if it falls into a pit on the Sabbath, will not lay hold of it and lift it out?" (2) "Of how much more value then is a man than a sheep?" The obvious reason for the questions was to stir the listeners to think through what Jesus was saying in order to come to the conclusion that Sabbath rules and regulations do not take precedence over the needs of people. After He spoke these things to them, He healed the man's withered hand. Verse 14 gives the response of the Pharisees. "Then the Pharisees went out and plotted against Him, how they might destroy Him." Their rules and regulations were more important than ministry.

Glory in past splendor ignores present decay.

Past experiences are surely important. From them a person learns more about themselves. But people live in the present not in the past. Dwelling on past achievements and splendor kept the city of Sardis from analyzing their present condition. Emphasizing the past causes one to ignore the present with the result that over time there is continual deterioration in spiritual development. You can be sure that a person who talks about spiritual activities in the past is a person who is snoozing spiritually in the present. That snooze will accelerate from a nap to complete sleep in a short period of time.

Jesus said to be alert and watch. In the letter to the Philippians, Paul wrote, "But one thing I do, forgetting those things which are behind and reaching forward to those things which are ahead, I press toward the goal for the prize of the upward call of God in Christ" (3:13b, 14.). We are to live in the present with an eye on the past and all the while, "looking for the blessed hope and glorious appearance of our great God and Savior Jesus" Christ (Titus 2:13).

CHAPTER NINE

Philadelphia:

The Church of the Open Door

Background

Philadelphia was situated on a major trade route from Pergamum and Sardis in the western portion of Asia Minor. The trade route linked Asia to Europe making Philadelphia a door to the east from these areas. Located approximately twenty-eight miles south east of Sardis, the city was in a river-basin of the Cogamis River, a tributary of the Hermus River. The Tmolus Mountains are located to the south of the city. To the north the terrain rises gently to the edge of a great plain called Catacecaume, which means "burnt land." Philadelphia was strategically located between three provinces of Asia Minor—Lydia, Phyrgia, and Mysia.

There is some debate over the establishment of the city. The preponderance of historians write that Attalus II Philadelphus (159-138 B.C.) founded the city.[306] The name Philadelphus (which in Greek means brotherly love) was given to him because of his deep devotion and love for his brother, Eumenes, king of Pergamum. The city was named Philadelphia in honor of the king. However, there is possible evidence that the city was organized prior to Attalus by trade guilds. Jones writes,

---

[306] Oxford Classical Dictionary

After 189 B.C. were built Philadelphia of Lydia, Dionipopolis and Eumeneia of Phyrgia, and Attaleia of Pamphylia. The first was almost certainly a native Lydean town reorganized; it still retained in later times the indigenous grouping by trades instead of the tribal system.[307]

In any event, the city does not have the historical background of the other cities having been the most recently founded.

The city was founded to be a "center of the Greco Asiatic civilization and a means of spreading the Greek language and manners in the eastern part of Lydia and Phyrgia."[308] The success of the city as a promoter of Hellenistic thought was great. By A.D. 19 the province of Lydia had become so inculcated with Hellenism[309] that the former language of the people was all but forgotten in favor of Greek.

The city was built on the edge of the Catacecaumene. The name of this plain was derived from the lava and ash of the volcanoes in that area. It was situated in a great seismic area. Strabo describes the area as "a plain covered with ashes, and the mountainous and rocky country is black, as though from conflagration."[310]

The location of the city had its pros and cons. The positive aspect of the ash and lava residue was the fertility of the soil. The city was a center for agriculture, particularly in grape production. Strabo writes, "the whole of it is without trees except the vine that produces the Catacacaumenite wine, which in quality is inferior to none of the notable wines."[311]

On the other hand, living near to seismic activity has its perils. Strabo writes, "And the city Philadelphia, [is] ever subject to

---

[307] A. H. M. Jones, *The Greek City From Alexander to Justinian*, (London: Oxford university Press, 1940 reprinted 1966), P. 17.

[308] Ramsay, p. 286, 287.

[309] An enthusiasm for or devotion to the Greek culture manners, and civilization introduced by Alexander the Great.

[310] Strabo, 13.4.11.

[311] Ibid., 13.4.11.

earthquakes. Incessantly the walls of the houses are cracked, different parts of the city being thusly affected at different times."[312] In A.D. 17 a great earthquake hit the area and destroyed Sardis and ten other cities. Philadelphia was spared total destruction but suffered tremors and aftershocks for a lengthy period thereafter. Strabo reports, "In Philadelphia, the city near it, not even the walls are safe, but in a sense are shaken and caused to crack every day. And the inhabitants are continually attentive to the disturbances in the earth and plan all structures with a view to their occurrence."[313]

The aftershocks were a constant reminder of the devastation that an earthquake can bring. The majority of the population left their homes in the city for fear of falling masonry and other material from the houses and buildings in the city. Those who decided to stay in the city were thought to be crazy as they waited subconsciously for the tremors and the feeling of having to flee quickly for open spaces where rocks and roof would not cave in on them. When the tremors came, they would by necessity flee.

When the earthquake of A.D. 17 destroyed the surrounding cities, Tiberius, emperor of Rome, sent money and aid to restore the area. He exempted Philadelphia from paying tribute for five years just as he had done for Sardis. Philadelphia was so grateful for his benevolence that they renamed the city Neocaesarea, the New City of Caesar. The new name was not in use after the reign of Claudius (A.D. 41-54) and the name reverted back to Philadelphia. However, in the reign of Vespasian (A.D. 69-79), Philadelphia once again demonstrated gratitude for the emperor's benevolence for favors granted and changed the city's name to Flavia in honor of the family name of the emperor. This name is attested by coinage discovered bearing the title Flavia.[314] Neither of these names lasted and by the end of the first century the city once again resumed the name Philadelphia. Today the city survives under the name Alasehir.

---

[312] Ibid., 13.4.10.
[313] Ibid., 12.8.18.
[314] Interpretors Dictionary of the Bible Vol 3, p. 782.

Exposition

And to the angel of the church in Philadelphia write,

> According to the *NIV Theological Dictionary of New Testament Words*, the name Philadelphia in the Greek combines the root word *phil*, meaning love or to be fond of, with the word *adelphos*, meaning brother. Of the approximate twenty-four words in the New Testament that have the root *phil*, Philadelphia is chief among them. The word appears as the name of a city in Revelation 1:11 and 3:7 (*philadelpheia*) but in Romans 12:10; 1 Thessalonians 4:9; Hebrews 13:1; 1 Peter 1:22; and 2 Peter 2:7 it takes on the meaning of brotherly love (*philadelphia*) while in 1 Peter 3: 8 it means fond of the brethren, i.e., fraternal; love as brethren (*philadelphos*).[315]

The city was so named because of the fondness, devotion, and loyalty that existed between Attalus, the founder, and his brother, Eumenes, the king. Polybius writes about a visit that Attalus made to Rome at the request of his brother, Eumenes. Attalus was warmly received by the Romans and soon learned that their kindness was a pretense to get Attalus to turn against his brother, that he might depose him as king. Their persuasion seemed to be working as Attalus agreed to appear before the Roman Senate to discuss the matter. In the meantime, Stratus, Eumenes physician, comes to Rome and speaks with Attalus. Stratus redirects Attalus' attention to the fact that he had already had the power and authority of the king, he just didn't own the title. Attalus was encouraged by these words and addressed the Senate on Eumenes' behalf as he been charged to do.[316]

Attalus was not only encouraged to defect from the loyalty and love of his brother, but the Senate took active steps to entice

---

[315] Zodhiates, p.75.

[316] Polybius, 30.1-3 *www.ukans.edu/historyindex/europe/ancient-Rome/E/Roman/Texts/Polybius/30*.html.* 2/8/03

him. It took a mediator, Stratus, to enter the picture in order to bring Attalus back to his sense of loyalty and away from a focus on his own situation. The church at Philadelphia needed such a mediator to remind them that their love and loyalty to the Risen Lord was not to wane but was to be encouraged and exhorted to be steadfast in the strength of the One in whom they had believed.

These things says He who is holy, He who is true, He who has the keys of David, He who opens and no one shuts, and shuts and no one opens.

Of the seven messages, this is the only message that doesn't describe the sender in images that are seen in chapter one. The closest thing to matching chapter one is the inference to the key of David in comparison to the keys of Hades and Death in 1:18.

He who is holy.

The word *holy* fundamentally signifies "separated" (among the Greeks, dedicated to the gods), and hence, in Scripture in its normal and spiritual significance, separated from sin and therefore consecrated to God, sacred."[317]

In Luke chapter one, the evangelist speaks of One to be born to Mary as "that Holy One who is to be born" (v 35). In Acts 3:14, Peter is preaching in Solomon's portico after having healed the lame man at the Beautiful Gate. He tells the people there, "But you denied the Holy One and the Just and asked for a murderer to be granted to you, and killed the Prince of life whom God raised from the dead, of which we are witnesses."

The Holy One to be born and the Holy One that was killed and raised to life is the same One who speaks to the church at Philadelphia. He who is holy speaks to them. He who is not of this world (John 17:14) but separated from it speaks to them to assure them that just as He is separate, so are they (John 17:16).

He who is true.

The word *true* here means true in the sense of real, ideal, genuine.[318] There is nothing false about Him. There are no

---
[317] Vine's, p. 307.
[318] Ibid., p.645.

pretensions. In John 15:1 Jesus tells the apostles, "I am the true vine." In 1 John 5:20 the apostle writes, "And we know that if the Son of God has come and has given us an understanding, that we may know Him who is true; and we are in Him who is true, in His Son Jesus Christ. This is the true God and eternal life."

The significance of the One who is true would not have been lost on the Philadelphians. They would have recognized that the speaker identified Himself in this way so as to communicate clearly that He was the authentic voice that could speak words of reality; words that meant something as opposed to the empty words of threat being uttered by the society in which they lived. Especially significant to them would have been the contrast between the lies of the synagogue of Satan (v. 9) and the Truth of the Risen Lord.

He who has the key of David.

In the Old Testament Book of Isaiah there was a man by the name of Shebna who was a steward with authority second only to the king. It's not exactly clear what Shebna did but whatever he did, it prompted the Lord to replace him as steward. He was replaced with Eliakim who is referred to by God as, "My steward" (Isaiah 22:20). God promised to clothe him with Shebna's robe, strengthen him with Shebna's belt, and commit Shebna's responsibility to him. In other words, he would become the steward second only to the king in authority. He would be given the key to the House of David which meant he had the authority to admit entrance into the king's presence or he could deny entrance into the king's presence. Isaiah reports that he "shall open and no one shall shut; and he shall shut and no one shall open" (Isaiah 22:22).

The sender of the message to the church of Philadelphia likewise has the authority alone to open and shut the admission to the kingdom of heaven. He even says in Revelation 1:18, "I have the keys to Hades and Death." In Matthew 28:18 He says, "All authority has been given to Me in heaven and on earth." No one shuts what He opens and no one opens what He shuts.

This five pronged description of the sender allows no room for misunderstanding. It clearly states that the initiator of the message is not of this world, is perfectly authentic, and has the power and authority to carry out the message He is delivering.

> I know your works. See, I have set before you an open door, and no one can shut it: for you have little strength, have kept My word, and not denied My name.

Once again the Risen Lord is perfectly aware of all the things the Philadelphians were doing. Their work was not going unnoticed. But what were these works? They are not elaborated on so there is no real way of knowing. However, since the Risen Lord has used historical settings and background to appeal to the other churches, there may be a clue in the historical background of Philadelphia. The early pioneers of the city of Philadelphia had a door of opportunity opened for them by Attalus to spread the culture and customs of Greece. And they walked through that opened door and did their part in Hellenizing the surrounding area. So too, the first-century Christians of Philadelphia had an open door provided to them by the Risen Lord to spread the gospel message, the truth as opposed to a lie, to their city and to all who would listen.

The concept of the open door was not new. Barnabas and Paul experienced God opening a door of faith to the Gentiles in Acts 14:27. In I Corinthians 16:9, Paul says that "a great and effective door has opened to me and there are many adversaries." In 2 Corinthians 2:12, Paul writes, "When I came to Troas to preach Christ's gospel, and a great door was opened to me by the Lord." Finally, in Colossians 4:3, Paul asks for prayer "that God would open to us a door for the word to speak the mystery of Christ." In every case, the door was either opened by, or expected to be opened by God. The open door was for the spread of the Gospel. Only God can open the door and the sender tells the Philadelphians that He has set an open door before them. According to Robertson the phrase *I have set* literally means "I have given." The open door is a gift of Christ.[319]

The works the Philadelphians have accomplished are works that were empowered and enabled by Christ. He knows their works. They have spread the gospel message just as they had been asked to do. He knows their works and explains to them in a manner

---

[319] Robertson, p. 665.

that they can understand that they accomplished those works only because He opened the doors of opportunity for them. Their dependence on Him and His enablement is the only reason the doors were opened and the works accomplished. Otherwise, the works would not be true.

What would cause someone to deny Christ's name? While not specifically stated, persecution is implied in the context. The reference to the synagogue of Satan makes one wonder if the persecution that was going on in Smyrna wasn't also happening in Philadelphia! The admonition to "hold fast what you have, that no one may take your crown," implies that someone is indeed attempting to do just that. If the Philadelphians were being persecuted, what activity were they involved in that would generate the persecution?

Since we are speaking in spiritual tones, spiritual warfare must enter the picture. Would Satan work in the heart of a non-believer to persecute a believer if that believer was not living a life honoring God? Probably not! There would be no reason for Satan to persecute a believer unless the believer was actively involved living their life for the Lord. Then Satan has a reason to work against the believer. Otherwise, Satan just allows the spiritual vitality that once characterized the believer to be slowly expended until they are as dead as the Sardis believer. Since Satan has no real opposition, there is no real persecution.

If this argument holds true, the church at Philadelphia was being persecuted. The reason for the persecution was probably due to the refusal of the Philadelphians to deny that the Christ that redeemed them. It seems unlikely that a believer undergoing persecution would need to be reminded that they had been redeemed by the blood of the Lamb and that they would spend eternity with Christ. That's all they have to hold on to. The conclusion by some commentators that the open door represents entrance into the Messianic kingdom seems unlikely unless that means that the non-believer will have the opportunity to take advantage of the offer of salvation as presented to them by those faithful Philadelphian Christians who walk through that open door of opportunity offered to them by Christ.

Jesus uses the word *see* to start verse 8b. In so doing, He is calling specific attention to what he is getting ready to say. The word used in this manner conveys the idea of being "seen or heard or mentally apprehended."[320] His purpose is to draw the listener's attention to what He is about to impart to them. It is amazing how even the smallest of words or thoughts in Scripture have an impact on what the Holy Spirit communicates through the human author. The same technique is used today. Many times when a speaker wants the audience to specifically hear a point about to be made, the speaker will say something like, "If you don't hear anything else I've said, listen to this." Some speakers simply say "listen" when an important point is made while other speakers repeat the point so that the audience doesn't miss it. The purpose is to highlight the point for emphasis. That is what Jesus is doing by using this word in this instance. He is directing the attention of His listeners by essentially saying, "Listen to Me!"

He goes on to contrast His strength in opening the door which no one can shut against the fact that the Philadelphians have little strength. He is trying to get them to realize that they haven't the strength in themselves to even open the door much less keep someone from closing it once it is opened. He not only has that strength but He willingly uses that strength for their benefit. He exhorts them to apprehend what He is trying to convey. The Philadelphians find themselves in a situation whereby they are being forced to make a decision whether to hold fast to the name of Christ or to deny that name. Persecution has come to them probably in the form of refusing to worship the emperor. The synagogue of Satan and those who claim to be Jews but are not are probably the chief source of the persecution. The other residents of Philadelphia are probably joining in the persecution as an attack against what they perceive as unpatriotic activity on the part of the

---

[320] Vine's, p. 59.

Christians. In the late 60s and 70s, flag burning became a sign of protest in America. All Americans didn't see this as a proper means of protest or freedom of speech. The majority of Americans saw it as an unpatriotic rebellious activity that needed to be corrected by the force of law. Sometimes violence erupted. The same scenario occurred in the cities of the Revelation, at the time of the writing of Revelation. The citizenry were grateful to the *Pax Romana* and saw the failure to worship the emperor as an unpatriotic act.

The Philadelphians were possibly reaching their limit with the persecution they were under and needed a touch from the Risen Lord just as John needed on Patmos. The touch of reassurance that the Lord was in control of their circumstances and that they needed to hold fast to what they believed. He had not failed them in the past and He would not fail them in their present circumstances or any future situation. His was the strength that had sustained them in the past and it would be His strength that would sustain them now and in the future.

Even with the little strength they had, they had to this point kept His word and had not denied His name. The idea behind denying His name infers a falling "back from a previous relationship with Him into unfaithfulness with the opposite meaning of holding fast or being faithful."[321] Denying the name of Christ was not an uncommon occurrence in the early Church. Emperor worship was thriving in the Roman Empire at this time especially under Domitian. Tenney writes,

> Although the worship of local deities persisted, the growing cosmopolitan consciousness in the empire prepared the way for a new type of religion, the worship of the state . . . The concentration of the executive functions of the Roman state in the person of one man had vested him with powers unprecedented in the history of the world. The fact that he was able to utilize those powers for the good of the empire created the feeling that there must be something divine in him.[322]

---

[321] Verbrugge, p. 174.
[322] Merrill C. Tenney, *New Testament Survey*, (Grand Rapids: Eerdmans, 1961). P.67.

Emperors were usually deified upon their death, an honor bestowed upon them by the Roman Senate. Tiberius was very uncomfortable about any attribution of deity or superhumanness to himself. On the other hand, Domitian, who was emperor at the time of this writing, became the first emperor to attempt to compel his subjects to worship him while he was still reigning. Refusal to worship the emperor was an unpatriotic act not taken lightly.

> The refusal of all Christians to participate in such worship precipitated violent persecution, for the Christian consistently objected to worshipping a human being. The polytheistic Romans, who could always add one more god to their list of deities, looked upon their refusal as a lack of proper recognition for the emperor and as a distinctly unpatriotic attitude. Between these two viewpoints there could be no reconciliation. The Christian attitude on this question of the worship of the state, or its head, is reflected in the Apocalypse, which reveals unmistakably the hostility between the claims of Christ and the claims of the emperor.[323]

Indeed I will make those of the synagogue of Satan, who say they are Jews and are not, but lie—indeed I will make them come and worship before your feet, and to know that I have loved you.

The church at Philadelphia did not renounce the name of Christ even in the face of such persecution. The Risen Lord again uses the word *behold* (KJV) or *indeed* (NKJV) to emphasize that He wants the Philadelphians to hear what it is He is saying. He makes a promise to them. He promises that those of the synagogue of Satan who are persecuting His people will be called to account. He will demonstrate His love for the Philadelphians by making those persecutors crouch at the feet of the Philadelphins and pay homage to them. The word used here is worship (*proskuneo*) which gives the sense of a "dog licking the master's hand."[324] In Isaiah 49:23 the prophet is writing about how God will remember Israel. He says, "Kings shall be your foster fathers, and their queens your nursing mothers; they shall bow down

---

[323] Ibid., p. 67.
[324] Zodhiates, p. 61.

to you with their faces to the earth, and lick up the dust of your feet. Then you will know that I am LORD." The idea in Isaiah and in Revelation is the same. Those that mistreat God's beloved will be humbled to the point of being placed at the feet of the believer and acknowledging their wrongful acts.

Christ does not intend the meaning of worship in this instance as the act of reverence toward God; for twice in Revelation, John is exhorted not to worship the angel but to worship only God (Rev 19:10; 22:9).

Because you have kept My commandment to persevere, I also will keep you from the hour of trial which shall come upon the whole world, to test those who dwell on the earth.

The church at Philadelphia had done all that it could to keep the word of the Lord. They were as faithful to Him as their limited strength would allow. The Lord did not judge them for what they didn't do, but He did commend them for what they did do. They kept His word and didn't deny His name even in the face of persecution. They persevered. The word used here for persevere "refers to the quality that does not surrender to circumstances or succumb under trial."[325] Because of their effort to keep the Lord's command, a promise is made to them. They will be kept from the hour of trial, which shall come upon the whole world.

This verse in its entirety has been a source of theological debate. The disagreement centers around how the promise will be carried out. One set of commentators sees the promise as the church at Philadelphia being protected during this hour of trial to emerge victorious at its completion. Another set of commentators sees the church at Philadelphia being removed from the hour of trial. The question becomes, "Will the Church be exempt from the events that are to occur during the hour of trial?" or "Will the church be delivered from the hour of trial?"

In order to analyze this verse, several questions need to be answered: (1) What is the hour of trial?(2) When will it occur? (3) Who does it affect? (4) What is its purpose?

---

[325] Ibid., p.964.

What is the hour of trial?

It is a period of time designed to test those who dwell on the earth at its occurrence. Jesus spoke of a time in the future in Matthew 24:21. He says, "For then there will be great tribulation, such as has not been since the beginning of the world until this time, no, nor ever shall be." He was speaking of a time of unparalleled judgment that would come upon the earth. In the Old Testament such a period of time was prophesied. Jeremiah 30:7 calls this time period, "the time of Jacob's trouble." Zephaniah 1:15 says, "That day is a day of wrath, a day of trouble and distress." Isaiah 34:8 calls it, "the day of the Lord's vengeance." Malachi 4:5 calls it the "great and dreadful day of the Lord." It is commonly referred to in the Old Testament as the Day of the Lord.

In the study of eschatology (last things) this period is referred to as the Great Tribulation. It is a period with a duration of seven years broken into two distinct parts of three and one half years each. The seven-year time frame comes from the seventy sevens of Daniel 9:24-27. The two, three-and-one-half-year periods come from Daniel 7:25; 12:7; Rev 12:14 where the phrase "time, times, and half a time" refers to a three-and-one-half-year period. Other verses in Revelation refer to a time period of forty-two months (Rev 11:2; 13:5) and one thousand two hundred and sixty days (Rev 11:3;12:6).

When will it occur?

When the Old Testament referred to the Day of the Lord it was obviously future. Jesus, speaking to His disciples in Matthew 24:21, spoke of the tribulation that was to come. In Revelation 3:10, the Risen Lord promises to keep the Philadelphians from this hour of trial which shall come. In every instance the timing of this event is future. If the hour of trial is the same event as the great tribulation that Jesus spoke of, then it still has not occurred and must be a future event. To date, there has been no event that was worldwide in scope that has had tribulation "such as has not been since the beginning of the world until this time, no, nor ever shall be." The hour of trial has not yet come but it is certain that it will in the future.

Who does it affect?

It affects those who dwell on the earth when it occurs. In other words, it is worldwide in scope. The phrase used in verse 10 to describe those whom the hour of trial will affect is "those who dwell on the earth." Those who dwell on the earth are spoken of ten times in Revelation using virtually identical wording (3:10; 6:10; 11:10 [twice]; 13:8; 12:14 [twice]; 14:6; 17:8). The phrase is not always identical but the meaning is constant. In 12:12, this same group of people are referred to as "inhabitants of the earth." In addition, an equivalent expression is employed in 13:12 and a similar, though ultimately ironic, usage is found in 14:6.[326] From the evidence presented, it appears that this hour of trial will involve all living beings on planet earth at the time of the occurrence.

What is the purpose?

The word used for trial in this passage is *peirasmos*. It means "temptation" or "testing." There needs to be a distinction made regarding this testing. "The meaning depends on who tempts. If it is God, it is for the purpose of proving someone and never for the purpose of causing him to fall. If it is the devil who tempts, then it is for the purpose of causing one to fall."[327]

The hour of trial is said to be for the purpose of testing those who dwell on the earth. The word for test is *peirazo* and can

---

[326] Information gathered from a paper presented to the Evangelical Theological Society by A. Boyd Luter and Emily K. Hunter, "The "Earth-Dwellers" and the Heaven-Dwellers": An Overlooked Interpretive Key to the Apocalypse," November 2002.

[327] Zodhiates, p. 946.

mean to prove in a good sense or in a bad one. In John 6:5, Jesus asked Philip, "Where shall we buy bread, that these many may eat?" Verse 6 tells us that He asked Philip that question in order to test him. Jesus already knew what the outcome would be. But by asking Philip the question, He forced him to come to the conclusion that there would not be enough bread anywhere to feed the multitude which was before them. By asking the question, Jesus highlights in Philip's mind the miracle about to be performed. The question tested Philip, the miracle assured him. In 2 Corinthians 13:5, Paul writes, "Examine yourselves as to whether you are in the faith. Test yourselves." These are examples of testing to prove in a good sense.

In Luke 8:13, Jesus is explaining the parable of the soils. He says, "But the ones on the rock are those who, when they hear, receive the word with joy; and these have no root, who believe for a while and in time of temptation fall away." The time of temptation in this instance is brought by Satan to disprove and harm. Satan solicits someone to sin by advertising his product in such a deceptive way that the person buys without thinking. There is no product guarantee. Such advertising in the business world would be considered false and against the law in most states because it promises something it cannot deliver. In fact the product Satan offers does exactly the opposite of what is promised.

The purpose of the hour of trial is twofold. God desires to have a relationship with His creation. He has given them every opportunity to respond to His love but to no avail. Now He allows Satan to bring adversity unimagined into their life in order to lead them to the conclusion they need the protection that only He can provide. Tim LaHaye in his book *Rapture Under Attack* states that the hour of trial is intended to shake man from his false sense of security. He writes,

> A stable world leads man to think that he can function independently from God. Earthquakes, plagues, and other physical phenomena from God will so shake man's natural confidence that when he hears the gospel through the

preaching of the 144,000, he will be more open to its offer of forgiveness and grace.[328]

In Revelation 14:6, God sends an angel flying in mid-heaven for all to see proclaiming the everlasting gospel. He is making every effort possible, natural or supernatural, to give every person the opportunity to respond to His grace.

On the other hand, God in His righteousness cannot tolerate sin. His justice demands that sin be punished. He has provided everything mankind could possibly need to have a relationship with Him. John 3:36b says, "he who does not believe the Son shall not see life, but the wrath of God abides on him." Paul tells us in Ephesians 2:3 that we are "by nature children of wrath." Not desiring a relationship with God, mankind is described by Paul as being "vessels of wrath prepared for destruction" (Romans 9:22). This hour of trial is a period of divine judgment. Isaiah 24:21 says, "It shall come to pass in that day that the Lord will punish on high the host of exalted ones, and on the earth the kings of the earth." "For behold, the Lord comes out of His place to punish the inhabitants of the earth for their iniquity" (Isaiah 26:21). This wrath is vividly described as the "winepress of the wrath of God" in Revelation 14:19.

Having answered the four questions, we can now turn our attention to addressing the issue of the Philadelphians being exempt from, or delivered out of, the hour of trial.

Both viewpoints hold that the church will enjoy the promise of protection. Both viewpoints hold that the hour of trial is synonymous with the tribulation period. The difference occurs as to what "keep from" means. Douglas Moo states "that spiritual preservation is clearly intended." "It seems best to think that in Revelation 3:10 Christ promises the Church at Philadelphia that it will be spiritually protected from the hour of trial."[329] Those

---

[328] Tim LaHaye, *Rapture Under Attack*, (Sisters: Multnomah, 1998), p. 64.

[329] Stanley N. Gundry. ed. *Three Views of the Rapture; Pre-Mid—or Post-Tribulational?*, (Grand Rapids: Zondervan, 1996), p. 198.

who hold this view see the Greek preposition *ek* (translated as "from") as implying protection within the hour of trial, i.e., the church at Philadelphia experiencing the horrors of the period by suffering no ill effects.

Jeffrey Townsend concludes just the opposite viewpoint regarding *ek*. He writes, "Sufficient evidence exists throughout the history of the meaning and usage of *ek* to indicate that this preposition may also denote a position outside its object with no thought of prior existence from the object."[330] Those who hold this viewpoint see *ek* as implying complete removal from the circumstances.

In both cases, the argument supports each group's belief in the timing of the rapture of the Church. The first group represents the idea that the rapture of the Church will occur at the end of the hour of trial. The Church will go through this tribulation period but will emerge victorious. The belief that the rapture will occur at the end of the tribulation period is called post-tribulational, i.e., after the tribulation. The second group represents the idea that the rapture of the Church will occur prior to the start of the hour of trial and that the Church will be removed completely from the experiences of the tribulation period. This view is referred to as pre-tribulational, i.e., before the tribulation.

The promise made to the Philadelphia church is that they would be kept from the hour of trial itself and not from the events of the hour of trial. David Winfrey offers these comments.

> [The postribulational view of] Rev 3:10 fails to provide any measure of comfort to the church in this period of trials. If God will protect the saints from the plagues he will inflict upon the ungodly, we may well ask why he doesn't protect them against those persecutions directed at them by Satan. If in fact the church will enter the great tribulation, it would seem that the Lord would provide something more in the way of protection for the church as she faces the most terrible

---

[330] Jeffrey L. Townsend. "The Rapture in Revelation 3:10," Bibliotheca Sacra vol. 137, July 1980.

> period of persecution in history. It seems a misuse of language to speak of those who are not divine targets (i.e., the church/tribulation saints) as being "protected" when in fact nothing is actually done to prevent them from suffering at the hands of Satan. It is a mockery to conceive of anyone being "comforted" (and surely that is the intent of the promise in Rev 3:10) by the fact that he is only the target of Satan. If while a believer is in the crosshairs of one sharpshooter (Satan) who fully intends to kill him, he learns that another (God) promises not to do the same, but will not however protect him from the other, what comfort is there in this? How can one rejoice over this "promise of protection"? What consolation is there in such "protection" if one is left utterly exposed to the "wrath of Satan and the Antichrist in the form of persecution"? Like the fine print in some insurance policies [this view] so limits the promise of persecution in Rev. 3:10 as to make it meaningless.[331]

Although not explicitly stated in this verse, the rapture of the Church is implicit. The promise of keeping the Church from the hour of trial, following a pre-tribulational view, leads to the conclusion that the Risen Lord will remove the Church from the tribulation period.

The first mention of the rapture of the Church is in John 14:1-3. The disciples are confused and troubled because Jesus had been telling them that He must go away. He comforts them with these words,

> Let not your heart be troubled; you believe in God, believe also in Me. In My Father's house are many mansions; if it were not so, I would have told you. And if I go and prepare a place for you, I will come again and receive you to Myself; that where I am, there you may be also.

---

[331] David G. Winfrey, "The Great Tribulation: Kept "out of" or "Through"?" Grace Theological Journal vol. 3, Spring 1982.

Just like the church at Philadelphia the disciples needed to be comforted. The Lord promised that He was going away but that He would come back for them so they could be where He was.

The Apostle Paul comforted the Thessalonians in 1 Thessalonians 4:13-17 by further expanding on this return of the Lord. In verse 16 he writes,

> For the Lord Himself will descend from heaven with a shout, with the voice of an archangel, and with the trumpet of God. And the dead in Christ will rise first. Then we who are alive and remain shall be caught up together with them in the clouds to meet the Lord in the air. And thus we shall always be with the Lord.

The Greek word *harpazo* used in verse 16 is translated "caught up" or "snatched." Literally, the word means "to seize upon with force."[332] When the New Testament was translated into Latin the Greek word *harpazo* was translated using the root word *rapto* meaning "to seize and carry off, snatch, drag, hurry away."[333]

It is from this word that we get the English word *rapture*. The word rapture does not appear in the New Testament. This message from Paul on the rapture is for the purpose of comforting one another.

In 1 Corinthian 15:51, 52, Paul elaborated on this event by calling it a mystery, i.e., something previously not revealed. He says, "We shall not all sleep, but we shall all be changed—in a moment, in the twinkling of an eye, at the last trumpet. For the trumpet will sound and the dead will be raised incorruptible, and we shall be changed."

From these verses, Jesus promises to come back for those who are His. He raises those who have died in Him, snatches those still alive from the clutches of the prince of this world to gather them to Him in the clouds, and just as the dead in Christ are given an

---

[332] Zodhiates, p. 892.
[333] Charlton T. Lewis., *An Elementary Latin Dictionary*, (New York: Harper & Brothers, 1891), p. 699.

incorruptible body, so to those alive at this point will be changed. In 1 Corinthians 15:53 Paul continues, "For this corruptible must put on incorruptible, and this mortal must put on immortality."

The church at Philadelphia was comforted by the promise of being kept from the hour of trial just as Jesus comforted His disciples with the promise of His return for them and just as Paul comforted the Thessalonians with the details of how the Lord would snatch them out of a hostile world to be with Him forever. So too, we are to comfort one another with these words.

Behold I am coming quickly! Hold fast what you have, that no one may take your crown.

Verse 11 begins with "Behold." Again, Jesus uses this word to continue to hold the attention of His listeners. Remember that these messages were not read by the recipient; rather, they were read to the recipient. Jesus has just promised to remove the Church from the hour of trial and now tells them "I am coming quickly!" Thomas writes,

> Christ promises to return soon to initiate "the hour of trial" on earth, but more relevant to those in the Philadelphian Church, to deliver them from their difficult circumstances. The placement of this fifth promise at this point is clear implication that deliverance of the faithful will occur in conjunction with His coming.[334]

The Philadelphians would wait expectantly for their deliverance at His coming.

This idea of expectantly waiting for the coming of Christ gives rise to what is called the Doctrine of Imminence. Simply put, this doctrine states that as far we know no event prophesied in Scripture must be fulfilled prior to the rapture of the Church. It is called imminent because Christ can return for His Church at any moment.

The intent of the doctrine is to teach the believer to be always ready for Christ's return by living a godly life in preparation for

---

[334] Thomas, p. 290.

His return. Paul writing to Titus says, "For the grace of God that brings salvation has appeared to all men, teaching us that, denying ungodliness and worldly lusts, we should live soberly, righteously, and godly in the present age, looking for the blessed hope and glorious appearing of our great God and Savior Jesus Christ." This blessed hope for which the Church awaits is the appearance of Jesus as He calls the Church to meet Him in the clouds. Some refer to this blessed hope as occurring at the Second Coming of Christ. But the Church will already be with Christ at that time and will accompany Him back to earth as part of that army "clothed in fine linen, white and clean" (Rev 19:14).

Regarding the imminence of this event Wayne Brindle writes,

> The fact that in Titus 2:13 Paul exhorts believers to look for the Rapture as the "happy," blessed hope (confident expectation) for the church, without any mention of preceding signs or tribulation, strongly implies the imminence of this event—that it can occur at any time . . . The exhortation to "watch" or "look" for what is the hope *par excellence* of the church loses its significance if it may not arrive "at any moment."[335]

The Risen Lord tells them to "hold fast what you have." They have little strength in themselves but great power in the promises Christ has made to them. He exhorts them to hold on to what matters. He will keep them and fulfill every promise that He made. Holding fast means not surrendering the eternal promises of Christ for the temporal allure that Satan presents whether it be in possessions or in comfort and ease. The victor's crown awaits. Let no one cheat you of your reward.

He who overcomes, I will make him a pillar in the temple of My God, and he shall go out no more. I will write on him the

---

[335] Wayne A. Brindle, "Looking for the Blessed Hope An Analysis of Biblical Evidence for the Imminence of the Rapture." Pretrib Study Group, Dallas, 09 Dec, 2002.

name of My God and the name of the city of My God, the New Jerusalem, which comes down out of heaven from My God. And I will write on him My new name.

There are four promises made to the overcomer in this verse.

I will make him a pillar in the temple of My God.

The Risen Lord promises the overcomer at Philadelphia that they would be analogous to a pillar. What significance could this possibly have? There are at least three ways of viewing this promise.

In Galatians 2:9 Paul wrote that James, Cephas (Peter), and John seemed to be pillars of the church. By that he meant that they functioned as leaders who helped uphold and support faith and practice in the church. They were the recognized leaders or elders. The church looked to them to supply needed support. Perhaps the Risen Lord was telling the Philadelphians that their perseverance placed them in a capacity for others to witness how they were upheld by the Lord and how they weathered the storms of life due to their unbending faith. A faith that had been given to them by the Lord but nevertheless strengthened by their diligence and the addition of virtue, knowledge, self-control, perseverance, godliness, brotherly kindness, and love (2 Peter 1:5-7). God gave them everything they had. Paul writes, "What do you have that you did not receive?" (1 Corinthians 4:7). But they were expected to add to what God gave them through diligence to these virtues, and they did.

When Solomon built the temple, there were two pillars made of iron that were placed on each side of the entrance. On the top of these two pillars were placed two iron capitals ornately crafted by Huram, a skilled artisan.[336] The pillars stood as testimony to God's security and strength that was available to Israel as she lived her life in obedience to Him.[337] The pillars were given names. The pillar on the right side was named Jachin which literally means

---

[336] See 1 Kings 7:13-32.

[337] John F. Walvoord and Roy B. Zuck. eds. *The Bible Knowledge Commentary*, vol 1. (USA: Victor, 1989), p. 502.

"He [Yahweh] Shall Establish." The pillar on the left side was named Boaz which literally means "In It Is Strength."

Perhaps the Risen Lord was telling the Philadelphians that though they had little strength, because they had believed His promises and relied on His strength, they would be like Jachin and Boaz. They would stand as testimony to God's security and strength.

Pillars are used to support the roof of a structure. To be a pillar would indicate a firm and permanent position. The Risen Lord could have been indicating to the Philadelphians that despite their experience with earthquakes creating instability in their city's structure, they could be assured that He would provide the overcomer with eternal stability and security. The world that they see may be shaken, even violently, but the overcomer will rest in His world of stability and security found only in Christ.

The Risen Lord promises the Philadelphians that they should go out no more.

The continuous threat of earthquakes and the aftershocks associated with them kept the citizens of Philadelphia in a state of flux. As was previously discussed, the citizens lived for the most part out of the city due to the fear of unstable structures as a result of the seismic activity. Those who chose to live in the city were seen as mad by the other citizens. The overcomer will not have to concern themselves any longer with the instability of life. They will be able to live in stability and permanence. They will stand despite the fact that all else has fallen.

The Risen Lord promises the Philadelphians that He will write on them the name of My God.

Writing on them the name of My God was equivalent to letting them know to whom they belonged. They were identified with God. Unlike those who claimed to be Jews and are not, but lie, the Philadelphians were authentic because they belonged to Him who is true.

The promise of having written on them the name of the city of My God indicates heavenly citizenship. Paul wrote to the Philippians that "our citizenship is in heaven" (3:20). By faith

Abraham "waited for the city which has foundations, whose builder and maker is God" (Hebrews 11:10). This heavenly citizenship was in the New Jerusalem which comes down from heaven from God. The overcomer would have residence in this new city as the reward for perseverance.

The Risen Lord promises the overcomer His very own name.

In the ancient city of Euromos located forty-four miles southeast of Ephesus, there are ruins of a temple to Zeus which have in recent years been unearthed. Thirty columns have been found. On the columns are placards noting the person that donated the money for that particular pillar to be constructed and put in use in the temple. The placard identifies the donor who could be said to own the pillar. The pillar did not construct itself but was constructed through the efforts of the benefactor. His name is on the pillar. So too, the new name of the Risen Lord written on the overcomer will identify the overcomer who is analogous to the pillar in the Temple of God. That new name will represent all that the Risen Lord is. It symbolizes the full revelation of His person and nature and identifies the overcomer as belonging permanently to Him.

The new name concept is not something new to the city of Philadelphia. You will recall that the city changed its name twice prior to this as a means of gratitude to two Roman emperors. They were grateful for the benevolence of these emperors for their help in the rebuilding process of the city. However, after a while, the city forgot this benevolence returning to the name by which they were familiar. The overcomer will not change their name but will be given a new name, which shall never be forgotten, identifying them with the eternal God.

The founder of the city, Attalus, when enticed by the Roman Senate to defect from his king and brother, was encouraged by Stratus, the mediator sent by Eumenes. Through this encouragement, Attalus stood strong and remained faithful. The Risen Lord is the mediator for the Philadelphians and through His strength and encouragement, the Philadelphians stood strong and remained faithful.

He who has an ear, let him hear what the Spirit says to the churches.

The Spirit calls out again for willing ears to listen and respond. The church at Philadelphia has only the promises of Christ to hold fast to. Their response to the Spirit results in their being kept from the hour of trial, their establishment as pillars in the Temple of God, their security in Christ, their citizenship in heaven, and a new name on which to rely.

CHAPTER TEN

Laodicea:

The Church of Disingenuous Belief

Background

The church at Laodicea was the last to receive the message from John. The city was located at the crossroads of two important highways and became the chief city in the province of Phyrgia. There were at least eight Greek cities founded in the third century B.C. by the Seleucids named Laodicea. This city was named for the wife of Antiochus II whose name was Laodice.[338] In ancient sources the city was called Laodikeia on the side of the Lycus to distinguish it from the other seven cities of the same name. The Lycus was a river, the valley of which ran through the city.

One highway connected Syria with Ephesus and was one of the most important roads in all of Asia Minor. This highway took travelers right through the city. The other road went from Pergamum south to the Mediterranean coast. Laodicea's location on these highways gave the city a perfect opportunity for material wealth. The city was famous as a financial center and became one of the wealthiest cities in the world. In A.D. 60 the same earthquake that struck Sardis and Philadelphia destroyed Laodicea. Just as Rome helped the other cities in Asia Minor rebuild after their cities were destroyed, so too they offered financial aid to Laodicea. However, Laodicea was so prosperous

---

[338] Barclay Revelation, p.137.

and proud they refused Roman aid and rebuilt the city entirely from their own resources. Strabo writes, "It was the fertility of its territory and the prosperity of certain of its citizens that made it great."[339] In A.D. 109 Tacitus wrote, "One of the famous cities of Asia, Laodicea, was that same year overthrown by an earthquake, and without any relief from us, recovered itself by its own resources."[340] It was this attitude of self-sufficiency that caused the citizens to rely upon their own resources and abilities. It didn't need Rome's help nor help from any other source.

Another industry that played an important role in the attitude and development of Laodicea was the garment industry. The sheep that were raised in Laodicea were famous for their black wool. "The country round Laodicea produces sheep that are excellent not only for the softness of their wool, in which they surpass even the Milesian wool, but also for their raven-black color, so that the Laodiceans derive splendid revenue from it."[341] The wool was spun and used to produce garments that were sold throughout the world. The civic pride that came as a result of these garments would not allow people of Laodicea to even think that they would ever be in need of any clothing for they could produce the world's finest garments and could easily clothe themselves.

The city was also well known as a medical center. Within the vicinity of the city was a temple to a god named Men Karou. In the temple was located a famous medical school which developed an ointment for the eyes. In the ancient East, a lack of water and less than desirable sanitary conditions caused considerable eye trouble. The sandy climate and the specks from the threshing floor often contributed to red and swollen eyes. The ointment or salve for which Laodicea was famous provided an answer for these eye troubles. *Tephra Phyrgia* or Phyrgian Powder, as it was called, was exported to the world in the form of a rolled tablet. When the tablet was crushed and mixed with water, the result was the famous eye salve. Hemer writes,

---

[339] Strabo, 12.8.16.
[340] Tacitus, 14.27.1.

We thus find considerable circumstantial reason for connecting the "eyesalve" motif with Laodicea. The city probably marketed exclusively and profitably an ointment developed locally from available materials, whose exact composition may have been kept secret from commercial rivals.[342]

The self-sufficiency of the city resulted from its prosperity. In 51 B.C. Cicero, the Roman politician and philosopher, was acting as governor of the province of Cilicia. Many of the letters he wrote to friends survive today. One such letter was written to Appius Claudius Pulcher in July of 51 B.C. In it Cicero informs the reader about his itinerary. The letter says, "On the 31st of July I expect to be in Laodicea; I shall remain there for a very few days to get some money due me on an exchequer bill of exchange."[343] Hemer writes that possibly Laodicea was the "proconsuls point of entry into the province and the natural place to draw the *vasarium*."[344] Laodicea would have been financially sophisticated so that foreign money could be exchanged for local currency. They had no financial needs as a result of their thriving industry, which was well diversified. "Laodicea ad Lycum [was] a city in Phyrygia . . . It became one of the most prosperous cities in Asia Minor and was the seat of a flourishing Christian Church as early as the apostolic age."[345]

There was however, a negative factor to living in Laodicea. The city water supply came from a spring approximately five miles to the south of the city. A system of underground aqueducts brought the water from a spring into the city. The water was tepid and dirty. The nearby city of Colosse, located ten miles to the east, was known for its refreshingly cool mountain streams and Heiropolis, six miles to the north, was known for its hot springs. The waters of

---

[341] Strabo, 12.8.16.

[342] Hemer, p. 199.

[343] Cicero, *Epistulae ad Familiaries*.

[344] Hemer, p. 191. Vasarium is the Latin word for money of a provincial governor, i.e. money owed to him as a result of his position.

[345] Henry Thurston Peck. *Harper's Dictionary of Classical Antiquities*, (New York: Harper and Brothers, 1898).

Heiropolis run in channels under the feet of the traveler. It is warm enough that steam rises from the ground. The water cascades down the hillside, which stands approximately three hundred feet high. The deposits from the water create a snowlike covering that can be seen from miles away. The ridge extends for nearly a mile. The white-capped hill is clearly seen from Laodicea.

Exposition

And to the angel of the church of Laodicea write,

It is generally thought that Epaphras was responsible for evangelizing the tri-cities of Colosse, Laodicea, and Heiropolis. Paul called him a faithful minister of Christ on behalf of the Colossaians (Col 1:7). He is described as having great zeal for the Colossians, "and those in Laodicea, and those in Heiropolis" (4:13). Paul also mentions him as a fellow prisoner in the closing verses of the letter to Philemon. The church would more than likely have been established during Paul's three-year stay in Ephesus. Acts 19: 10 says that "all who dwelt in Asia heard the word of the Lord Jesus, both Jews and Greeks." The date would have been circa 53-57. Not many years after this conversion, Laodicea would have experienced the devastation of the earthquake that destroyed the city.

There is no Scriptural evidence that Paul ever visited the city. In Colossians 2:1 he writes, "For I want you to know what a great conflict I have for you and those in Laodicea, and as for as many as have not seen my face in the flesh." Many commentators point to this verse as an indication that Paul never visited the city. But the verse doesn't say that. The verse states that Paul is struggling or laboring over three groups of people: (1) the Colossians, (2) the Laodiceans, and (3) those he has never personally met. Those who claim Paul never visited Laodicea connect the third group with the first two to conclude that Paul was never in either city. This could be correct, but, both cities are located on a major east-west trade route that would have made it difficult for Paul not to have visited there. On Paul's second missionary journey he reached Pisidian Antioch and continued his travels on the northern road that led him to Mysia and Troas. On his third missionary journey, Paul left

Antioch in Syria and traveled overland to visit the cities in Galatia which he had visited on his first journey. The trade route through that area forks in the near proximity of Pisidian Antioch. The northern fork goes to Mysia while the other fork travels through the Lycus Valley to Ephesus. On his second journey Paul took this northern fork because the Spirit forbade him to preach the word in Asia. Acts 19:11 says that on the third journey he passed through the upper regions to arrive at Ephesus. The NIV says he took the road through the interior to arrive at Ephesus. According to Turkish tour guides this road would have gone through Laodicea. There were no other roads on which to travel. The only other alternative would have been "through the goat tracks in the mountains."[346] Sherman Johnson writes,

> It is possible, of course, that on the so-called third missionary journey Paul went through the Hermus Valley on his way to Ephesus; but, as I have argued elsewhere, the most logical route for him to take was past Laodicea and down along the Meander River. A third possibility is that he came through the Cayster Valley, but this would have involved another mountain pass, and the towns along this route were not as important as those in the other two valleys.[347]

Paul instructed the Colossians to forward the letter he had sent them via Tychicus to Laodicea after they had read it. The implication is that whatever was written to the Colossians was equally applicable to the Laodiceans. Interestingly, he did not request they forward the letter to Heiroplois. In the city of Laodicea at the time Paul wrote this letter there was a church of Laodicea that gathered together for this letter to be read (4:16). Also, there was at least one church there that met in the home of Nymphas (NKJV uses the masculine) or Nympha (NIV uses the feminine).

---

[346] Personal correspondence from Hakan Bashar, Turkish tour guide.
[347] Allen Wikgren. ed., *Early Christian Origins*, (Chicago: Quadrangle 1961), p. 81.

There is a close association between the letter to the Colossians and the message to the church at Laodicea. The significance of that association will be pointed out, as the passage is exposited.

These things says the Amen, the Faithful and True Witness, the Beginning of the creation of God.

What is about to be said to the church at Laodicea is coming from a sender described in a three-fold manner. He is: (1) the Amen, (2) the Faithful and True witness, and (3) the Beginning of the creation of God.

The Amen

The word *amen* is a transliteration of the Hebrew into both Greek and English. Of the 129 occurrences in the New Testament, twenty-six of those occur in the Gospel of John where it is translated "most assuredly." It is the double amen to emphasize the strength of what is being said. In John 3:3, Jesus says, "Most assuredly [amen, amen] I say to you, unless one is born again, he cannot see the kingdom of God." "By introducing His words in this way, Jesus labeled them as certain and reliable and made them binding on Himself and on His hearers. They expressed His majesty and authority."[348] Identifying Himself as such assures the reader that His words are true, His prophecy reliable, and His outcome certain.

In Isaiah 65:16, the prophet writes about the "God of truth." Literally the words are the "God of Amen." The meaning there is essentially whatever God decrees or declares shall be true. This is the only occurrence in the Old Testament where amen is used as a name for God. In Revelation 3:14 the Risen Lord claims this title as the title He uses to identify Himself as the sender of this message. "Christologically, this title is significant since it attributes to Christ a title associated only with God."[349]

---

[348] Verbrugge, p.105.
[349] Aune, p. 255.

The Faithful and True Witness

In Revelation 1:5, John's greeting to the seven churches comes from "Jesus Christ, the faithful witness." As shown in the letter to Philadelphia (Rev. 3:7) Jesus claimed for Himself that He was true. The aspect of being both faithful and true denotes the reliability of Jesus to perform all that He says as well as the veracity of all those things that He speaks. He is both dependable and genuine. The aspect of being genuine contrasts sharply the lack of real belief on the part of the Laodiceans.

The genuineness of Jesus does not depend on His word alone albeit sufficient within itself. In John 8:18, Jesus claims that "the Father who sent Me bears witness of Me." At the baptism of Jesus (Matt 4:17; Mark 1:11; Luke 3:22) a voice came from heaven saying, "You are My beloved Son, in whom I am well pleased." [350] When Jesus was transfigured before Peter, James, and John a voice once again came from heaven saying, "This is My beloved Son in whom I am well pleased. Hear Him" (Matt 17:5). The Father witnessed to who Jesus is.

In John 5: 31-40, the evangelist lists the witnesses attesting to Jesus and His authenticity. They are John the Baptist (31-35), the works that Jesus performed (v 36), the Father (37, 38), and Scripture (39, 40). In John 15:26, 27, the Spirit of Truth is said to testify of Jesus and finally His very disciples will bear Him witness.

It was these two aspects of Christ's attributes that caused the Laodiceans to come to a knowledge of Him in the first place. It was only reasonable to point out to them that they think through why they call themselves followers. Believers are genuine because the object of their belief is genuine; not because of any inherent genuineness on the part of the individual. The Risen Lord is pointing out to them that this message is coming from the very core, or object, of what they say they believe.

The Beginning of the Creation of God.

---

[350] The account in Mark says, "in whom I am well pleased;" and Matthew says "This is My beloved Son."

In the letter to the Colossians which Paul clearly stated should also be read to the church of the Laodiceans, a plea was made that the recipients not be deceived with persuasive words. Paul was writing to warn them not to allow the false teachers to convince them that Jesus was something other than who He claimed to be. In 1:15, Paul writes, "He is the image of the invisible God, the firstborn over all creation." The firstborn over all creation and the Beginning of the Creation of God are similar in that they both refer to Christ as the initiator or originator of creation. He is the pre-eminent One, not the first in a continuous line of creation. He is not a created being but the initiator of the creation. Paul asserts that "by Him all things were created that are in heaven and that are on earth, visible and invisible" (Col 1:16). In his gospel, John writes, of Jesus being the *logos* or word. He writes, "All things were made through Him, and without Him nothing was made that was made" (John 1:3). He is the Beginning of the Creation of God because He was the initiator of that creation.

I know your works.

Zodhiates writes that works as used here "usually denotes comprehensively what a man is and how he acts."[351] Just as in the other churches, the Risen Lord knows everything about the Laodiceans. He is omniscient (all-knowing) and knows the thoughts of a man (Matt. 12:25) and the heart of a man (Acts 1:24). He knows what a man thinks and what the motives behind those thoughts are.

It is interesting to note that the Lord, knowing the works of the Laodiceans, finds nothing for which to commend them. He commended Ephesus and exhorts them for leaving their first love. He commended Pergamum and exhorted them for compromise. He commended Thyatira and exhorted them for allowing false teaching in their midst. He even told Sardis that He didn't find their works perfect. Yet to the Laodiceans, He has no commendation to give, only exhortation.

You are neither hot nor cold. I could wish you were cold or

---

[351] Zodhiates, p. 915.

hot. So then, because you are lukewarm, and neither cold nor hot, I will vomit you out of My mouth.

The idea of the Laodiceans being neither cold nor hot is an allusion to the water supply of the city. In full view of the city were the white-capped hills of Heiropolis where the mineral springs were known to be hot and medicinal. Laodicea had neither hot water as did Heiropolis nor cold water as did Colosse. Instead, due to the underground aqueduct that carried the water supply of the city some five miles from the source, the water in Laodicea was tepid or lukewarm. The Laodiceans were well aware of their water problem and they would not have missed the point the Risen Lord was making as a metaphor to their real life situation. They did not have a zest for Christ (hot) nor, at the other end of the spectrum were they so cold that spiritual things escaped them. They may very well have had thriving growth in their church. Attendance at services may have been regular and people may have spoken about spiritual matters. But they were doing so without Christ and as such were neither hot nor cold but lukewarm.

Regarding this lukewarmness, Boyer writes,

> The Laodicean church is not the theologically liberal church down the street, nor the apostate church of the end times. It is the Bible-believing church which possesses and upholds the light of the gospel, but which is conforming to the values of the world and refusing to get overly involved in the Lord's work. It is spiritually wretched and poor and miserable and blind and naked (3:17). It is lukewarm—not cold and unresponsive to the things of God, but not hot and "on fire" for the Lord who bought it. Rather it is somewhat in between. It is trying to enjoy the good things and to avoid the unpleasant things of both worlds.[352]

The Risen Lord expresses a wish that the Laodiceans were one

---

[352] James L. Boyer. *Are the Seven Letters of Revelation 2-3 Prophetic?*, Grace Theological Journal. vol 6. Fall, 1985.

or the other. The word *wish* or *would* means "if only." The thought is "if only it were true." It is not that Jesus doesn't know, it's His wish that it wasn't the way it is. If they were full of zest and hot for the Lord, they would first be seeking Him. Then they would seek what it is that He wanted for them. If they were cold spiritually, they would either have no desire for spiritual matters or they may even be adversarial to the Gospel message and toward believers who shared in that message. Either way, the Lord could deal with them. As it stands, however, they think they are believers but they are not. As long as they continue to believe this way, they face an eternity separated from God. The Risen Lord takes drastic measures here to graphically depict to them their real condition. He says He will vomit them out of His mouth. They are repulsive to Him. Aune states that the phrase "vomit them out of My mouth" "is a coarse figure of speech meaning utterly reject."[353]

It must always be remembered that the Risen Lord is reasoning with the church at Laodicea. He is addressing problems within the church which are serious and needs immediate and decisive action. It is as though He is grabbing them by the shirt and shaking them to get their attention. In Revelation 6-18, He will get the attention of all unbelievers in the same manner by literally shaking the very foundations of the world. Here He is dealing with a church that is called by His name but has no claim on Him because they are self-sufficient and not submissive to the Lord.

A Sunday school teacher went to visit a gentleman, who along with his wife, had come to class on a regular basis. During the course of the visit, the teacher asked the man about his spiritual journey. The man shared that he had been brought up in the church and even taught Sunday school for a period of time. Intrigued by the man's story, the teacher asked him to share the story of his conversion. The man said that he had been a Christian for as long as he could remember. The teacher pressed on to find some point at which the man could remember making a conscious decision to accept Christ as Savior and Lord. The man said that he

---

[353] Aune. P. 258.

could not recall a time when he made such a decision. The teacher impressed upon the man that Scripture says, "If you confess with your mouth the Lord Jesus and believe in your heart that God raised Him from the dead, you will be saved. For with the heart one believes unto righteousness, and with the mouth confession is made unto salvation" (Romans 10:9, 10). The man replied that he and the teacher would have to agree to disagree on that issue because he didn't see it that way. Clearly this man did not understand what a relationship with the Lord entailed but by the same token he thought he had one. The man came to only a few more classes then the teacher saw him no more.

It is not unusual any longer for people to be in church service every Sunday yet they have never made that decision to accept Christ as their Savior and Lord. They think they are saved but they are not. More and more stories are being told about ministerial staff, deacon chairmen, church trustees, and longtime members of churches who come to realize that they have been playing a game with God. They have been going through the motions of being a believer but they have never truly surrendered their life to Christ. This is the situation in Laodicea. They are pretenders and as such will be utterly rejected by Christ as though He vomits them out of His mouth.

In John 2:33-35 the apostle writes,

> Now when He was in Jerusalem at the Passover, during the feast, many believed in His name when they saw the signs which He did. But Jesus did not commit Himself to them, because He knew all men, and had no need that anyone should testify of man, for He knew what was in man.

Although it appeared outwardly that those who believed in His name were committed, Jesus knew their hearts and knew that they were not genuinely converted.

In John 12:42, 43, he writes, "Nevertheless even among the rulers many believed in Him, but because of the Pharisees they did not confess Him, lest they should be put out of the synagogue; for they loved the praise of men more than the praise of God."

If you asked the people described in John 2 if they were believers, they would assuredly answer in the affirmative. The same could be said for the rulers in John 12. The Laodiceans were no different. They thought they were believers but had never committed themselves to the Lord. This is what makes them lukewarm and not easily reached with the Gospel message. It is for just that reason that the Risen Lord excoriates them in order to get their attention.

Because you say, 'I am rich, have become wealthy, and have need of nothing'—and do not know that you are wretched, miserable, poor, blind and naked—I counsel you to buy from Me gold refined in the fire, that you may be rich; and white garments, that you may be clothed, that the shame of your nakedness may not be revealed; and anoint your eyes with eyesalve, that you may see.

The Laodiceans thought they were rich and had need of nothing. As was previously discussed, the city was extremely prosperous. They pretty much had what they wanted. They were self-sufficient. That was the attitude they took during the aftermath of the earthquake of A.D. 60. Rome offered financial assistance just as they offered to the other cities of Asia Minor. Laodicea refused the help and financed the reconstruction costs from their own resources. They carried this same self-sufficiency into their spiritual life. They did not know they were wretched, miserable, poor, blind and naked.

The word *wretched* means distressed. The Laodiceans were going through life as though everything was just fine when in fact they were distressed. Their situation was difficult; their condition was dangerous.

The word *miserable* means pitiable. The Risen Lord's heart was moved to pity these poor people due to their mindset of self-sufficiency. They thought they had it all together, but in reality they were pitied.

The word *poor* in this usage means abject poverty. They were poor and helpless. This describes a person so poor that they can only sustain themselves by begging. This is in stark contrast to the church at Smyrna. There the Risen Lord says, "I know your poverty." This church was destitute but the Lord says in reality, "you are rich." Here, the Laodiceans are rich materially but destitute spiritually.

They are blind. One of the successful industries of Laodicea involved medicine. The city was a famous producer of eyesalve. How ironic that the Risen Lord informs them that they cannot see. If they could, surely they would change their status. If they realized they were truly not believers, surely they would remedy that situation. The Risen Lord points out their blindness in stark words for the very purpose of drawing them to a conclusion that they are not self-sufficient and need to depend on the love of God and His plan for their life.

They are naked. This would have been quite a startling statement for a people famous for their woolen-garment industry. The word means stark naked and is intended to represent nakedness in the spiritual realm. Their righteousness was their own; not the imputed righteousness of faith.

Given this description of the church at Laodicea there could be no sense in which they were genuine believers. They were players on a stage who, as T. S. Eliot wrote, "prepare a face to meet the faces that you meet."[354] It was for this very reason that the Risen Lord advises the Laodiceans to take certain action. The word *counsel* here means to give advice. Synonyms for this word would be admonish, caution, warn, or exhort. The Risen Lord exhorts the Laodiceans to buy from Him what only He can provide. The gold refined in fire signifies all the impurities removed. There will be no more hypocrisy but an authentic faith. The wealth of a spiritual treasure takes the place of the material wealth about which the Laodiceans boast. This spiritual wealth is the same wealth the Lord

---

[354] T. S. Eliot. *Collected Poems: The Love Song of J. Alfred Prufrock*, (New York: Harcourt Brace, 1936), p. 12.

spoke to Smyrna about. It is a wealth that only Christ can give and He offers it to the Laodiceans.

He tells them to buy white garments that they might be clothed. The garments the Lord provides are white as a sign of purity. There is no stain of sin on them because they represent the imputed righteousness that only He can provide.

He tells them to anoint their eyes that they might see.

The three items He advises them to purchase from Him are antidotes to the debilitated condition of the Laodiceans. By accepting the prescription they will overcome the five infirmities listed in verse 17 and live. Failure to take the medication will result in eternal death.

As many as I love, I rebuke and chasten. Therefore be zealous and repent.

In his essay *Revelation 3:20 and the Offer of Salvation*, Daniel Wallace argues that the Laodiceans are indeed saved but perhaps in a backslidden state. One point that he makes toward that end is that the specific Greek word for love (*phileo*) is a "term that is never used of God/Jesus loving unbelievers in the NT."[355] Instead *agapeo* is the Greek word that speaks of this kind of love as used in John 3:16. But Verbrugge maintains that "the difference between these two words is not always maintained . . . the impossibility of a rigid distinction is clear."[356] As has already been discussed the words used by Christ addressing the Laodiceans as being wretched, miserable, poor, blind, and naked give clear indication that they are not genuine believers. The Lord loves them in the same sense that Paul expressed in Romans 5:8, "But God demonstrated His own love toward us, in that while we were still sinners, Christ died for us." The word used here is *agapeo* which would seem to corroborate Wallace's argument. However, that love was in place prior to any regeneration. Just as God loved the believer while still being an unbeliever in Romans 5:8, so too He loves the Laodiceans

---

[355] Daniel Wallace. *Revelation 3:20 and the Offer of Salvation*, http://bible.org/docs/soapbox/twist4.htm 2/28/03

[356] Verbrugge, p. 1305, 1306.

in their unregenerate state. He loves them enough to warn them of the dire consequences of continuing on in a life of unbelief.

Jesus' intent in calling the Laodiceans to account can be seen in the meaning of the word *rebuke*. It means "to reprove with conviction, which refers to effectual rebuke leading, if not to a confession, at least to a conviction of sin."[357] The rebuke has a purpose and that purpose is to drive the Laodiceans to Jesus in genuine conversion.

As a result of the rebuke, the Lord exhorts the Laodiceans to be zealous and repent. Robertson writes that "the Greek tenses here are a graphic picture of these commands, "keep on being zealous; and begin to repent."[358] Begin to repent indicates that they have not yet begun to do so and need to take their life in another direction different than they have been traveling. To repent for the Laodiceans means to turn away from their self-sufficiency and turn toward a dependence on God. An about-face is in order. The zealousness with which they are to do it contrasts sharply with the lukewarmness spoken of in verse 16.

Behold, I stand at the door and knock. If anyone hears My voice and opens the door, I will come in to him and dine with him, and he with Me.

As has previously been stated, beginning this verse with the word *behold* signals that the Lord wants to reason with the Laodiceans. He wants them to consider intellectually what he is saying to them for the purpose of making a conscious decision to take the action He recommends. He has stated His case and now comes the time for the Laodiceans to respond to what He has told them.

By standing at the door and knocking the Risen Lord is impressing on the Laodiceans that time is running out. He is at the very door. There is an urgency to the statement. John the Baptist preached a message of repentance and called the people of his day to take action. He stressed to them the urgency of the situation in Matthew 3:10 when he said, "And even now the ax is laid to the

---

[357] Zodhiates, p. 915.
[358] Robertson, p. 666.

root of the trees." By that he meant that judgment was imminent, i.e., it could come at any moment. James, the half brother of Jesus, exhorted his readers when he wrote, "Behold, the judge is standing at the door" (James 5:9). Once again this urgency to respond is impressed upon the listener.

Whereas the imminency of being at the door is stressed, so too is the fact that the Risen Lord is knocking. He could by all rights force His way into anyone's life. But He chooses to wait patiently for an invitation to enter. He invites those who are inside the house to open the door and receive him. Morris writes, "He is knocking, where the tense signifies not a perfunctory rap, but a knocking continued in the hope of a response."[359]

He says "if anyone hears My voice and opens the door, I will come in to him." The word *anyone* specifies the invitation is open to all who first, hear the voice and second respond to the invitation to open the door. Christ is not in the midst of this church. He is on the outside with a door separating Him and the members of this church. He is ready to enter but only at the invitation to do so. MacArthur expands the idea to include Christ's entry into the church. He writes,

> The invitation is, first of all, a personal one, since salvation is individual. But He is knocking on the door of the church, calling the many to saving faith, so that He may enter the church. If one person (anyone) opened the door by repentance and faith, Christ would enter that church through that individual. The picture of Christ outside the Laodicean church seeking entrance strongly implies that, unlike Sardis, there were no believers there at all.[360]

Tenney writes, "Christ outside the door of His own church seems to be an incongruous concept; yet that is exactly what this text implies."[361]

---

[359] L. Morris, p.83.
[360] MacArthur, vol 1 p. 83.
[361] Tenney, p. 67.

The idea of the Risen Lord dining with the one who hears His voice and opens the door has been seen in several ways by commentators. Some view this as an allusion to the Last Supper in the upper room, while others see it as an allusion to the Lord's Supper; and still others see in it a picture of fellowship with the believer. It seems best to see in this the idea of the Risen Lord having an intimate fellowship with the believer. He will come in and dine with the believer and the believer will be in the Lord's presence with all that it entails.

To him who overcomes, I will grant to sit with Me on My throne, as I also overcame and sat down with My Father on His throne.

Just as in the message to the other churches a promise is given to the overcomer. The promise is to sit with Christ on His throne, which He shares with the Father. Just as Christ overcame, He calls the Laodiceans to do the same and offers to reward the one who does by sharing His throne.

He who has an ear, let him hear what the Spirit says to the churches.

For the final time the Risen Lord speaks clearly of the need to listen and heed what is being said in these messages. It is important to remember that the Spirit is speaking to the churches collectively in each message. Otherwise the verse may well have said "let him hear what the Spirit says to this church." There is a clear human responsibility pictured here. The Spirit speaks. People are charged with listening, recognizing the voice of the Shepherd, and responding in faith to the message conveyed by the Spirit. To do less is not the role of the overcomer.

Application

So then because you are lukewarm, and neither cold nor hot, I will vomit you out of My mouth. How does this happen?

Wrong Premise

There are clues to the conditions found in Laodicea in Paul's letter to the Colossians. The reason for singling out this particular letter of Paul is due to his words toward the end of the letter. In 4:16 he writes, "Now when this epistle is read among you, see that it is read also in the church of the Laodiceans, and that you likewise read the epistle from Laodicea." Apparently whatever heresy Paul was writing about to the Colossians was affecting the Laodiceans as well. There is a close connection between these two cities.

In the letter to the Colossians, Paul tells them he is struggling for them. His concern is that they have a complete understanding of who Christ is. He warns them about this so that they will be aware of false teachers trying to deceive them with persuasive words. To counteract the false teachers, Paul exhorts them to conduct their lives in Christ as they had been taught. The false teachers were basing their arguments about spiritual matters on philosophy, human tradition, and the basic principles of this world. Paul tells them to base their spiritually on Christ (2:8). "For in Him dwells the fullness of the Godhead bodily; and you are complete in Him, who is the head of all principality and power" (v. 9).

Wrong Actions

After discussing the basis for their life decisions, Paul gets specific about what activities are apparently happening in Colosse and Laodicea. The false teachers have lured them into imposing on themselves dietary restrictions. In 2:16 he writes, "So let no one judge you in food or in drink." There is nothing wrong in imposing dietary restrictions as long as those restrictions are not to be considered for spiritual reasons. Jesus taught that "there is nothing that enters a man from outside that can defile him; but the things which come out of him, those are the things which defile a man" (Mark 7:15).

The false teachers have lured them into celebrations of religious feasts. There is nothing wrong with having memorial days marking significant events as long as there is an understanding that the celebration is a shadow of the event. The festivals they were celebrating were intended to point toward a future reality. The new moons, or Sabbaths, were not the reality. They merely pointed to the reality. They were Old Testament word pictures that pointed to Christ. Now, Christ had come and fulfilled those promises. He was the reality. It was no longer necessary to honor the shadow since the substance, or the reality, had appeared. The shadow has value no longer. Erdman writes, "Since those ceremonies were mere shadows and have been suspended, it may be concluded that they must be abandoned."[362]

The false teachers lured them into a false humility. They were pretenders. False humility is in reality pride. It is an artificial godliness. Jesus warned about this in Matthew 23:1-12. The Pharisees were characterized by Jesus as enjoying the praise of men, "But all their works they do to be seen by men" (v 5). This is a counterfeit spiritually. Those who operate according to this basic principle are pretenders.

The false teachers lured them into relying on personal experience rather than the reality of Christ. The NIV makes this plain stating, "Such a person goes into great detail about what he has seen, and his unspiritual mind puffs him up with idle notions" (2:18). Paul has already written in 2 Corinthians 12:1-6 about a vision of Paradise that he had been given by the Lord. However, he was quick to point out that he was also given a thorn in the flesh so that he might not become conceited or suffer from a bloated self-image due to the revelations given him. Those who make personal experience a test of spirituality have in fact "lost connection with the Head, from whom the body, supported and held together by its ligaments and sinews, grows as God causes it to grow" (2:19).

Wrong Conclusions

Paul writes, "Therefore, if you died with Christ from the basic principles of the world, why as though living in the world do you subject yourselves to regulations . . . according to the commandments and doctrines of men" (2:20-22). The Colossians/Laodiceans were obviously falling under the sway of this "new

---

[362] Charles R. Erdman., *The Epistles of Paul to the Colossians and to Philemon*, (Philadelphia: Westminster, 1933), p. 72.

spirituality" and deviating from "the gospel they had heard" (1:23). Paul reasons with them from a logical perspective. He wants them to think through the reason as to why they would abandon the freedom they have in Christ for self imposed regulations. He tells them, "Those things indeed have an appearance of wisdom in self imposed religion, false humility, and neglect of the body, but are of no value against the indulgences of the flesh" (2:23).

A Wrong Premise Leads to a Wrong Conclusion.

Does this mean the Laodiceans lost their salvation? Scripture teaches that a genuine believer is secure in Christ and can never lose their salvation. Whereas it does not mean they have lost their salvation, it does mean that the effect on future generations is stark. This is what happened in Laodicea. They did not heed Paul's warning. Approximately forty years later, the effect of the false teachers resulted in the Lord being so repulsed by the lukewarmness of the Laodiceans that He wants to vomit them out of His mouth.

The message to the Church today is to base their faith on the One who is Faithful and True and not the basic principles that are operative in the world. As simple as that sounds, its importance is profound. There is no other way. Paul writes, "For no other foundation can anyone lay than that which is laid, which is Jesus Christ" (1 Cor. 3:11).

BIBLIOGRAPHY

Books

Aune, David E. *Revelation*, 3 vols. Dallas: Word, 1997

Barclay, William. *The Revelation of John*, 2 vols., rev. ed. Philadelphia: Westminster, 1976.

Beasley-Murray, G. R., Herschell H Hobbs., and Ray Frank Robbins. *Revelation: Three Views*. Nashville: Broadman, 1977.

Ben Sasson, H. H. ed. *A History of the Jewish People*. Cambridge: Harvard University Press, 1976.

Benware, Paul N. *The Believer's Payday*. Chattanooga: AMG, 2002.

Benware, Paul N. *Understanding End Times Prophecy*. Chicago: Moody, 1995.

Berkouwer, G. C. *The Return of Christ*. Grand Rapids: Eerdmans, 1972.

Boak, Arthur E. R. *A History of Rome To 565 A.D.* New York: MacMillon, 1932.

Bock, Darrell L. ed. *Three Views of the Millennium*. Grand Rapids: Zondervan, 1999.

Boice, James Montgomery. *Genesis*, 4 vols. Grand Rapids: Baker, 1998.

Borland, James A. *A General Introduction to the New Testament*. rev. Lynchburg: University Book house, 1989.

Brauer, Jerald C. ed. *The Westminster Dictionary of Church History*. Philadelphia: Westminster, 1971.

Broadman, John, Jasper Griffin and Oswyn Murray. *The Oxford History of the Classical World*. Oxford: University Press, 1986.

Brower, Kent E. and Mark W. Elliott eds. *Eschatology in Biblical Theology*, Downers Grove: Eerdmans, 1997.

Bruce, F. F. *The Book of Acts*. *Grand Rapids*: Eerdmans, 1988.

Bucke, Emory Stevens. ed. *The Interpreters Dictionary of the Bible*, 4 vols. Nashville: Abingdon, 1962.

Bullinger, E. W. *Numbers in Scripture*. Grand Rapids: Kregel, 1967.

Butrick, George Arthur. ed. *The Interpreters Dictionary of the Bible*. 4 vols. Nashville: Abingdon, 1962.

Carson, D. A. ed. *From Sabbath to the Lord's Day: A Biblical, Historical, and Theological Investigation*. Grand Rapids: Zondervan, 1982.

Carson, D. A., Douglas Moo, and Leon Morris. *An Introduction to the New Testament*. Grand Rapids: Zondervan, 1992.

Couch, Mal. ed. *Dictionary of Premillennial Theology*. Grand Rapids: Kregel, 1996.

Doukhan, Jacques B. *Israel and the Church: Two Voices for the Same God*. Peabody: Hendrickson, 2002.

Eliot, T. S. *Collected Poems*. New York: Harcourt Brace, 1936.

Epp, Theodore H. *Practical Studies in Revelation*, 2 vols. Lincoln: Back To The Bible, 1969.

Erdemgil, Salahattin. *Ephesus Ruins and Museum*. Istanbul: Net Turistic Yayinlar A. S., 1986.

Erdman, Charles F. *The Epistles of Paul to the Colossians and to Philemon*. Philadelphia: Westminster, 1933.

Erickson, Millard J. *Christian Theology*. Grand Rapids: Baker, 1985.

Eusebius. *The History of the Church*. London: Penguin, 1965.

Flusser, David. *Jerusalem and the Origins of Christianity*. Jerusalem: The Magnes Press, 1988.

Gaeblein, Frank. ed. *The Expositors Bible Commentary* vols. 2, 12. Grand Rapids: Zondervan, 1981.

Grant, Michael. *The World of Rome*. New York: Mentor, 1961.

Grant, Michael. *The Rise of the Greeks*. New York: Charles Scribner's Sons, 1987.

Grant, Michael and Rachel Kitzinger. *Civilization of the Ancient Mediterranean: Greece and Rome*, 2 vols. New York: Charles Scribner's Sons, 1988.

Gregg, Steve. *Revelation Four Views A Parallel Commentary*. Nashville: Nelson, 1997.

Grudem, Wayne. *Systematic Theology*. Leicester: InterVarsity, 1994.

Gundry, Stanley N. ed. *Three Views on the Rapture: Pre-, Mid-, or Post-Tribulational?* Grand Rapids: Zondervan, 1996.

Guthrie, Donald. *New Testament Introduction.* rev. ed. Downers Grove: InterVarsity, 1961.

Gutzke, Manford George. *Plain Talk on Revelation.* Grands Rapids: Zondervan, 1979.

Hamilton, Edith. *Mythology.* New York: Mentor, 1940.

Harrop, Clayton. *History of the New Testament in Plain Language.* Waco: Word, 1984.

Hemer, Colin J. *The Letters to the Seven Churches in Their Local Setting.* Grand Rapids: Eerdmans, 2001.

Hendricksen, William. *More Than Conquerors.* Grand Rapids: Baker, 1940.

Herodotus. *Histories.* Hartfordshire: Wordsworth, 1996.

Hornblower, Simon and Anthony Spawforth. *The Oxford Classical Dictionary,* 3rd ed. Oxford: University Press, 1986.

Howard, Kevin and Marvin Rosenthal. *The Feasts of the Lord.* Nashville: Nelson, 1997.

Ironside, H. A. *Lectures on the Revelation.* New York: Bible Truth Press, 1930.

Jeremiah, David. *Escape the Coming Night.* Dallas: Word, 1990.

Johnson, Alan F. *Revelation.* The Expositors Bible Commentary, vol. 12 Grand Rapids: Zondervan, 1981.

Jones, A. H. M. *The Greek City from Alexander to Justinian.* London: Oxford university Press, 1940.

Josephus, Flavius. *The Complete Works* of Josephus, trans. William Whitson, Grand Rapids: Kregel, 1981.

Jurgens, William A. *The Faith of the Early Fathers.* Collegeville: Liturgical Press, 1970.

Kaiser, Walter C. *Exodus.* The Expositor Bible Commentary, vol. 2. Grand Rapids: Zondervan, 1990.

Keener, Craig S. *Revelation.* The NIV Application Commentary. Grand Rapids: Zondervan, 2000.

Keskin, Naci. *Ephesus.* Istanbul: Keskin, 2000.

Kim, Joochan. *Seven Churches in Asia Minor.* Korea: Okhap Publishing, 1999.

Knight, Kevin. ed. *The Catholic Encyclopedia*, vol. XIV Online Edition, 2002.

LaHaye, Tim. *Revelation Illustrated and Made Plain*. Grand Rapids: Zondervan, 1975.

Latourette, Kenneth Scott. *A History of Christianity*, 2 vols., rev. ed. Peabody: Prince Press, 1953.

Lewis, Charlton T. *An Elementary Latin Dictionary*. New York: Harper & Brothers, 1891.

Lewis, Daniel L. *3 Crucial Questions about the Last Days*. Grand Rapids: Baker, 1998.

MacArthur, John. *Revelation*. 2 vols, Chicago: Moody, 2000.

Martyr, Justin. *First Apology*. www.earlychristianwritings.com.
Dialog with Trypho. www.earlychristianwritings.com.

Meyer, Ben F. and E. P. Sanders. *Jewish and Christian Self-Definition*, 3 vols. Philadelphia:Fortress Press, 1982.

Morris, Henry M. *The Revelation Record*. Wheaton: Tyndale House, 1983.

Morris, Leon. *Revelation*, rev. ed. Grand Rapids: InterVarsity, 1987.

Mounce, Robert H. *The Book of Revelation*, rev. Grand Rapids: Eerdmans, 1998.

Origen, Adamantius. *De Principiis*. www.newadvent.org/fathers/04121.htm.

Pate, C. Marvin. ed. *Four Views on the Book of Revelation*. Grand Rapids: Zondervan, 1998.

Pausanias. *Description of Greece*. Trans. W. H. S. Jones and H. A. Ormerod. From the Perseus Project.

Peters, Joan. *From Time Immemorial: The Origins of the Arab Jewish Conflict Over Palestine*. Chicago: JKAP Publications, 1988.

Plutarch. *The Lives of the Noble Grecians and Romans*. Trans. John Dryden. New York: Random House.

Polybius. *The Histories*. Trans. W. R. Paton. From the Loeb Classical Library: Harvard University Press, 1922-27.

Poythress, Vern S. *The Returning King*. Phillipsburg: P&R Publishing, 2000.

Ramsay, W. M. *The Letters to the Seven Churches*, updated ed. Peabody: Hendrickson, 1994.

Reagan, David. *Wrath and Glory.* Green Forest: New Leaf Press, 2001.
Robertson, A. T. *Word Pictures in the New Testament.* Nashville: Holman, 2000
Runes, Dagobert D. *Pictorial History of Philosophy.* New York: Philosophical Library, 1959.
Sasson, Jack M. ed. *Civilizations of the Ancient Near East,* 3 vols. New York: Simon Schuster MacMillan, 1995.
Scherrer, Peter. *Ephesus The New Guide,* rev. ed. Turkey: Graphics, Ltd., 2000.
Suetonius, C. Tranqullus. *The Lives of the Caesars,* Trans. Alexander Thompson and R. Worthington, New York, 1983.
Simon and Garfunkel. *Collected Works. April Come She Will.* CBS, 1990.
Strabo. *Geography.* Trans. H. L. Jones from the Perseus Project.
Summers, Ray. *Worthy Is The Lamb.* Nashville: Broadman, 1951.
Tacitus, *The Annals.* Trans. Alford John Church and William Jackson Broadribb from the Internet Classics Archive.
Thomas, Robert L *Revelation, An Exegitical Commentary,* 2 vols. Chicago: Moody, 1992.
Tenney, Merrill C. *Interpreting Revelation.* Peabody: Hendrickson, 1957.
Vine, W.E. and Merrill F. Unger. Vines *Complete Expository Dictionary Of Old And New Testament Words.* Nashville: Nelson, 1985.
Verbrugge, Verlin D. ed. *The NIV Theological Dictionary of New Testament Words.* Grand Rapids: Zondervan, 2000.
Wall, Robert W. *Revelation.* Peabody: Hendricksen, 1991.
Walvoord, John F. *The Revelation of Jesus Christ.* Chicago: Moody, 1966.
Walvoord, John F. and Roy B. Zuck. eds. *The Bible Knowledge Commentary.* 2 vols. USA: Victor, 1989.
Wiersbe, Warren W. *Be Victorious.* Colorado Springs: Chariot Victor, 1985.
    Be Right. Colorado Springs: Chariot Victor, 1977.
Wikgren, Allen. ed. *Early Christian Origins.* Chicago: Quadrangle, 1961.

Wood, A. Skevington. *Ephesians*. The Expositor's Bible Commentary. vol 11. Grand Rapids: Zondervan, 1978.

Wilson, Marvin R. *Our Father Abraham*. Grand Rapids: Eerdmans, 1989.

Wuest, Kenneth S. *The New Testament: An Expanded Translation*. Grand Rapids: Eerdmans, 1961.

Zodhiates, Spiro. ed. The *Complete New Testament Word Study*. Chattanooga: AMG, 1991.

Articles

Boyer, James L. "Are the Seven Letters of Revelation 2-3 Prophetic?" *Grace Theological Journal*. vol 6. Fall, 1985.

Brindle, Wayne A. "Looking for the Blessed Hope: An Analysis of Biblical Evidence for the Imminence of the Rapture." *Pretrib Study Group*. Dallas 09 Dec, 2002.

Mundell, Robert A. "The Birth of Coinage." *Columbia University Department of Economics Discussion Paper*. January 2002.

Roberts, David. "On the Frankincense Trail." *Smithsonian Magazine*. October 1998.

Smith, Charles R. "The Book of Life." *Grace Theological Journal*. vol 6 Fall, 1985.

Tassel, Janet. "The Search for Sardis." *Harvard Magazine*. May 1998.

Taylor, Daniel. "Deconstructing the gospel of Tolerance." *Christianity Today*. January 1999.

Thomas, Robert L. "The Chronological Interpretation of Revelation 2-3." *Bibliotheca Sacra*. vol. 124 Oct, 1967.

Townsend, Jeffrey L. "The Rapture in Revealtion 3:10." *Bibliotheca Sacra*. vol 137 #547 July 1980.

Wallace, Daniel. "Revelation 3:20 and the Offer of Salvation." *bible.org*, 2/28/03.

Winfrey, David G. "The Great Tribulation: Kept "Out of" or "Through"? *Grace Theological Journal* vol 3. Spring, 1982.

Young, William J. "The Fabulous Gold of the Pactolus Valley." *Bulletin: Museum of Fine Arts, Boston*. (1972).

Printed in the United States
27014LVS00002B/51